Praise for Peter Karoff and
A Generous Life

"*A Generous Life* offers an inside look at philanthropy from a man who helped shape it. Peter Karoff's personal reflections reveal how the field has evolved during the last three decades, and will inspire funders and advisors alike to think more deeply about how we give."

—Darren Walker, President of the Ford Foundation

"It was among the greatest gifts of my life to be Peter's friend. We walked and talked all over the country as he imagined how donors could be more strategic in their giving. Why wealth with responsibility is the only path to wealth as well-being. He tried out his poems on me and they always sang. Now, in *A Generous Life*, you can hear Peter's voice as he sings out his love for his fellow humans—the essence of philanthropy."

—James "Jay" E. Hughes Jr., author of
Family Wealth: Keeping It in the Family and coauthor of
The Cycle of the Gift: Family Wealth and Wisdom

"Peter taught us philanthropy is the gift of who you are. It is a state of being that calls on our bravest and most authentic selves as we practice the art of giving. The lessons he imparted continue to resonate: to begin with the end in mind; to swing for the fences with big, hairy, audacious goals; to imagine the world we want through a lens of generosity.

Wherever you are on the philanthropic curve, Peter's presumption of hope in the 'great percussion of philanthropic possibilities' provides inspiration for the lifelong journey of becoming our best selves."

—Angelica Berrie, President of the
Russell Berrie Foundation and coauthor of *A Passion for Giving:
Tools and Inspiration for Creating a Charitable Foundation*

"If you were fortunate enough to have known Peter Karoff, to read this wonderful collection of his essays on giving is like reopening a conversation that was never quite finished. If you do not yet know Peter's work, you now have a ready access point. For all who love philanthropy, poetry, democracy, or just downright civic conviviality, this book will inspire you and challenge you to keep what matters alive."

—Phil Cubeta, former Director of the Chartered Advisor of Philanthropy® (CAP®) Program at The American College of Financial Services

"I am one of the lucky ones: those who were mentored by and simultaneously worked with Peter Karoff. And those actions were inseparable to Peter—he mentored everyone he worked with, and everyone he consulted he also mentored.

How grateful I am that Peter's voice and wisdom are now available to all. How much we, as one human family, need his reflections on the joy of generosity. Giving isn't only about impact, metrics, and results. Giving is more—it is the root to our finding purpose, joy, and identity in our time on this earth. There is no wiser guide I know of than Peter Karoff. My gratitude to those closest to him for bringing his writings together in a cohesive and approachable way. This gives those readers who weren't blessed to know Peter a chance to encounter him through this book and have his wisdom push them forward. Peter made me better. Anyone who reads *A Generous Life* will have the chance to be better too."

—Amy Goldman, CEO and Chair of GHR Foundation

"This compendium is a tribute to Peter and his exceptional humanness, and I am struck by how incredibly relevant his writings are for society today. To understand Peter and his work, begin your journey reading the wonderful tribute by Melinda Marble, and then peruse the topical chapters laid out thematically. And don't miss the first chapter's quote that conveys the 'essence' of Peter's beliefs:

'The potential for creative and original thinking and action is all around us. It often lives just below the surface of the everyday and with the right support can be stimulated, nurtured, mentored.'

Peter always hoped to spark your creativity and to have you enjoy your journey!"

—Sara Hamilton, Founder of Family Office Exchange

"As I paged through *A Generous Life*, I felt the extraordinary comfort of being in conversation with Peter once again. What a gift—in each chapter of this book, I found myself smiling and nodding, saying to myself, 'Yes! Absolutely!' I particularly love the practical bulleted lists, reflection questions, how-tos, and self-assessments. It gives me comfort that future generations of philanthropic advisors will benefit from a grounding in Peter's influence. His words serve as a reminder that rooting in love and responsibility, centering justice and generosity, and having meaningful conversations are signposts that they are on the right path."

—Elaine Martyn, **Senior Vice President at Fidelity Charitable**

"Peter's sage words remind us that individual giving is meant to be a deeply personal, heartfelt, and joyful journey—not simply a strategic exercise fueled by impartial metrics and PowerPoint presentations. In philanthropy, getting the balance right between one's brain and one's heart truly matters; if we are thoughtful, our giving can both make a substantive difference in the world and help us become a better version of ourselves."

—Thomas Tierney, **Cofounder of the Bridgespan Group**

A
GENEROUS
LIFE

A GENEROUS LIFE

REFLECTIONS on INSPIRED GIVING

PETER KAROFF

Edited and with an introduction by
MELINDA MARBLE

DISRUPTION BOOKS

Washington, DC

This book reflects the author's recollections of experiences over time. Some names and characteristics have been changed, some events have been compressed, and some dialogue has been re-created. Peter Karoff read widely and quoted freely in his many writings. We have done our best to source all quotes and references.

Published by Disruption Books
Washington, DC
www.disruptionbooks.com

Copyright © 2025 by The Philanthropic Initiative

All rights reserved, including the right to reproduce this book or portions thereof in any form whatsoever. Thank you for complying with copyright laws by not reproducing, scanning, or distributing any part of this book without express written permission from the copyright holder. For information, please contact the publisher at info@disruptionbooks.com.

Distributed by Disruption Books

For information about special discounts for bulk purchases, please contact Disruption Books at info@disruptionbooks.com.

The Philanthropic Initiative wishes to thank the James E. Hughes Foundation for its generous support in the publication of this book and distribution of the electronic version.

"Larger than Life," "A Hierarchy of Blessings," "Conscience," "Villanelle,"
"One Who Did Not Go Gentle," "Will," "Admonition" from *Parable* by Peter Karoff,
published in 2017 by WordTech Imprint, Cincinnati, Ohio.
Excerpt from THE COMPLETE POEMS OF PHILIP LARKIN by Philip Larkin,
edited by Archie Burnett. Copyright © 2012 by The Estate of Philip Larkin. Reprinted by permission of Farrar, Straus and Giroux. All Rights Reserved.
"The Ridge Farm" reprinted by permission from *The Hudson Review* 36,
no. 1 (Spring 1983): 75–110, https://doi.org/10.2307/3851337.
Copyright © 1983 by A. R. Ammons.
Excerpts from *The Redress of Poetry* by Seamus Heaney.
Copyright © 1995 by Seamus Heaney. Reprinted by permission of
Farrar, Straus and Giroux and Faber and Faber Ltd. All Rights Reserved.
Excerpts from *The Cure at Troy: A Version of Sophocles' Philoctetes* by Seamus Heaney.
Copyright © 1961 by Seamus Heaney. Reprinted by permission of Farrar,
Straus and Giroux and Faber and Faber Ltd. All Rights Reserved.
"In Those Years". Copyright © 2016 by the Adrienne Rich Literary Trust.
Copyright © 1995 by Adrienne Rich, from COLLECTED POEMS: 1950–2012
by Adrienne Rich. Used by permission of W. W. Norton & Company, Inc.

Cover design by Liz Driesbach
Book design by Kimberly Lance
Library of Congress Cataloging-in-Publication Data available.

Print ISBN: 978-1-63331-115-2
eBook ISBN: 978-1-63331-116-9

10 9 8 7 6 5 4 3 2 1

First Edition

CONTENTS

INTRODUCTION BY MELINDA MARBLE 1
    "Larger Than Life" 11

SECTION 1: THE CALLING 13
    The Opportunity of Philanthropy 15
    Your Whole Self 21
    The Wake-Up Call 24
    The Gift of Creativity 35
    The Generosity Scale 38
    Reflection 41
    "A Hierarchy of Blessings" 43

SECTION 2: EMBARKING 45
    The TPI Philanthropic Curve 48
    Translating Values into Practice 51
    True Wind and Apparent Wind 54
    Intersections for the Common Good 65
    The Fusion of Art and Science in Effective Philanthropy 75
    Reflection 89

SECTION 3: TROUBLE 93
    The Greek Chorus 95
    "Conscience" 102
    The Greek Chorus: Second Variation 104
    Reset: The New Name of the Game 112
    Parallel Tracks 116
    Hope Within the Shithole 123
    The Imagined Community (the Crime of Not Listening) 127
    Reflection 146

SECTION 4: JUSTICE   149

Standing Up   152
The Redress of Philanthropy   157
Sleepwalkers   160
"Admonition"   175
The Sociology of Wealth   176
In an Era of Scarcity   182
The Speech I Have Always Wanted to Give   192
"Will"   199
Movement Builders   201
Reflection   203
"Villanelle"   205

SECTION 5: COMING 'ROUND RIGHT   207

A Teachable Moment   209
Listen to the Voices   213
Who Is My Stranger?   227
The Magic of Philanthropy   240
Catechism for a Great Foundation   248
Reflection   251

SECTION 6: THE WORLD WE LEAVE   253

Reflections on Legacy   255
Sitting by a Still Pond   264
"One Who Did Not Go Gentle"   268

APPENDIX A: A BIOGRAPHY OF PETER KAROFF   269
APPENDIX B: PETER'S INSPIRATIONS   271
ACKNOWLEDGMENTS   273
NOTES   275

*To all those doers, donors, poets,
family members, friends, and colleagues who shaped
and were shaped by Peter's wisdom and ideas.*

INTRODUCTION
By MELINDA MARBLE

I met Peter Karoff more than thirty years ago. I'd recently moved to Boston early in a largely accidental career in philanthropy. To my surprise, Boston had fewer staffed foundations than the Bay Area at the time, and I'd found there was a demand for the kind of skills I'd built working for a community foundation and a regional association of grantmakers. I forget who told me to see Peter. All I know is I walked into a small office somewhere in downtown Boston, where I was greeted by a tiny woman with snow-white hair and the bright eyes of a particularly alert and intelligent bird. When I said I had a meeting with Peter, she simply pointed to a man seated on top of a desk in a partially furnished office. Things were messy—boxes all around—and the tiny woman's exasperation with this was almost palpable.

Peter started talking, and a cloud of questions filled the room. He was thinking of starting a business—or should it be a nonprofit? Could it be both? He had been a businessman, but maybe now he was going to be a poet. Could he be both? The business was going to tell donors how to spend their money more wisely. Was that a business? Could it be? Could it have poetry in it? When would he find time to write? Who was I? What did I care about? Was I interested in poetry? My stock rose when I said I liked to write. What role might I play in this new venture?

I heard a snort from a pile of empty boxes. Was the tiny woman making that noise? Later I realized that Catherine Corinha, Peter's longtime assistant, never hesitated to express herself in front of her boss.

"I've been listening to this stuff for twenty years now," she told me with a sigh as I left that day.

One of Peter's gifts, I came to know, was that he appreciated being taken down a peg from time to time.

I left that first encounter thinking that what eventually became known as The Philanthropic Initiative (TPI), whatever it was going to be, was a dumb idea. Why would donors pay for advice when so many would clamor to give it to them for free? And yet, I also felt immediately that I wanted to work there. There was something about the enthusiasm, the restless questions, and Peter's essential buoyancy that made me want to be part of whatever it became.

The following year I did go to work there. Being at TPI in the early days had a bit of the spontaneous, "Let's put on a show!" quality of a Mickey Rooney movie. We were figuring out this work as we did it, and it was scary and fun, the way any enterprise is when a band of smart, committed people are working together on something important. Peter always pushed us to listen to the client, to bring our full selves to the table, to reflect on what we were doing, and to share it as rapidly as possible with others. He always insisted we probe what was the right thing, the just thing, to do.

Peter also worried continually about TPI. Was it a business? Was it doing all the good it could do? It's rare to work with someone so aligned with his values, so attuned to his mission, so open to second-guessing. And it was a rare experience to work with talented, committed colleagues—Joe Breiteneicher, Bob Hohler, Leslie Pine, and Ellen Remmer, to name just a few—who shared this practice of restless questioning.

Later, I joined TPI's board where we had many long debates about whether TPI was a viable business. But under the leadership of Alan Broadbent, David Squire, Peter Nessen, Jay Hughes, and others, we also had some of the best conversations ever about how to support a gifted leader. It was characteristic of Peter to assemble a board of people who he admired and thought could teach him something—trusted advisors who had every kind of life experience imaginable, who were loyal but never afraid to push or question him, who were happy and excited to take on the big questions we faced. And Peter, with the help of an extraordinary staff, did build a business, and an entire field of advising. His specific philosophy of giving is what made TPI so successful.

A CERTAIN INTENSITY

As we learned from our clients at TPI, a vast amount of charitable giving is pedestrian, dutiful, a kind of rote "tax on life" for the donor who supports his church, her schools, or the search for the cure to their diseases. While the underlying reason for giving may be simple generosity, complex motivations often accompany it: guilt, the desire for visibility or ascension in status, the drive to strengthen a brand or business ties, and, far from least, a tax deduction. The ambitions behind the gift are sometimes grandiose or sometimes inappropriately modest and, in either case, seldom fully satisfied.

But for some donors, giving is more than that. It's a form of self-expression, a chance to honor the values and gifts that made the giver. It's also a journey and a return, a vehicle for lifelong learning that compels the giver to go deeper, to discover new worlds, and, along the way, to gain insights about himself. It's a chance for a second or third act in which to put one's whole self into an important enterprise.

For that giver, giving and receiving are seamless and satisfying experiences, though there are challenges and defeats along the way. That giver often achieves deep impact, and his generosity deepens over time as he understands more about the journey he's embarked on.

This book is for that giver—or for the person who wants to be—the one who brings her full gifts, the one who is changed by the gifts she makes. Peter Karoff was one of those people, and he helped countless others on their journey toward a generous life. This book collects some of Peter's extensive writings about his work with individuals, families, and corporations as he built TPI, a pioneering organization in the field of donor advising.

In his writings, Peter also drew on his lifelong experience of engaging in social issues, attempting to pull on the arc of the moral universe that Dr. Martin Luther King Jr. said is long but "bends toward justice." And he drew on his love and practice of poetry, encouraging donors to be brave, creative, and resourceful as artists, and to put everything they've got into the act of giving. He said:

> My slant on philanthropy is huge; it is the one where you put your whole self in. By huge, I do not mean big money, or even a monastic personal commitment, but I do mean *a certain intensity, ambition, and clarity of goals* [italics mine].

A brief biography, Appendix A, will provide more information on his life and work, but Peter described himself this way:

> I am basically a "peddler," a salesman, someone who loves to be loved and thus [is] intrinsically a mediator and finder of middle ground. It is in my genes. My great-grandfather sold sugar from a backyard mill in Shepatovka, a small village in the Ukraine, seventy kilometers east of Kiev. In America, my grandfather sold meat in a kosher butcher shop, my father sold hardware and stove grates from a small store until the first of the big box discount stores mowed him over like new grass, my brother sells stocks, my cousin toys, and so it goes. This profile is wrapped around a glass-half-full

conviction that all one needs to prevail is to have something substantive to say, to be true to it, and to use good words, which also happens to be Robert Frost's definition of a poem that works.[1]

At TPI, Peter used his good words to "peddle" philanthropy to great effect. It is no exaggeration to say that he convinced hundreds of individuals to begin or up their giving, and influenced the direction of billions of dollars in charitable assets. And this was his *second* act, after a career in insurance and real estate financing.

Peter was an effective peddler because he fervently believed that philanthropy is both a creative practice and an act of justice, and that both, like all generative endeavors, are refined over time. And, as in any worthy enterprise, going deeper into the work also requires going deeper into oneself. In other words, he believed that giving is a chance to find out what you're made of, that in practice and performance one can change the world a bit and emerge a different person than before. Peter referred to this process as becoming a "maker of gifts," and it was a bit different from the concept of strategic philanthropy that he helped to pioneer. As Peter said:

> For years, a choir of philanthropic players has been singing a similar tune: philanthropy should have measurable impact, meaning that grants should produce documented results and certifiable outcomes.
>
> My colleagues and I have contributed to that refrain, praising the benefits of strategic philanthropy, and trying to put it into practice. But I'll confess that the trend worries me. I am concerned that philanthropy is becoming too formulaic, too linear, too metric—in other words, that the emphasis on process is stifling creativity and squelching the very kind of social entrepreneurship

> that new generations of donors and grantmakers claim to favor.
>
> Process should be a servant of intuitiveness, values, instincts, and passions—and not the other way around. It's not that good analysis and demands for accountability are unimportant. It's just that, alone, they don't do the job. Also needed are creativity, curiosity, a willingness to take risks, a vision of possibilities, and a desire to form enduring relationships with grantees—the "secret sauce" of philanthropy that too often is missing in by-the-book grantmaking.
>
> A philanthropy of metrics and matrices is all well and good if it produces results. But my vote is for touch-and-feel grantmaking, a philanthropy spiked with the mystery ingredients of inspiration and imagination, a kind of philanthropy that gets under your fingernails.[2]

Peter believed that this "under your fingernails" philanthropy resulted in a unique alchemy.

> There is a gift within the gift—the greatest of gifts is when it transcends the evidence upon which it is based. Its mystery is the relationship between donor, recipient, and the community of interest being served, a dynamic that operates on multiple levels.

When he spoke, Peter often reminded his audiences that the word *philanthropy* means "love of humanity" and that it was first used in connection with Prometheus, who gave us fire when we were huddled in caves, cold and afraid of the dark. Love was always part of the secret sauce for Peter. Prometheus's loving gift of fire reminds us that giving is always a *choice*, a decision, as there is a choice in how we choose to pursue our gifts and our giving. Perhaps the boldest of all the inner questions we can ask ourselves whenever we want to begin again is this: What will I do with the gifts I've been given? Where will my love of humanity take me?

HOW *A GENEROUS LIFE* CAME TO BE

In February 2017, almost thirty years after Peter founded TPI and a decade after he had handed over daily operations and semiretired to Santa Barbara, I got a terse email from him asking me to call him to talk about an idea he had. I asked how he was and he said, "Dwindling." He had been fighting pancreatic cancer for a few years then, and was very clear-eyed about his situation. He asked if I would come out and spend a week with him going through his writings to see if there "might be another book in there." So in the last week in February, I got on a plane.

I arrived a day earlier than Peter expected and was warmly greeted by his daughter Deborah and her partner, Anna, and by a Peter who might have been dwindling but was not at all diminished. And we got to work. I hadn't spent much time with Peter in recent years, but it was immediately as if I were back in the early days of TPI and we were speeding in his car toward a client, talking excitedly, turning over the possibilities. Peter's driving matched his productive restlessness so that every trip, every conversation, was an adventure. And this was too.

In the days that followed, we ate soup and praised the merits of solitude; inventoried all the writing on his computer; watched episodes of *Shark Tank*; sorted a three-foot-tall pile of his writings, articles, and poems he loved and thought might be useful; noted our mutual good fortune of having good marriages and agreed that indeed all marriages, especially good ones, end in tragedy. We argued about which ice cream was better, McConnell's or Cabot's, and talked about books, his beloved family, philanthropy, poetry, social change—in short, we discussed the world we want and the world we leave. What a gift those conversations were.

During the week, the final galleys of his first published book of poems, *Parable*, arrived. I watched him open the package and hold it with fond delight, almost as if another grandchild had arrived. Every day, he would nod toward the stacks of papers in his study and ask me, "Do you think there's another book in there?" By the end of the week I was so happy to be able to share a first, rough outline of *A Generous Life* with him. Peter gave me permission to use that structure to knit and weave together his pieces, and permission to edit and append them.

A Generous Life was assembled from many short pieces written over twenty-five prolific years in the thick of his practice. I have tried to arrange these pieces—some full essays or talks he'd delivered, some fragments, and even poems—loosely, according to the stages of the philanthropic journey, and include them where they might be most helpful. The first two sections are encouragements or "ways in" to philanthropy that explore different motivations and implore prospective givers to reflect, pause, and understand philanthropy as a developmental process. Section 3, "Trouble," moves into a discussion of what obstacles might arise, both externally and internally. Sections 4 and 5 focus on the outcomes of philanthropy: Is it promoting justice and adding value to society? And then the final section contains some of Peter's deepest musings on how giving changes you and your legacy.

In the spirit of mystery and alchemy, what follows is not a how-to manual. It's a dreamer's guide, designed to give you ideas, similar to how an appealing cookbook whets your appetite and makes you want to go into the kitchen. Whether you are new to giving or far along in your journey, *A Generous Life* is intended to help you identify the causes you're most moved to fight for, prepare for when your efforts don't always go according to plan, and reflect on and evaluate the outcome of your giving to see how you can evolve.

As Peter once wrote:

> I like the metaphor that life is a journey—it is both within our consciousness and external in our experience. We are both an observer and an actor. There is poetry in all that we see and experience, even if we do not use that word. There is something to be learned from the practice of all that we do, even if we do not always understand it at the time.[3]

So some of the pieces that follow are about poetry, and some are about hard truths and difficult practice. They are best viewed not as a coherent, linear narrative, but rather as a set of reflections. You could read them straight through, or you can dip in wherever a topic or title calls to you. Peter's poems are also interspersed between sections. I have added reflection questions at the end of each section.

I hope that this book is like a good conversation, and that you talk back and think back to it as you read and consider the possibilities. Peter always did. Thinking about his remarkable life, the word *amateur* comes to mind. Not as in the fumbling efforts of an unschooled individual, but in the word's truest sense: someone who does something for the pleasure of it. It is a word whose root is, appropriately, *love*. Peter's open-hearted, open-minded embrace of whatever he was learning about is something to emulate. His drive, competitiveness, and energy were always harnessed to joy. Something about him seemed to declare, "How lucky I am to be in this place, at this time, with these people," a sentiment summed up by and brimming from his favorite word: "Terrific!"

During our time together in Santa Barbara, he said to me, "I've done everything I ever wanted to do," yet he lived his last weeks to the fullest, participating in board meetings by phone, offering advice to friends—still contributing, as if he'd been awarded a wonderful bonus.

Peter often quoted his friend John Abele, founder of Boston Scientific, on this topic. John said:

> Wealth, and being listed in *Forbes* magazine, is not what constitutes success. What you do with wealth is what defines you, and you never completely get there. The end goal is to provide value for society. That can happen in business, as I believe it happened at Boston Scientific, and it can happen in philanthropy . . . What is so unique about philanthropy is that it can act without some of the conventional restraints. Philanthropy can be a convener, an introducer, a bridge to common ground, and it can encourage others to expand the dialogue beyond the usual.

Looking back on our long friendship and work together, I've found in Peter's life a call, a reminder to be curious, to seek delight—whether in ice cream or the perfect phrase—in even the toughest times. He showed us, gave so many of us, permission to be ambitious but not grandiose, to be generous without being foolish, to make community and family the center of things, to worry a lot but have the time of your life. To give yourself fully to a life of joy and purpose, that was the important thing. "It may be possible," he said once, "to grow one's own soul." To grow the soul: that was his gift, to me, to you, to all of us. Please take it. He wanted you to have it.

LARGER THAN LIFE

When a good man dies
The earth nods, heaves a sigh
And goes right back to work.

Perhaps selling improvisations
Or taking on impossible odds,
Grandiose dreams by sheer force
Of will become reality.

Who ever would believe this script
In a world where the brisk business
Of birth, death, renewal and chance
Comes in on the money every time.

When a good man dies
The earth nods, heaves a sigh
And just goes back to work.

You can't trick fate
But you can mold it with passion,
Bend it by ambition
And turn it toward a better world.

SECTION 1:

THE CALLING

*You or I, when driven by great passion,
also have no choice, we must act.*

PETER KAROFF

The pieces in this section offer a way into philanthropy, posing questions and calls to action. The first, "The Opportunity of Philanthropy," is Peter's sales pitch, drawn from early lessons gained from practices at TPI, and enthusiastically exhorts us to engage. As Peter said:

> The potential for creative and original thinking and action is all around us. It often lives just below the surface of the everyday and with the right support can be stimulated, nurtured, mentored.

Peter always encouraged clients to start by probing what drives them, their values and passions, as an actor might ask of a role: What motivates this character? "Your Whole Self" urges us to bring not just money but all our gifts, resources, and connections to the act of giving.

Why are some generous and others are not? What keeps us in the game? "The Wake-Up Call" goes deeper into motivation, addressing it as part of the "mood to find greater meaning" and discussing the challenges of "[making] wealth a positive."

Peter fervently believed in philanthropy as a path to soul-growing. "The Gift of Creativity" makes the case for philanthropy as art as well as science, urging donors to identify what they are compelled by and to act on it in deeply personal ways. Peter argues that "the rare gift, like the rare poem, is one of imagination and transcends the heart and the mind"—a powerful call to bring the values and visions we cherish to our giving. This piece is about becoming a maker, a *macher*, the Yiddish word for an influential person, perhaps, through giving.

Finally, in "The Generosity Scale," Peter provides a gentle self-reflective quiz designed to help us probe how justice and generosity are central in our daily lives.

The Opportunity of Philanthropy

Your fortune is rolling up, rolling up like an avalanche!
You must keep up with it! You must distribute it faster than it grows.
If you do not it will crush you and your children,
and your children's children.

REV. FREDERICK GATES[1]

Philanthropy is my business. It is an odd business, and to say you are in it sounds like an oxymoron. We started The Philanthropic Initiative years ago with the unabashed objective to make the world a better place. When we started TPI there were very few philanthropic advisors, but the seeds for such work were planted long ago, when Frederick Gates, a Baptist minister, met lifelong Baptist John D. Rockefeller. Gates became central to Rockefeller's business and philanthropic work, and over a period of thirty years beginning in the 1890s, he supervised the distribution of about a half billion dollars, an astounding, unprecedented philanthropic commitment.

When we started TPI, we didn't know if anyone would want to hire us. It turns out there is a huge market of people who want to make their giving more strategic and more satisfying. All of us who work at TPI believe with our hearts and our minds that philanthropy can make a difference in finding solutions to major social problems.

What have we learned?

- We have learned that philanthropy goes beyond charity and is rooted in the universal human tradition of helping others help themselves.
- We have learned that the best philanthropy is based on passion, and as James Joseph, former president of the Council on Foundations, said, "Without it, giving is an empty act."
- We have learned that philanthropy is more satisfying when you flip the process of reacting to requests from others and become proactive to what interests you.
- We have learned that you do best when you focus on fewer issues, perhaps even one.
- We have learned that the most satisfying thing of all is when you involve yourself, as well as your money.
- We have learned that philanthropy can be creative, bold, brave.
- We have learned that what drives the philanthropic process are your values, and those values provide the context for everything one does.

The journey that is strategic philanthropy starts with this question: What are your values, your family's values?

It is interesting how hard a question that is to answer, and that outside of church or temple we seldom even frame such questions. Our society and our lifestyles place tremendous pressure on families. Many feel that the nuclear family as our parents knew it is very much at risk and, as a result, the observance of ethical values is undermined. One of the challenges facing every family is to work hard to not allow that to happen. That is what TPI's work with families is all about.

Why are so many people drawn to explore philanthropy?

- Some wish to be a citizen of the earth and want to learn more about what that means.

- Some believe passionately in equity and justice for all people.
- Some want to learn how to involve their children—or parents—in a shared family enterprise.
- Some are seekers of what has been called "a shred of hope" in an otherwise dangerous and turbulent world.
- Some wish to rationalize their wealth, and determine its meaning and how it can be used for themselves, for their children, for the world.
- Some have no choice, no ethical, emotional, or psychological alternative than to be in a place where women and men give of themselves to each other.

Here are some wonderful lines from Philip Larkin's poem "High Windows":

> Rather than words, comes the thought of high windows:
> The sun-comprehending glass,
> And beyond it the deep blue air.[2]

The sight of a window somehow becomes something fundamental to the poet, to where he or she is in life. The philanthropist does the same thing. The raw material—the critical needs that face our communities, our country, the globe—lie like the leaves, seemingly endless and complex before our eyes. We all struggle with what our response should be, can be. Do we ignore, for our own sanity, the litany of problems that the media parades before us every day in that flat, curious blend of voyeurism, despair, and hope? Or do we take it as part of our human job, to think hard enough about those things we believe are important, to learn about them, to become competent to make something happen, to apply our resources to make a difference? Each of us must pick our own spot.

For the wealthy, you don't get too far down this road without bumping up against the meaning of wealth. As Peter Goldmark adapted words from the noted philosopher Pogo: "For some people, wealth is an insurmountable opportunity! All you need is imagination, will, and a ticket to the adventure."

Here is a quote from a client: "Inherited wealth creates tremendous freedom, freedom to do what you want to. What I want my philanthropy to do is help others have that kind of freedom."

What our client was saying has been framed before in other ways. In Maimonides's eight grades of charity, the last grade is "to forestall it all by enabling your fellow humans to have the right to earn a livelihood."[3]

Freedom, opportunity, enabling: These are huge, uplifting words. Yet, one of the more discouraging observations TPI made in its early years is what I have come to call the "marginalization of philanthropy." It is not that those with wealth do not give—they do—but the amount in relationship to the resources is frequently not material, and the process is often casual. In 1991, eight out of ten wealthy individuals who died that year left nothing to charity.[4] Overall, those with higher incomes give less, on average, as a percentage of their income than those with lower incomes.[5]

Why is it that some are generous, and others are not? These are not abstract issues. The allocation of an individual's fortune between society and the family is a fundamental wealth issue. In TPI's work with families, we sometimes don't get beyond the issue of how much to leave to the children and how much to leave to a family foundation or other charities. It has as much to do with what one believes is best for children and grandchildren as it does with philanthropy.

We have learned that the effectiveness and satisfaction of the philanthropic process can dramatically influence those decisions. Why should you consider giving more to the family foundation if its giving is lackluster and without connection to what you believe is important? The reverse is true as well, and some of our clients who have seen the power of radical strategic philanthropy have changed their view, and their estate plans, to reflect those views.

The amount of one's giving is one aspect and the process is another, and it is here that TPI spends most of its time. We have been developing with our clients an evolving notion of strategic philanthropy. That means you cannot sit at the dining room table on December 31, sort out the stack of charitable requests you have been saving all year, and consider yourself a strategic philanthropist. You need to engage, do the homework, and find the connection between these requests and what you believe in.

It is interesting that the process of doing this work is in and of itself useful in the development of the donor's identity. John Gardner has said:

> Your identity is what you've committed yourself to. If you make no commitments, you are an unfinished person. Freedom and obligation, liberty and duty, that's the deal! You build meaning into your life through your commitments—whether to your religion, to your conception of an ethical order, to your loved ones, to your life work, to your community.[6]

In poetry, the biggest sin is to tell, and not show. In philanthropy, the biggest sin is to "talk the talk" without "walking the walk," to be satisfied with feeling good but not really doing any good. In TPI's perfect world, the results of your philanthropy are real product results that can be defined and measured.

There are many opportunities in all this for families. Here are just a few:

- Philanthropy can be a wonderful bridge between the generations. It establishes a forum for communication that can establish a family purpose and team spirit.

- It can foster a greater sense of self-worth and a reduction in the sense of separateness from the larger world that people of wealth often experience.

- It is a way to view money as a blessing, instead of something else.

- A family foundation can be a way of passing on values from one generation to the next. It can be a powerful tradition that keeps a far-flung clan together.

- It can be a mechanism to stimulate sibling cooperation on issues outside the business side of the family, and a way to have fun and learn together.

We suggest you begin to think strategically and ask yourself, and maybe your family as well, some questions. They can be as simple as these posed by David Rockefeller:

> What do you care about?
> What is important to care about?
> What is my community?
> What do I want to leave behind?

Your Whole Self

Last month, I walked on the beach each afternoon in Santa Barbara, enjoying some perfect late summer days. The shore birds were into their roadrunner act, racing the waves as the tide ran up the beach, long legs and long beaks busy amid the rich nutrients from the sea. And I thought that these lovely creatures would live out their days in the same simple pursuit, and not be faced with much in the way of "new knowledge" with which to contend. Unless, of course, the massive oil rigs offshore, the very same that at night present sparkling beacons flickering in and out of the Pacific fog, break apart in some violent storm and desecrate this pristine place.

Assume philanthropy is a kind of table one sits at or a room one enters or a house we inhabit. We enter these spaces with different levels of commitment and participation. We enter based on our particular take and, since we only know what we know, that interpretation is heavily weighted with our experience and worldview. I have been on more than thirty nonprofit boards, for example, and thus have seen firsthand how success and failure play out in different ways. That is often useful, but I sometimes think that body of experience gets in the way, makes me less open to new, fresh ideas. I tend to think I know it all when I really know very little.

What we bring to the table, our "old knowledge," can be positive and it can be negative. As we get older, or at least as I get older, certainty fades, nuance enters more and more, and rightness and truth seem increasingly less clear. I think this is often the result of the confrontation between "old knowledge" and "new knowledge"—the desire not to change our thinking and our ways amid the constant, in-your-face evidence that the facts and circumstances of life have been altered.

Indeed, the evidence of this is all around us. Just watch the latest TED Talk speaker whose brilliant ideas, outstanding production, dominant market share, star performance, and revolutionary process is evident in every field of human endeavor. Whatever the domain, new knowledge constantly pushes and challenges the status quo, and today this occurs at a dizzying rate of speed.

Such events are also part of the natural flow of each succeeding generation as it comes of age. The challenge of one generation toward another—the most recent version of *King Lear, How Green Was My Valley, The Sopranos*—animates much good literature, movies, daily media coverage, and even family foundation boards.

It is the human species alone that is blessed or cursed with the knowledge business. What is different for the present generation is the pace of change, and the increasing inability to deflect or postpone grappling with new knowledge.

That has not always been the case. In their portrayal of an idyllic rural life, the great English landscape painters captured a time that seemed to be, for centuries, timeless. You feel that timelessness in the typical, recognizable, eighteenth-century painting of the village scene, the one with the boy loading hay into a wagon while a young girl looks on. Looking at the painting, you feel, you just know, that he will grow up, live his life, marry the girl in the painting or her cousin, have children, and work the land, all without confronting immense change. Fast forward to the nineteenth century, and all hell and the industrial revolution breaks loose. And as it did again in the 1990s, with the e-economy and tech revolution, when "kids" became smarter, richer, more powerful, and ruthless overnight. They appeared to be taking over the world, and new knowledge was developing so fast that many of us were left in the dust, unable to turn on our newly complicated television sets. I fully expect the next wave of youth-led revolution to hit us before the ink has dried on this page—another obsolete metaphor in the age of laser printers.

These strong external forces swirl around us in a blur, make us uncomfortable, challenge our thinking, our worldview, our priorities. They make our own claims at expertise suspect.

And the options for dealing with change feel suspect too. One option is to bury our heads in the sand and live "securely" in a gated community. How inconceivable such a notion seems after September 11! As I write these words, security, for me and for my grandchildren, is impossible to define.

Another option is to make a token contribution of self, a kind of nod in the direction of change that at least suffices for casual, cocktail party chitchat. Still another, and what I would want to do, is to open yourself up, apply your old knowledge in new circumstances, and dive in with your whole self.

My slant on philanthropy is huge, it is the one where you put your whole self in. By *huge*, I do not mean big money or monastic personal commitment, but I do mean a certain intensity, ambition, and clarity of goals. Let me note that I use the word *philanthropy* only because I haven't found a better one. Maybe you, the reader, can think of one, something about love and goodness, perhaps something about duty.

The Wake-Up Call

Paul Simon's *Graceland* came out in 1986. Do you remember 1986? In "The Boy in the Bubble," he talks about those moments that inspire you to change your life; what I would deem "wake-up calls."

For reasons that I can't fully explain, these lyrics had a lot to do with why I started TPI. You see, I had a wake-up call. For me it was not religious in the conventional sense, but it clearly was spiritual, although at the time I would not have called it that. It was not based on any great insight into how the world could be a better place, although I guess there were a few ideas floating around. It was not based on any clear idea of how to contribute to the greater good, except knowing that I was not the only one with a strong yearning to do so. You see, we had not done very well in the hero and heroine department. As you know, too many of the few heroes we had were ruthlessly taken away in a manner that seemed impossible in the America we had grown up in. And too many of our would-be heroes did not and, alas, do not now, seem to measure up.

But there it was, and it was part of my wake-up call, which by the way wasn't some seminal moment, or brilliant flash of light. It had been building for a long time. It took more than thirty years of living as a husband, a father, a provider (a.k.a., a plain vanilla businessman), a part-time writer, a donor, a privileged member of the city in which I live—in essence, as an elite, before I was finally ready to throw my hat in the ring. Like many, I have been involved in various community activities and am deeply affected by suffering, by inequity, by unfairness, and by beauty. For years, the picture of my beautiful and smart children, and the life I was able to give them, was juxtaposed with the very different picture of equally beautiful and smart, but very poor and disadvantaged, children. These were pictures of something not right, echoes of the philosopher Allen Wheelis's line "some things are not permitted," and over time they drew me in more and more.[7]

The motivation to start TPI was also affected by a fascination with why some people are generous, and others are not; why some companies seem to do the right thing, and others are stuck in the sand. TPI has been on an entrepreneurial mission to see if the wealthy, however that is defined—individual, family, corporate, or community—could be encouraged to answer the wake-up call; to see if they could measure up.

As I write these words, they seem dangerously close to hubris, but like all high-risk ventures, which is what TPI was, you need a little of that or you never get out the door.

These wake-up calls are representative of the mood of the society in which we live. There's a mood to find greater meaning in our lives. It has been estimated that roughly half of Americans are on a hunt for a higher purpose, a search for values, for connection, for community, for spirituality. For a purpose beyond work, beyond the sound bites of the evening news, away from the information-overload, the minute-by-minute spinning world that we inhabit. This yearning for engagement runs across the divide of wealth and class. To what extent this awakening is being driven by our affluence versus other aspects doesn't really matter. Without a doubt, this mood establishes a new receptivity to take the call. In the words of Allen Wheelis: "We are driven to find meaning and find it by discovering a necessary relation between our lives and some larger purpose."

My guess is that most of you would not be reading this if you were not drawn in one way or another to a larger purpose. The bigger question for our community, however we define community, and for our society, is how to bring more people into this room.

The Canadian group called Barenaked Ladies—introduced to me, naturally, by my then-seven-year-old grandson Jacob, who likes the name of the group as much as he likes the music—has a song called "If I Had a Million Dollars." The lyrics say this would make them rich, but they are mostly wrong—these days, having a million dollars does not make you rich.

It is interesting, though, how wealth fascinates; it fascinates those who have it and those who do not. Wealth is not value-neutral even though in theory it could be. Wealth is hot, even though it is supposed to be cool. Wealth is concrete, but in our minds it is a fantasy. Wealth frees us from economic worry and should relax us, but it often does the opposite. We worry about losing it, about being taken advantage of, about being loved for our money instead of ourselves, about it ruining our children's lives. For some, wealth reduces confidence and self-worth and, for a few, it creates guilt. In a nutshell, wealth is supposed to be fun and often it is not.

An existential view of wealth would say all of the above is nonsense and that how we respond and react to our wealth is a matter of will. Wealth is what we make it and while I believe that is true, how to make wealth a positive and not a negative is not simple. It is not simple for us or for our children.

I don't know any way to begin dealing with these questions without determining what wealth means to you and what your relationship is to it. In the words of Emily Dickinson, we all bring a "certain Slant of light" to that determination.[8] Here is one slant that we heard in July from another American entrepreneur:

> When *X* and I started the company, we never dreamed it would be so successful or that we would end up with such incredible amounts of money. I don't need it, and my kids don't need it. I think of myself as "guardian" to the wealth and intend to give away as much as I can while I am here, and then have my kids continue the process after I'm gone.

I can't tell you how many people have told us, "I never dreamed I would have this much money," but the use of the word *guardian* is intriguing. It is very close to *steward* and the concept of *stewardship* that formed the basis of Andrew Carnegie's "The Gospel of Wealth" in which he restated the scriptures: "All man's possessions are but a loan from the Creator of the universe."[9]

Carnegie's "Gospel," written at the turn of the century, became the standard of wealth and responsibility for a whole generation of wealth-creators. Today, we do not have an agreed-upon gospel of wealth and, as Paul Simon correctly stated, we are more loosely affiliated and less homogeneous. There seem to be patterns emerging that promise a good deal, but it is really too early to tell.

Let's say you have come up with your answer to what wealth means—what's next? Well in our experience the first two questions are as follows:

- How much makes sense to leave to the children, and how much is too much?

- How much should we give, and can we afford to give, back to society—to philanthropy writ large?

For many of the people we have met, the allocation question *is* the question, and the answers are not written in any book. They are highly individualized and based on a complex set of factors that relate to how family legacy is defined, as well as an assessment of the human capital within the family. If you think your kids are competent and can handle things well, it is one thing. If the reverse is true, then it is another. We encounter these scenarios time and again, and often conclude that the next generation is far more competent to handle their affairs than their parents think.

How much can you afford to give away? Claude Rosenberg, one observer of this field, has written about this question with surprising conclusions. Rosenberg offers an example for an individual who is sixty years old with an $18 million net worth who, on average, gives away $75,000 a year. He then runs a series of exercises that "proves" that this person can increase his giving to $750,000 a year and still accomplish every single one of his financial goals. If everyone in this room and all the others like us around the country followed Claude's advice, giving would increase by more than $100 billion a year.

Obviously, financial security is paramount but resolving what that means is often complicated by a mindset, especially when the wealth has come very fast. The balance sheet is in a new place, but the individual's or family's mindset is often fixed on a time when the financial situation was very different. For example, the thirty-five-year-old tech executive with $18 million in stock who just finished paying off her college loans last year has great difficulty bringing her net worth into perspective.

The primary driver of these decisions is what might be called one's *values*, and coming to grips with what they are is frequently a bit of an adventure in itself. We always begin our interviews with these questions: What are your personal values? What are your family values? Are they the same or different? What are your community values? Those questions usually stop the conversation, and what we get is silence, squirming, and a fair amount of awkwardness. We just don't talk about this kind of thing, but once we have broken through the dialogue it is usually revelatory.

For example, what do we want for our family? We all want a happy family, which by the way is defined in the OED (Oxford English Dictionary) as "a collection of birds and animals of different natures and propensities living together in harmony in one cage."[10] I will leave it to each of you to bring that metaphor home!

What do we want for our children? A healthy life that is satisfying and productive, an ability to give and receive love and to sustain long-term relationships, and enough confidence and strength of character to deal with the inevitable vicissitudes of life. We also want them to be caring and responsible citizens. Some of us want them to believe in God and live according to religious principles. *In other words, what we want for our children has nothing to do with money.*

While there are many bridges between having money and what we want for our children, one of the most effective is philanthropy; a family-giving process that takes what is best about the family and connects it to those issues that are important to you.

Last month in Missoula, Montana, I heard about another wake-up call answered. A woman who had inherited a very large sum of money had recently established a foundation. The board included her husband, a close friend, and two trusted advisors. The woman has two daughters, ages eleven and thirteen, and one of her major objectives is to include the girls in the foundation. When pressed to explain what her goals were, she said, "I think of the foundation as my 'third child,' it is that important, and I want my daughters to come to know this other 'sibling' as well as they know each other. I want the foundation to be both at the kitchen table and deep inside the psyche of our family life."

The more we talked, the "third child" concept became clearer. She is very concerned about the impact of wealth on her kids and views the foundation as a way to give meaning to the wealth, a way for the children to get a lesson in values, to get to know their community—not just the privileged aspect of which they are a part. She hopes the foundation will help her daughters come to terms with their wealth, something that she herself has found difficult. She believes this is a way for the family to learn together, to have fun together, and to grow together.

With that said, everything else about the foundation's mission, goals, and focus fell into place. Everything was driven by her value-driven desire to include the children.

My guess is these notions had been brewing in her mind for some time, and that by being back home in Montana, a place she loved, and sitting around a room with the people who are the most important to her, it just came out—it was a wonderful moment.

What the right family-giving process can do, within a foundation, a donor-advised fund, or simply around an annual budget, is invaluable. It can:

- bind the family together;
- create an elevated common ground within the family;
- bridge the world of those who have and those who do not;
- create an opportunity to give back and make a difference;
- foster intergenerational dialogue and respect;
- make the notion of legacy real;
- provide intellectual and spiritual satisfaction; and
- be a way to have fun!

It is easy to say the "right" giving process, and sometimes hard to do. Here are a few of the key ingredients needed to make a great family-giving process possible:

- Committing to be and act as a collective, one with a broad, long-term vision that is inclusive of individual interests but at the same time goes beyond those interests. It is where $1 + 1 =$ more than 2. In essence, families should engage in a commitment to accommodate each other—which of course is the secret of any successful relationship.

- Addressing the inevitable family dynamics, especially the generational dynamics, like the loving but dominant dad and/or mom. Addressing the inherent dilemma of letting go or of letting go too much and thus not appearing sufficiently engaged—of wanting the kids to play in the charitable sandbox, and not giving them any sand.

- Dealing with the sibling "stuff" that might have more to do with the teddy-bear fight of twenty years ago, or the competition for love and attention, than the issues on the table.

- Deciding, clearly, how children's spouses, unfortunately often referred to as "outlaws," will be treated. Are they invited to the table or not? This is a big policy decision that, for some families, is no problem but for others is difficult and perplexing.

- Recognizing that differences in interests sometimes track the generations. As one donor put it: "It's what happens when the giving moves from the museum to the Amazon. What do you do?"

- Most important, in our view, is having a process that engages family members, meets them where they are in life, and doesn't set demands—stated or unstated—that are unrealistic or make people feel guilty, and turned off.

One of our more interesting clients has made his money in the development of less-invasive medical equipment. What he wanted for his family foundation was a "less invasive" system that would allow his children, who were all at different places in life, to enter the foundation process on their terms. In this case, there are two parents and three children, a total of five family members. Each member has a share to distribute with a sixth share kept for communal giving. If a family member does not want to use his/her share in any given year, it drops into the communal bucket. The only rules are that family members share the what and the why of their gifts. They also utilize TPI staff to perform due diligence as needed. There is no pressure, and what is done in one year does not affect what is done in the next year. It has been a great system for this family that has allowed the youngest to set her own pace, and gradually build interest and enthusiasm for the gift-giving process.

All of this means that the roles and responsibilities of family members, as trustees or board members, need to be realistic and clear. It also points to making trustee training and learning a high and continuing priority.

Mark Gerzon, a wise and talented writer who discussed society and life, wrote these words:

> Every community (every person) has a buried treasure. These hidden assets are the unexplored differences that lie just below the surface of beauty, complexity, and value to be fully appreciated—and enrich everyone.

There are "buried treasures" in ourselves, and in our families, and a great giving process enables us to discover them.

We raise children out of our instincts, not out of our rhetoric. As one of our very wise clients said a few years ago, "There is no protection from a smart daughter!" Preaching doesn't work—action does. It is hard to exaggerate the pleasure and satisfaction we feel when our children succeed, when the family succeeds. Philanthropy, often teased out of whole cloth, is a buried treasure that goes far beyond the dollars involved. It is the essence of legacy for ourselves and for the world in which we live.

When we first organized TPI in 1989, we had no idea that the immense amount of wealth in the system, in essence all the money that had been built since World War II, would almost double in ten years. We also had no idea that there would be such an explosion of interest in philanthropy.

It doesn't take a genius to connect the money and the mood and walk across the street to the world of citizenship, community involvement, service, and philanthropy. But when we do, another set of operating and process questions emerges:

- How do I make gifts that make a difference?
- How do I know the impact, the results, of those gifts?

For the last twenty-five years, my colleagues and I have been talking about a new language around the domain of philanthropy. The words we have been using are hardly new: philanthropy that is strategic, philanthropy based on your values and on your passions, philanthropy that suggests the donor is also an investor whose return is based on a combination of the heart and the mind. Other words are useful, like *venture* philanthropy—or at the very least *venturesome* philanthropy—and, perhaps most important of all, a philanthropy that is aligned with the donor's belief system.

So how do you get there from here? How do you become more strategic? Here are a few simple steps:

1. Take a deep breath and step back; think about and articulate your values and your passions.

2. Determine a governance process and allocation of funds within the family that acknowledges individual needs and differences, if it's a family philanthropy.

3. Determine areas of focus and learn more about them through research, needs and gaps analyses, discussion with experts or those on the ground. Build on the "due diligence" of other donors interested in the same things you are.

4. Establish goals and decide what kind of donor you want to be (i.e., venture capitalist, steward, or change agent).

5. Create guidelines and criteria for grantmaking and proactive ways to surface the kind of opportunities you want to fund.

6. Begin to build relationships with grantees and other partners who can advance the work, including structuring a shared learning process.

7. Reassess and evaluate the process from time to time.

I will leave you with three things—the first is a definition of philanthropy I like a lot from Peter Goldmark in his last report as president of the Rockefeller Foundation: "Philanthropy is the practice of applying assets of knowledge, passion and wealth to bring about constructive change."[11]

The second is the hope that you will answer your own wake-up call, that you will define what being a "guardian of wealth" means to you, and that you will consider the notion of a "third (philanthropic) child."

The last is some wonderful words about legacy because the more I think about these things, the more it comes to that. They come from a Senegalese writer named Baba Dioum.

> In the end
> We will conserve only what we love
> We will love only what we understand
> And we will understand only what we have been taught.[12]

The Gift of Creativity

The poet William Butler Yeats wrote of feeling a poem in the marrow of [his] bones.[13] Yeats spoke to that moment when the poet from deep within joins the imagination and mystery of the creative process, and the workings of the mind surge forward. The result is a "gift" from the poet to the larger world. It is a gift of intimacy, and thus carries personal risk to the poet who sends it out into the world with great trepidation, with the earnest hope it will be understood, admired, and perhaps loved. A poem, like every other form of art, aims to transcend the literal, the figurative, and even the spiritual. If it succeeds as mystery, and as imagination, then it is a rare gift indeed.

I think that the heart of the motivation for generosity comes from a very similar place within the individual. The yearning of the poet to write the poem, or of the artist to paint the picture, is to say something important. The poet literally has no choice when the vision, the image, the insight, or the story becomes so compelling that the only option is to find expression. The yearning of the individual to find meaning in life, to be a good person, to find ways to say something important about those things we care deeply about, is just as powerful. You or I, when driven by great passion, also have no choice but to act. The instinct is equally as deep within us as it is within the poet.

The difference is in the articulation. The poet writes a poem and, when it is finished, feels for that moment great satisfaction—completion. A kind of harmony is in the room, a sense of having risen to a demanding challenge, having done a good thing.

The nonpoet makes other kinds of gifts. They may be ideas, influence, credibility, advice, access, money, or personal commitment for an hour or a lifetime. They are whatever we have at hand. We make these gifts for many reasons: because we are asked, because we are angry, because we want to cure a disease, because we see someone suffering, because we see something beautiful and want to preserve it, because we cannot live with something that is unjust. It comes out of our life experience and is based on our response to and assessment of a need, and our realization that we can do something about it. It is what we call *philanthropy*.

Those gifts, like that of the poet, are launched into the public domain always with trepidation, and often with great risk. The rare gift, like the rare poem, is one of imagination, and transcends the heart and the mind. When we have done a truly generous thing we, too, feel great satisfaction.

I remember seeing the Kirk Douglas movie in the late '50s depicting the life of Vincent van Gogh. It was at a time when I was young and raw, and I was deeply moved by the depiction of Van Gogh's tortured artistic drive. I cried over the sheer force and beauty of the creative process, how it both propelled and consumed the artist. It was the revelation that out of vulnerability, out of a desperate life situation, the artist was compelled from the marrow of his bones to paint his pictures. It spoke to me with great force—there is a path of higher purpose in life, something that is excellent, something more than the "I," and we are all irrevocably drawn toward it. It has driven me, and I believe it drives you who is reading this piece.

The essential lesson is that the human spirit—vulnerable, insecure, limited, hurting, tentative, afraid as it is—remains indomitable. Perhaps that is what the arts do better than anything else. They turn us, with heightened sensibility, to our own humanity. I think that reaching out to others, giving back to society—generosity in all its dimensions—turns us in exactly the same way, but goes one step further.

The potential for creative and original thinking and action is all around us. It often lives just below the surface of the everyday and with the right support can be stimulated, nurtured, mentored. A gifted giver has a nose for signs of excellence even when they are unformed and just beginning to stir. A gifted giver, like the artist, puts the pieces together and out of the mysterious puzzle that is life makes something coherent. This makes the link between the creative process and generous behavior complete. Great art hits a nerve. Great acts of generosity, of philanthropy as it is broadly defined, hit a nerve as well. The art of philanthropy, at the end of the day, is the gift of high expectation and opportunity. It is a gift of creativity.

There is an advantage in this art form. You don't have to be a Yeats or a Van Gogh to produce high-performance generosity. Robert Frost's three-part definition of a good poem is relevant: Did the poet have anything to say, was he true to it, and did he use good words? We might ask: What do we most believe in, did we act on those beliefs, and did we execute at the highest possible level? The very process itself, a mix of strong vision, mission, and execution, has a simple genius of its own, one that is accessible not to the select few but to the many.

I love thinking about things in the context of the creative experience. I like the surge of intensity, passion, commitment, and even obsession that joins the heart and the mind in the making of things. These are the elements that make us emotionally and intellectually engaged, make us alive to what swirls around. It is how we wake up out of the somnolence of the everyday and how we go deep into our humanness. I think it always comes out as a "gift" to the larger world, sometimes as a poem or a painting, but more frequently as something else.

It is interesting how those who we think of as gifted are, at the end of the day, themselves the "makers of gifts," and it is through that process that the artist realizes their meaning. I think it is the same for each of us in our own search for meaning—we are most fully realized as a "maker of gifts."

The Generosity Scale

What we mean by *being generous* clearly goes beyond philanthropy, and I have recently been thinking a lot about the broader concept of generosity as it relates to individual behavior.

The concept of generosity is a bit like a cloud. It is a subject that is difficult to wrap up or distill in ways that are meaningful or useful. Yet the fascination of developing some kind of measurement or standard is very strong. What one would most like to do is create not a dictum, but a template that others could use for their own individual purposes. In essence, I'm suggesting the creation of a contemporary and applied version of the Sermon on the Mount or Maimonides's eight levels of charity.

A useful Generosity Scale would have two primary elements: 1) an inclusive, multifaceted format that could be easily added to or subtracted from, and 2) in keeping with the American tradition, a way of keeping score.

Well, here goes! As you read the following eight bullet points, rank your sense of the *truth* of the text as it applies to you on a scale of one to ten, with one being the lowest and ten being the highest. Make as many entries as you wish. The total is your score, even if you are the only audience.

- You wish to be, and you may actually be, a good person. And by *good* I mean that you say hello to strangers you meet (even on elevators), you listen to others with consideration even when you disagree, and you do not interrupt. Your opinions, however strong, do not color your openness to other views (even if you do not change your views). You exercise authority and control carefully and dispassionately, especially with those who are vulnerable. You are honest and fair and do not attempt to live other people's lives for them, even your children's.

- You give of yourself on an ongoing basis to help others in the manner that is the best use of yourself. You make a concerted effort to think and care about people and things other than yourself, and you support and promote those, in public and private life, who you believe are generously minded, including those with whom you work and live.

- You will not tolerate injustice, bigotry, racism, or unfair treatment wherever you find such actions or behavior, including among friends, neighbors, colleagues, and elected officials. And despite the fact that you are usually quiet or may be afraid, you will speak out with conviction and courage even when there is only a whisper or vague possibility that injustice exists.

- You share financial resources beyond what is deemed the norm. Your giving does not create dependency but the reverse. While you may want and receive recognition, gifts are not made for the sake of recognition. You apply qualitative standards to gifts but are careful to not be arrogant. You look for ways to reinforce those aspects of society that reflect your values and passions. You are particularly interested in adding to collective community capital, however you may define it.

- You are consistent in how your moneys are invested to make sure that you are not supporting businesses that operate against your fundamental values. You encourage businesses to adopt ethical and responsible policies and practices.

- You work for or lead an organization that is, in all respects, ethical; supportive and respectful of others; fair; welcoming to diversity of gender and race; committed to policies that conserve, preserve, and protect the environment; and functioning at the highest level of corporate responsibility to all of its stakeholders.

- You live in a country, state, community, neighborhood that is fair and that honors, respects, and supports its diversity. Your community treats all of its citizens—especially those of color and those who are most disadvantaged—without discrimination in regard to housing, public safety, and education, and allocates its resources appropriately to support those policies.

- You take all this very seriously, and support others who do as well.

Now add up your score, and reflect on where you would like yourself and others to be. It may perhaps be even more interesting to think about this text, and then make up your own!

Section 1 Reflection

Questions for Individuals

- What does wealth mean to me?
- In what ways am I generous?
- Do I think of my giving as a creative process or as a duty or both? What would I like it to be?
- Do I think of giving as a search for meaning?
- In what areas of life am I a maker of gifts? Where is my greatest contribution? Where would I like it to be?
- What inspires me to be generous?
- What discourages or dampens my generosity?
- How does my current giving reflect that inspiration and/or those obstacles? Where would I like it to be more closely aligned?
- Do I believe in the things to which I am giving?
- What gifts are joyful for me?
- What is the story I want to write about my philanthropy? How might it be told twenty years from now?

Questions for Families

- What is our family's definition of "wealth with responsibility"? How do our passions and values drive that definition? What guiding principles would help us be true to ourselves?

- What public persona do we have today, and what do we wish to present to the outside world in the future? Being anonymous and invisible is not an option in our web-based environment where information is easily accessed, so how do we become more intentional in communicating that public persona?
- How do we, as a family and as individuals, truly engage in the broader world? What does engagement mean regarding time, talent, experience, contacts, networks, and financial resources?
- What are the bridges between our isolation, our privilege, and others who do not have those resources?
- What role does strategic philanthropy play for us, and how do we develop the competence and governance for a great philanthropy?
- A family's investment philosophy and policy can also be a bridge. How do we integrate our values and principles into a comprehensive investment philosophy and policy?
- How expansive a role does impact investing play? Where are the lines between socially responsible investing and traditional philanthropy?
- How can we engage the rising generations in developing our family's guiding principles about wealth and social responsibility?
- How do we prepare and educate family members around these questions? How do we manage the guilt syndrome or the feeling of being somehow different, and the fear of being a target?
- Are there issues and dynamics within our family that might surface as we practice giving together? What are they and how might we address them?
- How can we make philanthropy joyful and fun for family members?
- How do we measure and evaluate progress and results on the above?

A HIERARCHY OF BLESSINGS

The blessing of being a seeker
Metamotivation strives within

The blessing of individuation
Oh conscious unconscious be whole

The blessing of knowing each other
When I and thou become complete

The blessing of selective memory
You forget what you have forgotten

The blessing of God's presence
She is defrocked and disruptive

The blessing of silent sacred places
All you hear is the vibration of the soul

The blessing of community
The sacred shining city on a hill

The blessing of doing the work
Dive deep your whole self in

The blessing of hope the great gift
Of being able to give

Final blessing is the first blessing
Our love our love of our family
Of the bitter-sweet world

SECTION 2:

EMBARKING

The philanthropic journey is part experiential, part intuitive, part spiritual. As that experience evolves, the hope is we grow and learn. The hope is that we become more fulfilled. The hope is that we have in fact made a difference.

The work calls for growing our souls while we seek to transform society.

PETER KAROFF

The pieces in this section are about something Peter revered: reflective practice. They are intended to provision you with food for thought as you set off on your philanthropic journey; as you strive to, in Peter's grand words, achieve your philanthropic destiny. They are also intended to help you remember to pause, to look back on where you've been, and to gather energy to move forward.

Save, perhaps, the refugee's sudden flight, every journey starts with dreaming, planning, choosing one's vessel and navigational instruments, and packing. But—and this is also true for human development—the trip seldom goes as planned. We often start with a rough idea of where we want to go, with the sketchiest of maps. We may make false starts and need to backtrack. As our confidence and knowledge of the terrain grows, we may grow bolder, and we will certainly encounter the topics covered in Section 3 called "Trouble."

Early in TPI's history, Peter and staff began to map the evolution they saw in many of their clients, with the thought that understanding philanthropy as a developmental process might comfort those struggling with their giving and encourage them to be aspirational.

Peter wanted clients to understand both that they were embarking on a unique journey, one with no clear road maps, and that there were stages that could be understood and noted. "The TPI Philanthropic Curve" outlines those stages. He understood that, like parenting a toddler, it can be comforting to read something that lets you know you are not alone in your voyage, that others have passed this way before.

"Translating Values into Practice" represents Peter's belief that all the dilemmas that challenge our values in life present themselves in philanthropy as well. Will we be true to those values in our giving? The answer, according to Peter, depends on whether we are open to "[working] on our own stuff," examining our biases, knowing what we don't know, and managing our egos.

"True Wind and Apparent Wind" is about navigating philanthropy through "disruptive headwinds." It is an extended metaphor in which Peter asserts that "the bottom line is you can't get there in a sailboat—there being anywhere—relying only on true wind," which, in his metaphor, is the "simple moral presumption of doing good." He argues that real navigation depends on "factoring in all kinds of complicated influences that hit you right in the face," and on identifying and steering around the moral hazards that threaten good work. As he says:

> The central tension—between philanthropy's true wind and apparent wind—is that philanthropy is private action in public space. It starts with what is most personal, and most private—our values and passions—and moves to a transaction, of money or time, that is enacted in public. This combination of a public and private persona is distinctly American.

In "Intersections for the Common Good," Peter extolls the beauty and necessity of the pause that every crossroads affords. "Intersections are way stations in our journey, as in the philanthropic journey," he said. It is about the importance of becoming a reflective practitioner, but it is also about the importance of intersectional organizations, ones that allow different constituencies to come together in a common cause. Written as a speech for the Greater Kansas City Community Foundation, it makes the case for community foundations as intersection builders, but many of its insights are applicable to individual donors and family foundations. Peter closes this piece with a vision of what open-source philanthropy—giving directed by both real and apparent wind—might look like.

In "The Fusion of Art and Science in Effective Philanthropy," Peter challenges the dominance of the management sciences in philanthropy, calling for balance and understanding of how processes of both measurement and judgment are critical to the work. He delves deeper into the idea of the reflective practitioner, outlining questions donors and trustees can use to periodically interrogate their work, their assumptions, and their values.

This section closes with reflection questions and an exercise called "Your Moral Compass," which was designed to help you articulate your values, influences, and vision for your giving.

The TPI Philanthropic Curve

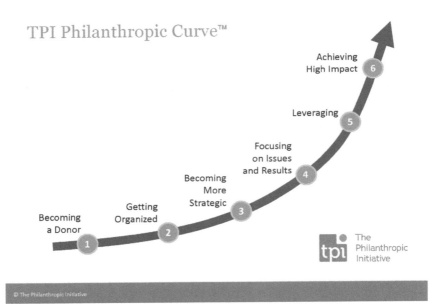

Level One: You Become a Donor

A complex combination of personal and religious values, family background, business and social pressures, ego, and heartfelt response to the world around you motivates you to become a donor. Giving becomes part of your way of life, your position in the community, your yearning to be a good person. Over time, giving becomes somewhat automatic, demands on you increase, and you are on *many* lists. Your gifts, with few exceptions, are distributed in small amounts to an increasing number of organizations. Sound familiar?

Level Two: You Decide to Get Organized

The goal is to get control of the giving process, instead of the process controlling you. You review what you have done over the last several years, and think about what gifts have given you the most satisfaction, and what really interests you. You decide to be less reactive to requests, learn how to say no, begin to determine priorities, develop criteria, and make fewer but larger gifts.

Level Three: You Become a Learner

You realize that you don't really know enough about the issues that interest you. You roll up your sleeves, do some research, visit your community foundation, talk to experts in the field and with other donors, make site visits to relevant organizations, and survey the literature.

If you cannot do all this, you hire someone to do it. Out of that process comes a clearer focus and a clearer understanding of the issue, and the organizations you support reflect that focus. You have now made a distinction between the gifts you must make and your real philanthropy.

Level Four: You Become Issue- and Results-Oriented

You want to maximize giving and increase the chances of making a difference. You are more concerned with results, with evaluation. You look harder at the underlying issues, and the ways your available resources can be best applied. You invest in the most talented nonprofit entrepreneurs. Gifts to organizations focus on building their capacity. You have become increasingly proactive and, rather than simply responding to requests, you go out, or have someone else go out, to search for and fund the best people and organizations.

Level Five: Your Philanthropy Is Leveraged

You develop and fund custom-designed programs that meet specific programmatic objectives. You collaborate with other donors and participate in public–private partnerships. You attempt to create models that can be replicated, and ones that will attract other private and public resources. You have become increasingly competent about the issues, about what works, and about what can really make a difference.

Level Six: Alignment, Engagement, Growth

Your values and interests are aligned. Your philanthropy is among the most exciting and satisfying things you do; it is a vehicle for community good and personal growth.

The truth is that each of these levels can satisfy the yearning we have to give. One's total giving is almost always a portfolio that accomplishes many goals, and thus is, by definition, multilevel. TPI does most of its work with those who want to move from one level to the next. Professionalizing, or making the process more sophisticated, doesn't take away from the joy and satisfaction of giving or change where you give. It simply reinforces the impact of those gifts and increases the chances that your gifts count. The objective is to help your individual philanthropy achieve its destiny.

Translating Values into Practice

Here I want to provide food for thought about the translation of values to the practice of values. In other words, how do you put into place guidelines to help you navigate situations where values are, in one way or another, at risk?

The articulation of values is an important step in the process of sorting out what we believe in, and it is not easy to do. Values are hard to get your arms around—the words that we use, such as *love, courage, gratitude, compassion, equity*, etc., are complex with many meanings and interpretations. They are truly thirty-thousand-foot words, and while useful as an overlay and context for a belief system, in and of themselves do not provide a practical guide for the way one acts or responds to the facts and circumstances of specific situations. And yet, values come into play all the time as we go through our day-to-day life.

Values drive the culture of the workplace, especially how we relate to our coworkers and those we market to or those we serve.

Values are foundational for families—how we treat our spouses or partners and, perhaps most important of all, the behavior and expectations a family has for and from their children. There is nothing more challenging than kids who constantly push at boundaries and test their parents. I remember a comment at a family meeting when the mother, frustrated by good arguments from her three daughters, said, "There's no protection from a smart daughter!" And as the father of three daughters, I can testify that is true!

Lastly, values form the basis for how a society is defined, and how it is governed. The platforms of both the Republican and Democratic parties, in preparation for their conventions, are replete with pronouncements of what the party stands for—in essence, what its values are (whether either party's actions actually reflect those values is an open question). On a local community and neighborhood level, values are in play and tested all the time.

Here are some stories from my own experience that are real-life examples of values in action:

Your sixteen-year-old daughter has been invited to a birthday party for a friend where beer will be served. You do not know the friend's parents but they will be at the house, presumably monitoring the consumption of beer. *Do you let your daughter go to the party?*

You are at a dinner party and one of the guests makes a series of anti-Semitic comments. You are Jewish. Only the hostess knows that, and she is sending you nonverbal signals to let the comments pass. *Do you say nothing, confront the guest, or just get up and leave?*

You are part of an ambitious effort to build five hundred units, on ten sites, of low-income housing in your city, and most of them are in the poorer parts of town. The project has become controversial. You are facilitating a community meeting at your children's middle school. It does not go well. Lots of raucous, racist, and angry discussion. When the meeting is finally over, two men you do not know come up to you and say: "We know who you are and where you live. Don't forget that." And they walk away. *Do you stay involved with the project, continuing to play a leadership role and facilitate open community meetings, or do you step back or even drop out?*

You are president of the state mental health association. The association has thirty-seven chapters around the state. One of its major programs is an excellent health insurance plan that is very important to the local chapters. The long-term executive director asks to meet with you in private and informs you the health plan has a $3 million deficit and unless that is made up will go bankrupt, which could put in jeopardy the association itself. The deficit has been building for several years.

No one else in the organization, including the board, knows about the problem. The ED asks you to not tell anyone as he thinks he has a way to cover the deficit, and if he succeeds no one else needs to know. *Do you wait and see if the ED can resolve the issue, agree that if the issue is resolved no one needs to know, or call an urgent meeting of the board?*

My response to these situations varied. For some I was true to my values and for others less so, but in every instance I grew and learned. If there was a principal lesson, it was how frequently these kinds of situations are nuanced and not straightforward.

I first encountered this in 1968, when Dr. Martin Luther King Jr. was assassinated and, along with others, I formed an organization (FUND) that partnered with the Boston Black United Front to raise money and consciousness about racism in our community. FUND raised $3 million over a three-year period with a unique fundraising approach. We held 7 a.m. breakfasts all over Greater Boston. Our message was radical for its time when the terms *Black Power*, *racial justice*, *prejudice*, and *equity* were not in the air, and were certainly not a subject for kitchen tables of newly remodeled suburban kitchens. Those were extraordinary sessions and FUND did more than one hundred and fifty, of which I facilitated about forty. What I, and my colleagues, finally learned to do was to present these concepts and our pitch in ways that were true to the underlying values, but did not scare the hell out of those around the table.

We also learned something else that many organizations do not understand. The first thing we as a board needed to do was to "work on our own stuff." We had to do a deep dive into why we were on this mission and whether our motivations were grounded and authentic.

In the process, we learned a lot about ourselves, which deepened our commitment to a thoughtful group process and our ability to have meaningful conversations that benefited the organization.

True Wind and Apparent Wind

From a 2010 speech to the Santa Barbara Yacht Club

"Moral Dimensions: True Wind and Apparent Wind in Philanthropy" is a risky title for a talk in any room, but especially so in a room full of sailors. It is risky because every time you build a case on a metaphor, and that is what I am going to do, it is a little like the problem of the hammer and the nail—if the only tool you have is a hammer, then everything looks like a nail. That said, I love metaphors, so please bear with me.

The title is risky because the term *moral dimensions* is politically and ideologically charged and, outside of church and temple, not in everyday use—and certainly not at a yacht club forum lunch. It is also risky because the difference between true wind and apparent wind, while on one level very simple, "continues to mystify many people who have been sailing for years," according to Steve Colgate, a noted sailor and writer.[1] Lastly, the title is risky because philanthropy—a very big word indeed—means different things to different people.

So let's begin with some definitions. And all you sailors please listen closely to see if I get this part right.

Apparent wind is the actual flow of air upon a sail. It is the wind as it appears to a sailor on a moving vessel. It differs in speed and direction from true wind that is experienced by a stationary observer.

Colgate states that apparent wind "is the combination of two winds: the one derived by the boat moving through the air and the wind produced by nature—the true wind."[2]

Colgate gives the example of standing in a convertible. "It is a calm day, so there's no true wind. As the convertible starts forward, you will begin to feel a breeze on your face that increases as the speed of the car increases ... This is apparent wind. Now imagine yourself in the same car heading north and there's an easterly wind of 10 mph blowing. This nature-produced wind from the east is what we call *true wind*. It is hitting the right side of your face. As the car starts forward you will not feel two different winds, one on the side and one on the front of your face, but a resultant wind coming from an angle forward of the true wind. What you feel is the apparent wind."[3]

Sailors need to calculate apparent wind in order to determine the best point of sail, especially in racing. Modern instrumentation—transducer, anemometer, and wind vane—help make these calculations, but in practice they are very complex.

The bottom line is you can't get there in a sailboat—there being anywhere—relying only on true wind.

Before I get into more trouble with those whose navigation skills are way beyond mine, here is my case right up front: True wind in philanthropy is based on the simple moral presumption of doing good, but the reality is you really can't get there, you cannot accomplish your noble goals, without factoring in all kinds of complicated influences that hit you right in the face. Some of these influences are within us; some influences lie shrouded in fog on the course we have chosen to take; some are a direct result of how we give, the very process and attitude we choose; and some represent pushback from the communities and recipients of our philanthropy.

The apparent wind of philanthropy is a combination of our good intentions and the unexpected/unintended consequences of our actions. It is what we experience. You cannot separate the two. Unlike sailing, we do not have instrumentation to help us stay the course. We are dependent on our moral compass, and our common sense. Sometimes, that moral compass gets lost. And sometimes we check our common sense at the door.

Everyone has a moral compass whether we call it that or not. Michael Gazzaniga at the University of California, Santa Barbara (UCSB), has done research that proves our brain has an "interpreter" with a moral dimension—an instinctive sense of right and wrong—and that we are essentially wired to know the difference.[4]

Society is hugely divided on what constitutes right moral action on a whole range of issues and we, as poor mortals, are conflicted as well. What is a true moral position or action to me may not be at all true to you. The question of "whose morality?" looms large.

There is great debate as to whether there are universal moral truths. The philosopher Kant believed that moral action becomes true only if it can be universalized beyond what you or I think.

All moral considerations begin with our obligation to others, and moral struggles typically demand that we resist favoring ourselves to the exclusion of others. That is especially relevant to a donor with strong views of how things should be done.

Moral compass is based on moral imagination—the best definition of which I have seen comes from Robert Wright, in his book *The Evolution of God*: "Moral imagination is the capacity to put ourselves in someone else's shoes." And empathy on that level is exactly what defines philanthropy.[5]

In sailing, there is no value differential between true wind and that generated by the forward movement of a vessel—they just are what they are, while in philanthropy moral judgments and opinions are all over the place.

I believe that the true wind of philanthropy lies in civic virtue, in deeply held convictions. The word *philanthropy* is based on the Greek word *philo*, the root meaning of which is *a strong affinity for love*. To be philanthropic is to express that love through your means—money, time, and your self.

In practice, that is what we do when we make a gift to help someone in need, or support the work of theater and the arts, or enable kids to learn how to sail who would otherwise not have that great fun and joy.

Charity is the basis for philanthropy. Charity comes out of our heart. It is the emotional response to the needs of the community and world in which we live, and it is a central aspect of the spiritual journey in every major religion. American philanthropy, as distinct from charity, has always been a combination of the heart and mind in "the search for the best in people, their organizations, and the [relevant] world around them."[6]

The central tension—between philanthropy's true wind and apparent wind—is that philanthropy is private action in public space. It starts with what is most personal, and most private—our values and passions—and moves to a transaction, of money or time, that is enacted in public. This combination of a public and private persona is distinctly American. The opening lines to the first poem in Walt Whitman's "One's-Self I Sing" from *Leaves of Grass* express it perfectly.

> One's-Self I sing, a single separate person,
> Yet utter the word Democratic, the word En-Masse.[7]

That "separate person" is the American citizen-actor we so yearn to be—confident, independent, entrepreneurial—a Californian in all respects and probably a sailor, too, yet deeply concerned and committed to community. When that kind of person turns to philanthropy, the resulting disruption is very dynamic.

Let me ask this question, because it bears on all these themes: Why do you think some people are generous and some with the same capacity, or even more, are not?

The Center on Philanthropy at Indiana University found that the most important motivations for charitable giving by high-net-worth households were meeting critical needs and giving back to society, both of which have true moral dimensions and social reciprocity, which is quite different (i.e., if you support my cause, I will support yours).[8] A recent article in *The Economist* cites a study that found that donors "do good because it makes them look good to those whose opinions they care about" (i.e., image motivation).[9]

None of this is a surprise. The reality is that many successful fundraising efforts are based as much on ego gratification and recognition as on programmatic impact. Motivation is never entirely pure, but that is the human condition.

Today's donors are intentional, have focus, and demand measurable results. Donors want to not only feel good about their philanthropy, but they want proof they have made a difference.

They are cautious, however, about highly analytic strategic philanthropy. One concern is that donors can be too controlling. There is also a concern that overreliance on data and measurable results makes donors less likely to take actions that are hard to measure, and thus, more risk averse.

When we get caught up in too much process, it is easy to lose sight of the moral questions. Who to serve and who not to serve? How to stand up and be counted when it is important to do so? When relevance becomes a servant to rigor, we lose our way.

This new kind of engaged donor can find themselves at the center of lots of disruptive headwinds. Sunday's *New York Times* had a big article about the troubles at the Aspen Music Festival, where activist donor–board members have clashed with the artistic director and the musicians—very painful for all concerned and terrible press for a distinguished organization.

When we get caught up in those kinds of things, and anyone who has been on enough nonprofit boards has had variations of that kind of experience, we easily forget the noble reasons we are on those boards.

In the '80s I was president of the board of the Massachusetts Association of Mental Health. It was during a time of great upheaval: deinstitutionalization, the closing of the big hospitals, and the beginning of the community mental health system. At one of those endless board meetings, late, late at night, the board was having a huge, loud argument. All of a sudden, one of the members—the dean of the school of social work at Simmons University—pounded on the table and said,

"Hold it, this is not good for our mental health!" It brought us back to why were in the boardroom to begin with.

One of my friends loves to say, "No good deed goes unpunished." And he has lots of examples.

A very wealthy man in Madison, Wisconsin, saw the need for a new arts center, optioned what he felt was a perfect downtown location, and immediately hit a storm of objections ranging from project scale, traffic, design, and resistance from other arts organizations. After a year or more of bitter wrangling, the donor was quoted in the press as saying, "I'm going to give $100 million to Madison for a new arts center whether it wants it or not!"

A little bit of hubris? Sure, but what happened in Madison—and, by the way, the arts center was finally built and is a huge success—happens all the time in every community.

You are an advocate for more low-income housing, or supportive housing for the homeless, or a day care center for children, or a youth center to help combat gang violence—all perfectly well-intentioned and needed projects that no one argues against, except for NIMBY, not in my back yard. It is always a moment of truth for a donor; do you stand up and be counted when powerful headwinds make it very tough to do so?

There are also broader societal tensions. Frank Karel, a wise observer of philanthropy who worked for both the Robert Wood Johnson Foundation and the Rockefeller Foundation, expressed it this way: "Philanthropy does not rest easily on the bosom of the American society."

It was true when John D. Rockefeller wanted to establish the first foundation in America and was met by fierce resistance from a skeptical Congress who did not trust this robber baron's motivation. It is part of the American love–hate relationship with wealth that has only intensified with the troubling, growing gap between the rich and the poor.

Bill Gates, Melinda French Gates, and Warren Buffett have issued a challenge to billionaires in particular, and the wealthy in general, to give away at least half of their wealth. If all those on the *Forbes* 400 did so, it would amount to $700 billion.[10] As a point of reference, Americans last year gave $300 billion to charity. As someone who has spent twenty-plus years working to promote philanthropy, this high-profile push for more giving is very exciting. You can go to the Giving Pledge website (www.givingpledge.org) and see statements from forty billionaires who have taken "the pledge," and I am pleased to say that some of TPI's clients are among them. Yet the reactions in the field and in the press have been mixed.[11]

From a practical perspective, there is a concern that the nonprofit delivery system doesn't have the capacity to handle that kind of increase. There is a bigger concern that concentrations of philanthropic dollars in the hands of a small number of individuals, no matter how smart or how well motivated, will overly influence the social agenda—a kind of "big box" philanthropy—without transparency and public input. That concern is fueled by the larger question of exactly what the American society gets in return for the tax advantages that the charitable sector enjoys? Specifically, the billions in charitable income tax deductions is that much less for the government. There have already been reversals in many parts of the country on the real estate tax exemption for nonprofit organizations—something that is just assumed.

There is more of that kind of pressure on philanthropy to come, including a sorting out of what role philanthropy should play, what role government should play, and what role the market economy could play in the resolution of social dilemmas.

All of this ups the ante for philanthropy to avoid what are called *moral hazards*—the term economists use for decisions/actions with good intentions but that go off course and hit the rocks. In my view, the biggest moral hazard for philanthropy is when it breaks the golden rule to "do no harm."

The Rockefeller Foundation in the '70s funded a large-scale DDT effort in Africa to fight malaria. The result was devastating environmentally. One unintended consequence was the elimination of cats and other natural enemies of rats, whose numbers dramatically increased. It took years to reverse those problems.

John D. Rockefeller set the standard for wise philanthropy in many ways, and intuitively understood this concept. One great story was when Dr. Bill and Dr. Bob, the founders of Alcoholics Anonymous (AA) came to see the then-richest man in America to ask for support for their fledgling organization. Mr. Rockefeller listened to them, and a week later invited the two men back, so they were very, very hopeful. But what Mr. Rockefeller had decided was to not make a grant. AA, then and now, was based on peer-to-peer support and spiritually based self-realization. That is its essence and he wisely understood that turning it into a typical, nonprofit, professionally staffed organization would destroy it. He was proven right and his non-gift was the greatest gift he could have given.

I have a good friend, and TPI client, who has a favorite saying: "The best way to kill a good idea is to try to improve it"—a soft kind of criticism of too much analysis, of too much donor intrusion in the operations of nonprofit organizations.

Sometimes, the wind can get pretty rough at sea, and the same is true in philanthropy.

The Annie E. Casey Foundation, a national foundation that is based in Baltimore, is remarkable in many ways. It has focused on persistent poverty and poor families for many years, which are what one of my colleagues calls the "wicked issues." Their early efforts to mount programs in cities across the country were abject failures. The foundation was perceived as arrogant, not having done local homework, and promoting programs that were counterproductive. Perhaps even more remarkable, the foundation admitted its failure, published the lessons learned, and relaunched their national work with families and children that has become a model for the rest of the field.

Failure is almost never discussed by foundations. Several years ago, I had the opportunity to give a talk to the Gates Foundation staff entitled

"Catechism for a Great Foundation." The question-and-answer period was led by Patty Stonesifer, then–Gates Foundation president. She had one question: How do you deal with failure? Almost all their major programs, on global disease prevention and on public school reform, had run into unexpected roadblocks. Here is the largest private foundation in the world, with access to the smartest experts in the world, coming up short in its ambitious and noble efforts. That social change is incremental at best is a lesson every donor learns,[12] but I was impressed with the humility, self-awareness, and openness of the discussion—something that is not normative in the field and needs to be.

According to Independent Sector and the Foundation Center, in 2002 only 11 percent of philanthropy in the United States went to poverty or social justice issues, and the percentages are even less globally.[13] The impact of the recession globally is huge—one out of seven people on the earth suffers from pervasive hunger, an increase in the past year of one hundred million people![14]

Here are a few ideas of how to navigate philanthropy's apparent wind and be a great donor:

- Integrity of the philanthropic process begins when we become a listener and a learner about others who are different, about the issues, about what works and what doesn't. Great donors learn how to listen deeply to the community.

- Great donors believe that integrity of purpose for any social action is based on one simple condition: "If it isn't good for the community, and only good for the donor, it isn't worth doing."[15] Anyone who doesn't understand that runs the risk of having a chair thrown at them someday. Sometimes that chair is literal, sometimes it is mud on your face, and sometimes it is because you have broken the rule to "do no harm."

- Leadership matters. It matters across cultures, it matters across time, and it matters greatly. Virtually all lasting significant social change comes from leaders working in intersecting networks of influence. Great donors work hard at identifying and supporting leadership.

- Great donors focus on more than problem-solving and investment return. They make the time—as hard as that is—for reflection and scenario-planning on the long-term reality of what will take, in most cases, decades to accomplish.

- Great donors, irrespective of size, resist their core bureaucracy, remain nimble, and bring energy into a room, as opposed to taking it out.

- Great donors do more than ask the tough questions; they really want honest answers, even if those answers counter and disrupt the very assumptions the donor holds.

And lastly, the heart and soul of great philanthropy flows from our values and passions. The work calls for growing our souls while we seek to transform society.

I believe those dictums are true, and also this one: "When all is said and done the only change that will make a difference is the transformation of the human heart."[16]

The practical visionaries I interviewed for my book *The World We Want* got it right. Here is what they said:

- Acknowledge that people know what they need. Help individuals find their own power and take control of their own destiny.

- Seek out the assets that every community has, build on them, and celebrate. Make heroes of those who do this work.

- Find the alignment between self-interest and the common good. When there is none, push back and stand firm.

- Break out of the box. Use all available resources and innovation from every sector—business, citizen, government, nonprofit—to get the work done.

- Do whatever it takes—disruption, confrontation, jujitsu, logic, data, advocacy, and traveling the parallel tracks. The tactics and strategies are endless.
- Abandon comfort. Raise the bar. Put your whole self in and hold the moral conscience of your community dear.
- Open it up; open yourself up. Provide building blocks for others to make their own dreams come true.
- To truly love, you must touch.[17]

All of these put together make up the point of view of the ethical and moral relationship we seek.

Let me end with these wise words from the Tao Te Ching.

> The Tao of Leadership:
> Go to the people
> Live among them
> Learn from them
> Start with what they know
> Build on what they have
>
> But for the best leaders
> When their task is accomplished
> Their work is done
> The people will all remark
> We have done it ourselves.[18]

Intersections for the Common Good

These comments have three themes: intersections, social dilemmas, and what I call *open-source philanthropy*.

So much of what happens in life is at the intersection, the place where things come together, sometimes abruptly and sometimes in a stream. It is that moment of inspiring synthesis that has the potential to become sweet. That is the moment when the greater good, personally or as a society, is within reach. I think we in the United States need a pause right now. It would be a good thing if our society that is so divided could take the kind of time-out that seems to be so useful for my grandchildren. What we would love to have is that sweet moment in time—the space for miracles to happen.

Intersections are never isolated events, which is why Robert Frost, in his poem "The Road Not Taken," wrote, in addition to the line that is so well known, this one: "Yet knowing how way leads on to way."[19] Everything we do, or do not do, influences what comes next.

How one handles the intersections of life determines how some people end up at a dead end and how some people end up in a wonderful place, how a society moves forward or moves backward. Intersections are part of the connectivity of things, of the continuum of what is called *flow*. Intersections are way stations in our journey, as in the philanthropic journey.

The philanthropic journey is part experiential, part intuitive, part spiritual. As that experience evolves, the hope is that we grow and learn. The hope is that we become more fulfilled. The hope is that we have, in fact, made a difference. We gravitate, without even realizing it, to others who have similar objectives in the same way all of you are here this evening. It is part of the flow.

The Greater Kansas City Community Foundation has become a place where the intersections that punctuate the philanthropic journey are held up under a bright prism of light. The Foundation, and the recipient communities with which it works, ponder, dissect, worry, dream, create, plan, and—often with great trepidation—act in what they hope is the public interest. It is part of the network for good that is everywhere, but especially here in Kansas City, because this organization has become quite special. It has made immense progress since I last visited. Why do I say that?

Community foundations are in the community organizing business. The best of them take the lessons of Saul Alinsky and work them to ambitious goals that have potential to be transformational. Community foundations are a stunning idea that are only at the beginning of their potential growth and influence based on two kinds of capital: financial and intellectual. Of the two, it is the intellectual capital that is by far more important. That capital is made up of knowledge and understanding of the major social issues facing a community, the mapping and evaluation of the strengths and weaknesses of the nonprofit infrastructure of the community, and the understanding of the roles of government and the market economy on the issues the Foundation wants to address. The fundamental question becomes what role can philanthropy play in addressing those issues? It is the question every donor asks.

For most community foundations, intellectual capital is poorly developed. The imperative to fundraise dominates the situation and, even if it doesn't, asset growth, which is easy to count, is very seductive to boards and staff. Kansas City is in a unique position because the Foundation has a growing amount of intellectual capital available.

The Foundation's Impact 2014 document entitled "Community Leadership Area Grantmaking" is a great template around which to develop a strategic philanthropic action plan. Combined with the Donor Edge software, the Foundation has both the information and the tools. It is as good as any I have seen anywhere in the country.

The question becomes what are Kansas City donors and would-be donors going to do with that information?

The Philanthropic Initiative (TPI) has worked in this space for many years. We have learned that the adrenaline really gets going when a donor goes to the next level of knowledge and understanding, the next level of strategic thinking, the next level of innovation and creativity, the next level of impact, and most importantly—without which one is on the wrong track—the next level of attitude that respects, empowers, listens to, and meaningfully engages the community.

We have learned that the best philanthropic work comes when research on issues like racial equity, community development, health and life sciences, children and youth, and arts and culture provide donors with the context and direction for their philanthropy.

We have learned that the best work is at the intersections of ambitious vision, informed by change from the bottom up, combined with leadership from the top that utilizes outside catalysts for change. Where the introduction of new ideas leads to strategies that create visibility and welcome broad public support, and which ends in building the widest possible coalition to sustain the effort.

The best philanthropic work is when someone or some family realizes a lifelong dream. The best of this work is when a family finds the intersection between their values and passions and the community. The best of this work is when a corporation finds a meaningful intersection between its objectives as a business and a critical social issue.

In these intersections, a smart community foundation becomes a powerful philanthropic tipping point and that has become the case in the Kansas City region.

Philanthropy is private action in public space which in and of itself is a social dilemma. Social dilemmas are defined as the problem of the one and the many. The dilemma arises when individual rational behavior leads to a situation where everyone is worse, not better, off.

For philanthropy, it poses this question: In an increasingly political and media-intensive world, what governance, accountability, transparency, attitude, and action are appropriate and right for charitable organizations, individual donors, and private foundations?

Social dilemmas are fundamentally tensions between cooperation and competition, and the choices that must be made at every turn. One famous social dilemma is "the tragedy of the commons"—when a common grazing area is overgrazed by farmers who show no restraint, or when fishermen deplete the stocks so no one can fish, or when someone pushes their beliefs too far and does not accommodate others.

In 1950, the RAND Corporation created a game called the Prisoner's Dilemma that pits one prisoner's self-interest against another. If both prisoners rat on each other, they both go to jail. If only one rats, then the other goes to jail. If neither tells on the other, they both go free.

We face variations of social dilemmas and the Prisoner's Dilemma all the time. Funding vaccine treatment for measles means that funding for something else, the AIDS vaccine, for example, may not be available. As a result, the community with measles and the community with AIDS compete against one another.

The Greater Kansas City Community Foundation faced a social dilemma when it decided to focus its work on five big issues in the community—racial equity, community development, health and life sciences, children and youth, and arts and culture—out of a much longer list. That was not an easy decision and it took courage to make it. Every donor faces similar issues. Each action one takes forecloses other actions. The process is an ongoing negotiation between and among the many alternative ideas on the table. Once focus is established, the negotiation shifts to one of implementation, how to concretize the idea, establish realizable goals, determine the best strategies, and then how to measure and evaluate the results.

What is interesting and new is that in many domains the old model of competitiveness, the survival of the fittest, is "being replaced by new models of collaboration."[20] The growing movement of "cooperative studies" is based on the evidence that cooperative arrangements, interdependencies, and collective action in biology, sociology, commerce, and society are changing the world. The economics of peer production, of collective action, especially the power of distributed computing, have radically shifted the equation. The big example, of course, is the World Wide Web, which is owned by no one but has provided the platform for this immense amount of economic development and wealth creation, and is changing the way we live. The proliferation of blogs, of web-based political and community organizing, are what many people believe is a new wave of democratization—but that also holds the potential to damage democracy.

Especially promising to me is the explosion of open-source technology, which no one owns but everybody can use, of which Linux is the earliest, best-known adaptation. Those of you who work in technology live in a world where your biggest competitor today may become your strongest ally tomorrow. Technology has learned that to yield is more profitable than to resist.

I think there is an equally burgeoning movement toward what I call *open-source philanthropy*. It is in the design of more effective systems of collective social action, with less segmentation of issues and more holistic ways of solving problems. It can best be seen in the increased focus on collaboration as the most powerful and leveraged means for the resolution of social issues. It can also be seen in new attempts to look at whole-system partnerships that have the potential to change the paradigm of social action. I am part of two such efforts, one that is looking at sustainable food production and another that has the goal of eliminating child malnutrition in two provinces in India. These are huge ambitions whose moment in time has come, but are they any different than what you want for your community and what we all want for our country?

Open-source philanthropy funds efforts that bridge rather than divide, that bring more dialogue into situations that are in conflict, that cross silos and support attempts to bring those who are unlike each other "into meaningful work and experience together, and encourage and nurture increased collaborations among competing organizations doing the same."[21]

Giving and learning circles are an example of an open-source approach to philanthropy, and they are popping up everywhere. Social Venture Partners, where younger and newer donors make $5,000 annual commitments that go into a pool for community-giving, is now in twenty-four cities. Giving circles come in all sizes—fourteen families in Boston invested $11 million in a pool to work on a few big social issues in that city. In many ways, the Greater Kansas City Community Foundation is itself a variation of a large and complex giving circle.

This represents a big change for donors. It is a trend that pushes against the fierce individualism that has been the trademark of American philanthropy. It is a classical social dilemma. Is the donor willing to trade the opportunity to do something unilaterally for the greater potential that would come out of a collaborative action? It is not a new question in the American experience; witness the opening lines of the first poem in Walt Whitman's great book of poetry *Leaves of Grass*:

> One's-Self I sing, a single separate person,
> Yet utter the word Democratic, the word En-masse.[22]

No community foundation in America has been more successful in attracting donor-advised funds than Kansas City. But if all eight hundred donor-advised funds do their own thing, and this aggregation of significant philanthropic capacity fails to address the critical community issues facing the region, the net impact on the fabric of life here will be less. The challenge, and the opportunity, is to make a compelling case, through research and education, that those needs deserve attention.

An open-source philanthropic mission is one that is developed from a 360° perspective. A 360° mission would distinguish organizational self-interest from the public interest. A 360° mission would have less emphasis on what "I"—the foundation, donor, nonprofit organization—want to do, and more emphasis on the broadest possible interpretation of the issue for the people being served, on what works for the community. A 360° review of mission and operating procedures would ask these questions:

- Have we carefully thought through the implications of our actions on others, including possible unintended consequences?
- Do we avoid simplistic solutions to complex problems, issues, and social systems?
- Are there opposing views to what we want to do? Is there merit in that resistance?
- Are we respectful and sensitive to other cultures and beliefs different from our own?
- Are we sufficiently on guard against hubris and excessive personal and organizational ambitions?
- Are we absolutely committed to integrity, and to avoiding conflicts of interest, including between the personal and family relationships of both board and staff?

And overarching all is this question: Is our mission the right one, and are we true to it? I think trust is earned when we address the "imperatives," those critical issues in our society about which we are and should be passionate. That is where philanthropy comes alive. This is open-source philanthropy.

Let me ask this question: What do you think is the biggest social dilemma we face as a society?

Here is my answer: It is my fear that a society as deeply divided as ours will not face and resolve the serious domestic and global issues that challenge us. My fear is that we have created a huge, contemporary version of a tragedy of the commons. In the pursuit of what we individually believe is right and wrong, we run the risk we will be left with less than what we started with.

American philanthropy's values have always been based on the commons, on concepts of mutuality, on inclusion, on access, on opportunity, on the making of level playing fields. American philanthropy is based on the great rhetoric of America. It is why philanthropy is positioned to be a powerful articulation of citizen voice, one that gives form and clarity to the issues that engender our confusion.

For philanthropy to be the kind of leader that I think our society badly needs, it must begin with addressing the important questions around governance, accountability, standards, principles, and transparency. It will help us earn trust in what we do, but it is at our greater peril if we ignore other questions that make up the intersections between our rhetoric and our action.

These are some of the questions I began to address in my book *The World We Want*:

- In a vision for a better world, what are the conditions needed to realize that vision? What are the obstacles? What parts are realistic? And what ideas, strategies, and actions can make it so?

- Is there hope in the yearning so many Americans have expressed for something more out of life—call it values, faith, spirituality, or community—and the potential for reaching common ground across the huge ethnic, racial, and ideological divides in our society?

- Has the American culture of materialism, greed, and self-referential behavior become so pervasive that we are numb and indifferent to inequity, injustice, and issues like persistent poverty?

- Does philanthropy, as it is being practiced in America today, actually hinder the development of an advanced and progressive society in which everybody benefits?
- How much of philanthropy is self-referential, motivated by self-improvement and personal salvation, thus really benefiting the giver more than anyone else?

Some questions are the "stick," and they force us to think. I think we need the answers much more for ourselves than for others. There are other questions for philanthropy that are closer to the "carrot," such as these:

- What really makes philanthropy special? What draws us in *and* what could draw others in?
- What does this incredibly rich and idiosyncratic field, this pluralistic, philanthropic universe, this third sector, mean in today's world?
- We mess around and think creatively, but so what? Are we working around the edges of issues? Why are we not outraged more often?
- How do we turn powerful visions into practical strategies for leadership, and even transformation?
- How do we learn to think beyond money, services, and programs and to the convening and organizing of communities of interest?
- How do we keep from falling in love with the rhetoric of our own importance? Or put another way, how do we transcend personal ego?
- How do we believe more in ourselves? How do we resurrect the value of maturity and wisdom?

I do know what would resolve the tragedy of the commons:

- A society that has enough common sense to understand (and bravery to admit) that good will and building bridges are neither naïve nor dangerous.

- A "we" that represents a broad and open public purpose and supports a citizen-driven process that inhabits the public commons and that has the humility to fund the structures of an open society.

- Philanthropy dedicated to the promotion of citizenship and civic values, and to the education of society, especially the young.

- A philanthropic sector willing to roll up its sleeves and seriously address the critical issues in America and around the world—especially poverty, but others as well.

This is what I mean by open-source philanthropy.

The Fusion of Art and Science in Effective Philanthropy

What is going on here?

The theologian H. Richard Niebuhr famously wrote about this concept, saying: "We are 'answerers' who must first ask—what is going on here?"[23] Niebuhr believed this to be the central question of human existence. We want to know whether what we do means anything, and if that is true generally in life, it is certainly true in philanthropy.

For many good and proper reasons there is, within the field, a strong focus on results, on impact, and on what overall has been termed *effectiveness*. At the same time, there is concern that an over-reliance on data, metrics, and evaluation is somehow in opposition to a mission-centered approach to philanthropy. Terms like *hyperrationalism* and *managerialism* seem counter to creativity and may potentially inhibit risk-taking. We aspire to certainty, but there are many nuanced influences on effectiveness that are difficult to capture, and that are sometimes elusive. The effectiveness movement is not new. It goes back to the early days of American philanthropy when the Rockefeller Foundation, the Carnegie Foundation, and the Commonwealth Foundation began to practice what was then called "the scientific method of philanthropy," defined as follows:

1. Getting the facts right by research and/or surveys;

2. Identifying the problem clearly and precisely;

3. Studying a number of potential options for action;

4. Identifying those whose help would be needed or whose opposition must be neutralized in order to achieve the objective, and only then:

5. Developing a plan of action that includes a clearly defined objective, benchmarks of progress, and methods of gathering data to evaluate accomplishments.[24]

If that sounds familiar, and I'm sure it does, it is because these are the identical elements of strategic philanthropy and all of its cousins that continue to build upon the concept—high-impact philanthropy, venture philanthropy, social entrepreneurship, philanthrocapitalism, and other made-up phrases like "collective philanthropy" that encompass these central ideas. Why this got lost over the last ninety years, if it did, and had to be reborn again, is not clear. Nonetheless, we are drawn to anything that can help us figure out "what is going on."

It is science that is associated with certainty, and art that is associated with softness and disruption. It is a fundamental left-brain (logical, analytical, and objective) and right-brain (intuitive, holistic, and subjective) differentiation.

The resulting tensions between the terms *art* and *science* of philanthropy have created a false dichotomy that pits two domains against each other when they are, in reality, complementary. When this dichotomy is taken apart from the perspective of the goals and practice of philanthropy, it becomes evident that the terms *art* and *science* have more in common than is generally understood, and that making the differentiation clear, determining how each adds value, and measuring accordingly can greatly enhance and expand our understanding of effectiveness.

It is hard to know what is going on.

Leslie Pine and I are meeting on Thursday with the trustees of a long-term foundation client to try to wrestle to the ground exactly what the role of evaluation is in their giving portfolio. In preparation for that meeting, Leslie wrote the following:

There is no denying that the types of goals and strategies supported by many foundations can be extraordinarily difficult to evaluate. The resources needed to conduct rigorous evaluations can be significant, and the pitfalls and challenges to meaningful evaluation can be daunting. Below are just a few of the hurdles and challenges that arise in many situations.

- What is measurable is not always what is most important—and, in some cases, what is measured (perhaps because it is measurable) can influence outcomes to the detriment of the program.
- Determining causality can be difficult or impossible— a variety of external factors can influence grant outcomes.
- Change may occur over a very long time horizon— and the findings of shorter-term evaluations can be misleading.
- Getting honest feedback from grantees and others can be a real challenge for foundations.
- Foundations may feel committed to existing strategies and grantees, and can find it very difficult to approach evaluation work with a "beginner's mind" that challenges certain beliefs, assumptions, or loyalties.
- Limited time, attention, and resources are among the most commonly cited barriers to conducting evaluations and using results to reflect on foundation strategies.

These challenges are, in and of themselves, a reflection of those aspects of philanthropic work that we sense as true but cannot really measure. Hence the term *beginner's mind*.

What is the beginner's mind? Here is one slant—from the Buddhist master Nan Huai-Chin:

> We do not see the full process of coming into being of social action: we do not see its descending movement from thought and consciousness to language, interpretations, and relationships. We see what we do. We also form theories about how we do things. *But [we] are usually unaware of the place from which we operate when we act.*[25]

I think that this observation expresses what drives a lot of what we do in every sphere, but try selling it to an analytical, results-oriented donor or foundation executive!

So let's deconstruct a bit, and in so doing, acknowledge that it will be tough going to make a case for art because, as in all domains, there are assumptions of hierarchy, and there is no question that in philanthropy science is viewed as far stronger than art. The very existence and success of groups like Grantmakers for Effective Organizations and the steady stream of how-to books and articles on being a better grantmaker have helped drive a culture around the theme of scientific effectiveness. Even more to the point, this is what occupies our time in the work itself; it is all driven by the aim for results as we try to button things down and penetrate the mystery.

What Do We Mean by *Science*?

State of knowing; knowledge as distinguished from ignorance or misunderstanding. Knowledge or a system of knowledge covering general truths or the operation of general laws especially as obtained and tested through scientific method. Such knowledge or such a system of knowledge concerned with the physical world and its phenomena. A department of systematized knowledge as an object of study. Something (such as a sport or technique) that may be studied or learned like systematized knowledge. A system or method reconciling practical ends with scientific laws.[26]

Closer to the practice of philanthropy are the terms *management science* and *decision science*, which came out of a discipline that applies advanced analytical methods to help make better decisions. It is often considered to be a subfield of mathematics. The goal is to arrive at optimal or near-optimal solutions to complex decision-making problems that are often concerned with determining the maximum (of profit, performance, or yield) or minimum (of loss, risk, or cost) of some real-world objective.

Philanthropy has borrowed from these themes the utility of process standardization so that the work can be more easily measured and generate useful data.

What Do We Mean by *Art*?

Here is a passage from the poet Percy Bysshe Shelley that addresses both the challenge and the potential of those influences that come under the realm of art:

> For the mind in creation is as fading coals, which some invisible influence, like an inconstant wind, awakens to transitory brightness the power from within, like the colour of a flower which fades and changes as it is developed, and the conscious portions of our natures are unprophetic either of its approach or departure. Could this influence be durable in its original purity and force, it is impossible to predict the greatness of its result.[27]

I very much like these phrases—"purity and force" and "the greatness of its result"—because that is what all of us involved in philanthropy would like to see happen. At the same time, we want to be in control.

There is something reassuring in data and something disruptive in the kind of free flow that the Shelley quote implies is central to artistic endeavors. But the actual definition of art is far more concrete.

Art is skill acquired by experience, study, or observation. A branch of learning. An occupation requiring knowledge or skill. The conscious use of skill and creative imagination especially in the production of aesthetic objects.[28] Art is often described as "judgment-based work," "craft work," or "professional work."[29] None of this precludes evaluation and, in fact, art is measured and valued all the time based on agreed-upon criteria. Even when within the art there are elements that are mysterious—what the poet Rilke called the "unsayable"—those are acknowledged and valued as such.[30]

Some definitions cross over and apply equally to art and science. For example, a man of science is a man skilled or learned in any discipline, art, or craft. Interestingly, science was originally associated with the seven medieval "liberal arts": grammar, rhetoric, logic, arithmetic, geometry, music, and astronomy.

The Plot Thickens

What further complicates this discussion is philanthropy's unique DNA—a set of underlying principles and assumptions and abstract elements—which, while neither art nor science, fall more within the realm of art.

To begin with, TPI has long believed that philanthropy is fundamentally an articulation of values and passions, and we have witnessed how powerful it can be when those elements are joined with a strategic process, and how empty it can be if they are not.

Love of humankind is the root meaning of the word *philanthropy*. While some have tried to make a science of love, it doesn't quite work. There are other assumptions—words we use all the time in vision and mission statements such as *passion* and *compassion, inspiration, imagination, intuition, instincts*, and even *wisdom*.

Even more fundamental are the ethical and moral assumptions that are at the core of philanthropy. Yet, measuring the integrity of purpose and the integrity of process and practice is typically not part of what we evaluate.

I remember a poignant comment at a Philanthropy New York workshop some years ago, when a foundation program officer said, "We have all these great sounding words in our mission, but they have nothing to do with what I actually do every day." If we are subsumed by the sheer busyness of the work, and a dominant focus on the science of the work, we become distanced from the higher ground that brought us into philanthropy in the first place.

Exploring the Dichotomy

Helpful in looking at this dichotomy is the influential work of Donald Schon, who was at MIT for many years (and was also a West Newton neighbor of mine). Schon had remarkable influence on the theory of learning—naming for the first time the "learning society" that we have become—and also on practitioners who are "reflective in action" where the work is "susceptible to a kind of rigor that is both like and unlike the rigor of scholarly work and controlled experimentation."

Schon argued that for the reflective practitioner "the knowledge inherent in practice is to be understood as artful doing." Schon warned against a practice where "relevance is subject to rigor." Process should be a servant to principles, not the other way around. Schon called this process of reflection in action "thinking on our feet," and believed that it provides a "double loop" form of learning. In practice, it helps avoid major problems because we never have a full understanding of things before we act, and learning while we do is the essence of what has become knowledge management.[31]

When Should a Process Be Art, Not Science?

In an article in the *Harvard Business Review*, written by Joseph Hall and Eric Johnson, entitled, "When Should a Process Be Art, Not Science?" the authors make the case that the movement to standardize processes has gone overboard. Some processes require an artist's judgment and artistic process cannot be rigidly controlled and should be managed accordingly.[32]

The conditions of artistic process exist where "inputs" and "outputs" to the process are variable, and where variations in outcomes are natural, and viewed by customers as a good thing. Hall and Johnson say, "Art is needed in changeable environments ... when raw materials aren't uniform and therefore require a craftsperson's adjustments and when customers value distinctive or unique output..."[33] An example is Steinway, where no piece of wood is the same and each piano's soundboard is distinctive, and fine-tuned to the exact specification of the buyer, in this case the concert pianist.

Another example, far removed from music, are MinuteClinics that operate hundreds of walk-in medical offices. Care is provided by nurses and physician assistants who follow a standardized, step-by-step process to treat common ailments supported by software that is constantly updated. At the same time, clinicians have the freedom, and are encouraged, to provide a personal customer experience that is viewed as an artistic, nonstandardized process. MinuteClinics continually evaluate the line between art and science.

If the process is deemed artistic, employees need to be trained differently, require a different infrastructure, and are encouraged to, in Donald Schon's terms, think on their feet. These variations inevitably lead to more mistakes, more failures that need to be tolerated and turned into the kind of double-loop learning that improves effectiveness.

The authors of the article suggest a matrix that differentiates between 1) mass process geared to eliminate variation; 2) mass customization that accommodates customer-driven variation—like Dell or BMW, which allow customers to "build" their own product; and 3) artistic process that leverages variability and creates variations as needed.

What is important is to separate the artistic process from the standardized one and treat each according to its needs. Many aspects of manufacturing a piano can be standardized, while "perfecting the sound and feel of the pianos is an art."[34] A surprising number of fields have these artistic characteristics, including leadership training, auditing (the broad principles of standards require understanding and judgment), hedge fund management, software development, account relationship management, business development, and industrial design. All of these require what Schon called *reflective practitioners*.

The authors ask three questions: Where will art add value? How should art be supported? How should artistic process evolve? They suggest these steps:

1. Identify what should and should not be art.
2. Develop an infrastructure to support art.
3. Periodically reevaluate the division between art and science.

The article concludes that both art and science are important. Art allows for flexibility, creativity, and dynamism that a purely scientific approach cannot replicate. Artistic approaches can also create differentiation that cannot be easily copied, or outsourced.[35]

What comes to my mind is the extraordinary work done when organizations have been intentional about creating a culture and infrastructure that nurtures reflective work and produces measurable results—think Bell Labs, Xerox PARC, and Disney Imagineering.

We do not have the equivalent reflective space in philanthropy, and we need it.

Diving Deeper

Let's circle back to love—maybe the thorniest, or the mushiest, of all the wonderful elements and principles behind philanthropy. How can you tell—how do you know a gift, or a service, is an act of love, and does that make it more effective?

Dennis Littky, the cofounder of Big Picture Learning and a charismatic and inspired teacher/educator, has found that the single most important factor in kids' learning is "whether they believe that they can."[36] That kind of influence from a gifted teacher to a student is profound. We can and do measure the academic progress of the student, but it is harder to quantify a gifted teacher's impact on the student. Sometimes though, it is not hard to see.

A TPI colleague has worked for many years with a client who supports a wide range of small, grassroots organizations, and many, many, talented and deserving young people. He will only do so if he has met these kids personally and listened to their stories. I asked my colleague to describe what goes on between the donor and the student. She explained, "Compassion is certainly part of it, but as I watch him with the kids I think it goes beyond that. If I had to boil it down I would say it is admiration he most feels for their 'scrappiness' and desire to make something good out of their lives. Maybe he feels connected to them because he sees in them the qualities that he hopes he has himself demonstrated in life, and those he admires most in other people: hard work, determination, passion. Pride is also part of it. He always tells the students how proud he is to know them and it is so incredibly genuine and sincere each time he says it."

So here is this guy, sitting there beaming, and here are these kids rising to his hope and high expectations for them—it is exactly the kind of philanthropy that one wants. These exchanges are the essence of what Martin Buber called dialogue—the narrow ridge, the place where we meet another. This is the "I-thou" relationship where the image of the self is incomplete without the image of the other. [37]

These are very powerful influences.

The literary critic Harold Bloom, in his books on the anatomy of influence, defines influence as inspiration, and as literary love. Bloom's view—and this is very interesting—is that "the overwhelming presence of love is vital to understanding how great literature works."[38]

He explains that the poet within the poet in the greatest of poems is the poetry itself—and not something else—namely "influence, which figures everywhere in life, becomes intensified in" the process of making and reading poetry.[39]

He writes, "But strong critics and strong readers know we cannot understand great literature if we deny literary love to the writers or readers. *Sublime literature demands an emotional not an economic investment* [emphasis mine]."[40]

My take from Bloom's insight is remarkably specific to all the Dennis Littkys out there, and to all the donors, who practice the art of philanthropy.

There is a gift within the gift—the greatest of gifts is when it transcends the evidence upon which it is based. Its mystery is in the relationships between donor, recipient, and the community of interest being served—a dynamic that operates on multiple levels.

One level is contractual and may be spelled out in considerable detail—a multiyear grant/contract to a youth organization based on research, data, and measurable evidence. Let's call it science. But it is the relationships between the parties at interest that makes or breaks the success of the program. These relationships flow between the organization's staff, the youth involved in the program, parents and extended families, powerful peer groups, all of which intersect within a community culture. These are the influences of a pretty complex system that is part cognitive and part noncognitive. And therein lies the "love factor." Therein lies the art.

I agree with Harold Bloom, and I agree with our client—you cannot have a great gift if you deny the donor, or the recipient, philanthropic love. Sublime philanthropy demands an emotional investment, as much as an economic and process investment.

Parker Palmer, in *Healing the Heart of Democracy: The Courage to Create a Politics Worthy of the Human Spirit*, writes that "the word *heart* points not merely to our emotions, but to the core of the self, that center-place where all of our ways of knowing converge—intellectual, emotional, sensory, intuitive, imaginative, experiential, relational, and bodily, among others. The heart is where we integrate what we know in our minds with what we know in our bones, the place where our knowledge can become more fully human."[41]

What an interesting juxtaposition of words—*heart, bones, knowledge, more fully human*—I think this leads to a philanthropy unbound!

What I am thinking of is the TPI client who loved reading, and credited his mother's love of reading with the highly successful person he became. The reading programs his foundation funds—now expanded to the whole STEM universe—are a direct expression of his values.

Fusion of the Art and the Science

Let's try to pull some of this together. To begin with, there are existing bridges between the art and the science of philanthropy. Take the following as examples:

- The 2010 report from Grantmakers for Effective Organizations (GEO) called "Do Nothing About Me Without Me" offers several perspectives on engagement.[42]

- Heifetz's, Grashow's, and Linsky's concept of adaptive leadership where "the stakeholders themselves must create and put the solution into effect since the problem is rooted in their attitudes, priorities, and behavior. And until stakeholders change their outlook, a solution cannot emerge."[43]

- Human-centered design from global design firm IDEO is when organizations "develop a deep and intuitive understanding of client and customer needs in order to create 'human-centered' products and services."[44]

- Embracing empathy from Dev Patnaik who says, "The ability to empathize and have a 'gut' connection to the people you serve allows an organization to do truly transformative work."[45]

- Catlin Fullwood's notion of participatory evaluation, which she explains by saying, "We are not talking about feedback—we are talking about ownership—ownership of the questions, the data, the analysis, the application of the findings."[46]

Angelica Berrie, in her book *A Passion for Giving*, co-authored with Peter Klein, writes: "A good philanthropist needs this capacity for deep listening, to cultivate a culture of creative receptivity that allows the opening of minds and hearts to grantees who 'keep us on the path.'" Our ability to listen enables change when we are transformed by what we hear and can act from a larger whole.[47] Angelica and Peter reference Otto Scharmer who, in his book *Theory U*, quotes violinist Miha Pogacnik on the four levels of expanded listening that "moves your listening and playing from within to beyond yourself."

> Listening 1: Downloading (reconfirming your habits of thought)
>
> Listening 2: Factual listening (listening by paying attention to facts and noticing new data)
>
> Listening 3: Empathetic (really feeling how another feels, with an open heart to connect directly with another person from within)
>
> Listening 4: Generative (experiencing a subtle profound change that transforms the listener through communion, with a deeper sense of knowing and self to access knowledge of your/the best future possibility)[48]

Conclusion

What are the steps to make the fusion of the art and science of effective philanthropy a reality?

- Begin with naming where one perspective begins and one leaves off. Going through the exercise is, in and of itself, clarifying. Identify what should and should not be art, and how it adds value.
- Develop an infrastructure to support art—periodically reevaluate the division between art and science.[49]
- Artistic work should be evaluated with the same degree of intensity as scientific work, but requires a different kind of reflective metric that would include anecdote and story, and intuitive and emotional interpretation.
- Ask a different set of questions:
  - What is "going on" in the work that you intuitively feel but cannot easily measure?
  - What is our emotional investment in the work we do and is that manifested?
  - What are the reflective metrics that would help you better understand what is going on?
  - How well and how deeply have we listened, and to whom?
  - Do our actions reflect our values? How do we test this?
  - Is there integrity in our purpose?
  - Is there integrity in our process?

Add it all up and we have a more complete picture of the whole. Add it all up and we have elevated the discourse around effectiveness. Add it all up and we have left behind the rhetoric, the silly arguments, and moved the field of philanthropy to a better place.

Section 2 Reflection

Formative Values

- List three to five formative experiences in your life. How did they shape your core values?
- List three people (they can be individuals you know, historic figures, or characters in a novel or movie) who have strongly influenced you. What values did they transmit to you?

Your Values Today—Personal and Philanthropic

Review the list of values below and circle five to seven that are most important to you personally at this stage of your life. Feel free to write in others. Then circle five to seven that you feel are most important for your philanthropy to reflect at this stage of your life. Are they the same or different?

Acceptance	Entrepreneurship	Mastery
Achievement	Equality	Merit
Acknowledgment	Expertise	Open Communication
Adventure	Fairness	Opportunity
Agility	Faith	Peace
Arts	Flexibility	Personal Growth
Beauty	Freedom	Preservation
Change	Generosity	Pride
Collaboration	Happiness	Privacy
Comfort	Harmony	Respect
Commitment	Health	Responsibility
Community	Honesty	Security
Compassion	Humility	

Conservation	Innovation	Self-Expression
Courage	Integrity	Self-Reliance
Creativity	Involvement	Service
Democracy	Justice	Stability
Dignity	Knowledge	Stewardship
Diversity	Leadership	Truth
Education	Love	Wise Use of Resources

Your Moral Compass

The goal of this exercise is to draw or write (in fifty words or less) a vision of your moral compass. In their work on moral intelligence, Fred Kiel and Doug Lennick propose that north on a regular compass represents integrity on a moral compass; south represents forgiveness, east represents compassion, and west represents responsibility.

These four principles are honored by people across races, religions, and genders in some form.[50]

A moral compass is part of one's moral biography. "*Moral biography* refers to the way all individuals conscientiously combine two elements in daily life:" their personal persona and their public persona (i.e., their role as a citizen-actor).[51]

Let's take another example. A sign above my desk reads: "Those who spread sunshine to the lives of others cannot keep it from themselves." How do I strive to do this?

Treat others with dignity and respect. Do unto others as you would want to be treated. Look for the good in everyone, even those who may not look like, act like, or share the same beliefs as you. At the core of everything, uphold your integrity by staying true to your word. Interlace service to others into daily life. Strive to be a role model to the next generation.

Your Vision Statement

In a paragraph or page, articulate a vision for your giving that

- reflects your values and moral compass;
- creates a concrete picture or image;
- represents future accomplishments;
- is positive and inspiring;
- presents a unifying theme;
- encourages you to stretch your expectations and aspirations; and
- describes what you want to see in the future and defines your "mission accomplished."

SECTION 3:

TROUBLE

Confusion is not what one expects from experience.

PETER KAROFF

Of course, there is always trouble. As the boxer Mike Tyson once said: "Every man has a plan until he gets punched in the face."[1] A chronic worrier, Peter spent sleepless nights and long hours with clients parsing the difficulties, the moral dilemmas encountered in the simple-sounding business of "doing good."

Many of Peter's troubles were stirred up first by that frenemy, his loud, persistent, and ever-present conscience. The first two pieces in this section conjure up his internal "Greek chorus" of doubt and dread about various enterprises. Those voices will be familiar to anyone who's encountered complexities in the course of trying to get something done. They are, in Peter's words, part of the hazards of "our moral imagination pressing back against the real world in all of its disruptiveness."

"Reset: The New Name of the Game" was written during the financial crisis of 2008, but its measured, practical advice for donors seems fresh and relevant in today's uncertain political times.

"Parallel Tracks" draws lessons from the work of one of Peter's earliest and favorite clients, John Abele. It is about finding ways around difficulty to achieve purpose. And "Hope Within the Shithole" is a strangely ebullient argument for a clear-eyed assessment of reality as the first step for getting out of the muck.

"The Imagined Community" starts as an idyll, an evocative piece centered in his beloved West Newton, about what community and home meant to Peter. But it takes a darker turn as he explores the fragility of communities and organizations faced with change. He cautions us against "the crime of not listening" as we go about our philanthropic business.

The section closes with a sort of incantation and reflection exercise called "Bridges to Reconciliation," which points to how our internal troubles—and even some in the outside world—might be resolved through work on ourselves. As Peter says, "Trust begins at home, with our confidence not only in ourselves, but also in the communities of interest that make up our world."

The Greek Chorus

I often hear the voices of a kind of Greek chorus as I go about my life and work. They come from two directions: one is from inside my head or heart, and the other is from what, on some days, seems like the whole bloody world—sometimes literally bloody. These persistent voices are a kind of surround sound and, of the two principal themes, there is far more *open wailing* and not enough *wise sympathetic comments*. The Greek chorus of which I speak has one unfailing characteristic: It always tells it like it is—no sugarcoating, no denial, no romance. It has absolute integrity; it only tells the truth. It is never new news to me, this truth, but that doesn't make it any easier. To say this is annoying, difficult, painful, confusing, fascinating, and revelatory all at once would be accurate.

There are times when the chorus drowns out everything else, roaring in rage at the outrageous. There are times when these voices speak in a whisper or a murmur, bemused, considered, reflective, and there are times when they are present but ominously silent in who knows what way—anger, disapproval. And then there are those occasional moments when the chorus clucks like a chicken or tut-tuts like an old granny on the porch on a hot summer evening in her rocking chair. Such a multiplicity of wide mood swings seems to flourish in everyone with a brain, even the most confident among us.

I get a little tired of hearing this noise all the time, as though I didn't have enough on my plate, as though there were not enough critics in the house and outside as well. Who needs to have a chorus hanging on every word, listening in on every thought? It isn't fair!

Here they come, gathered in their magisterial blue robes, with more relish than usual, by the way, for the early evening synopsis of the day's events. You might as well listen in. I am trying to relax with the paper and a scotch and water. Fat chance!

> *You tried to dodge it, Coward*
> *Your action detrimental, Coward*
> *What you claim to care, Coward*
> *Where's your staying power, Coward*
> *If you can't stand the heat, Coward*
> *Backbone missing stand up, Coward*

Give me a break! As always, these guys tend to dramatize things. Let me tell you what's happening. No question, it could be one of our best projects; seventy-five units of low-income housing on a tract of land just north of the Ashmont T station. I love the idea and it would literally turn the neighborhood around. We have been funding the community development corporation (CDC) that wants to develop the project over the past year and have about $250,000 into the deal. Now things have gotten messy, screwed up. I'm in the middle and have exposed our foundation to boot. The CDC is embroiled in a huge internal fight over control. The neighborhood demographics have changed and it is now primarily Hispanic where once it was predominately African American, and the two groups are at loggerheads. City hall is supporting one of these factions and putting fuel on the fire.

> *You knew that, knew that, knew that*
> *Saw it coming, saw it coming, saw it*
> *You never said a word never*
> *Afraid of even one word*

The executive director has been accused in the press, unfairly in my view, of being power-hungry, not sensitive to the new Hispanic voice, and of diverting funds to his own benefit. The last accusation is absurd.

He is not a good listener
That man doesn't listen
Steamrolls over people
Could of should of told him
Where were the brown faces
All those endless meetings
Where the hell were you
Saw it coming saw it coming

Last week there was an article and our foundation was described as well-meaning, but naïve. The other trustees nearly died.

The signs along the way
Your job was to ask questions
Whose time were you wasting
Saw it coming saw it saw it

The AG is now investigating—which is a lot of bullshit. I believe the organization and the ED will get a clean bill of health.

So you hope hope hope
You've been a dope so hope
Get off it move beyond
What's right what's substance
Whose eyes which beholder

All right, I could put the foundation on the line. The board of the CDC has asked the foundation to advance funds as a bridge loan, some $1.1 million, until such time as the situation sorts itself out.

You fade in and out
How incomplete you are

This is not a bloody laboratory
This is re-al-i-ty baby re-al-i-ty baby
Big-time if you get a next time

The mayor called me personally and requested us to help and indicated he would do everything he could to make sure we were made whole. The assumption is that the permanent lenders would come in and take our loan out. I don't know what to do.

Shoot yourself in the stupid foot
Try something new very new
Think it through and through
You are not the biggest big shot
Calm down take it slow

This is way outside our foundation guidelines, much riskier than anything we have done.

What are you chicken shit
Risk capital right
Prudent man or gutless
They call it opp-or-tun-i-ty
Big-time if you get a next time

I declined to be interviewed by the reporter from the *Globe*. Our foundation prefers to be anonymous and has a policy against publicity of any kind and this is the worst of all—getting in the middle of an ethnic issue. We don't belong there.

What world are you in
We live in the middle of ethnic issues
Face it man you belong there
Policy or not like or not

The problem is that the option to acquire the property is about to expire. The owners have another buyer waiting in the wings who has no interest in housing. If this window of opportunity is lost, there will be no housing in that neighborhood for a long time. Two years of work by a lot of people will go down the drain, our $250,000 with it. Once again, expectations raised and then not fulfilled. It happens over and over again.

> *The argument is complex*
> *We acknowledge your hesitation*
> *Think credits and debits and merits*
> *But for goodness sakes grow up*
> *Stop moaning and sighing*

My dilemma is both political and financial. On the merits of the situation, we should continue to back the plan but I am nervous about our reputation. It isn't as though we are at fault or anything, but I am greatly conflicted. I do not think I am a "coward" but I wonder. Maybe I should stand up, stand our ground.

> *Calm down the world will not end*
> *You may deserve the benefit of doubt*
> *You can still do the right thing*
> *There is always a right thing*

I should have confronted this long ago. I need to be honest and agree to do the deal only if the ED and the CDC board commit to mend fences, and open up to the other voices in the community. Will they listen?

> *Rough seas ahead*
> *Gird your loins*
> *Keep the wind in the sail*
> *And you will prevail*

How about this for a news release:

> The ABC Foundation is pleased to announce the acquisition of the Barker Mills property in Dorchester for the purpose of building seventy-five units of low-income housing. The property will be held by the Foundation until such time as the various community groups who represent the interests of the neighborhood have worked out their differences. The Foundation has also made a grant to the XYZ CDC to engage the Public Conversations Project, experts in conflict resolution to work with the community factions involved.

It isn't always about you
You and your kind
There is a missing link
Go deeper

Right! News release:

> The XYZ CDC is pleased to announce that a bridge loan has been received from the ABC Foundation that will allow the acquisition of the Barker Mills property in Dorchester for the purpose of building seventy-five units of low-income housing. The property will be held in escrow until such time as XYZ has worked out the differences with the various community groups who represent the interests of the neighborhood. To facilitate this "community listening" process, XYZ has engaged the Public Conversations Project, experts in conflict resolution. XYZ CDC is excited about this opportunity and grateful to the ABC Foundation for their support and belief in the project and in our community.

You did it you stood up
When it counted most
Spirit away spirit away

That's it for tonight, guys. I'm exhausted and going to go to bed.

CONSCIENCE

Caught in the dangerous traffic between self and universe.
STANLEY KUNITZ[2]

I carve out a small space, a nest
Of sorts and lie my conscience down.
As a gift it bears little resemblance to
The madness around me, those who think
They know everything, those who despair.

My own absurd, hesitant, presumption is hope.

I watch the Osprey hunt the harbor at dusk,
It soars and glides to a frantic wing-beat
And like an acrobat hangs in mid-air
As flashes of silver scales below
Signal time to make a precision dive.

My own hesitant presumption is hope.

As an infant flails, wails, loss of womb,
Its wet, loud, pronouncement—I am here!
My conscience, not newborn, nor single-
Minded like the Fish Hawk, hears the cry
Of the wounded heart.

My own presumption is hope.

Even as deadly fog shrouds the backstage
It is no match, these awakenings are legion,
New dimensions of spirit and soul
Rise from sweet hearth and beloved earth,
Feminine and Divine.

My own hope
Lies in Mahler's 1st, from minor to major,
From darkness to Frère Jacques. So rise
Tired traveler, renew, seek secret places,
The great percussion of possibilities within.

The Greek Chorus: Second Variation

Children are children
Shame on you shame
On the backs of children
You have no business
Doing business there
Where profiteers
Or worse and worse
Run rampant
Shame on you shame shame

It's amazing to me how simple it may seem, how quick to judge you people are, how to the casual observer, it looks like we are callous, unfeeling, and without ethical boundaries of our own. That's the real issue, you see—it would be much easier if we were without ethics, and just flat out mercenary, but we are not. It is ironic that we of all companies are even in this position. If it didn't hurt so much it would be laughable.

What did you expect
A polite thank you
They are foreigners
For God's sake
You are naïve

God, I wish you people would cease and desist with these stupid comments. It only confuses and exacerbates a complex situation.

This is the background:

We came late into the soccer ball business in the '90s, and by that time the industry was pretty much centered in the Sialkot region of Pakistan. The same fingers that can weave rugs turned out to be just right for stitching soccer balls. In fact, the stitching tradition goes back to when the British horse saddle manufacturers in the mid-1800s were established in this very same region.

> *Ah ha*
> *Corporate kingdom*
> *One kind of imperialism*
> *Just like another*
> *Admit it admit it*

I admit nothing but that we wanted to do business there only if we could do so under terms consistent with the values and protocols we had established around the world. I thought we had done that but what happened in those villages caught us unawares. I agree it shouldn't have, but it did. It was embarrassing for the company, and let me tell you after twenty years of putting my all into this work, it was very, very discouraging—although this was hardly the first time.

> *It didn't surprise us*
> *We told you so*
> *They will cheat*
> *They will steal*
> *They will lie*
> *You should have known*

All right, enough already! I'm proud that we were the first major footwear company to focus on human rights and labor issues, especially child labor, and have been out front ever since. In fact, it is not an exaggeration to say that it was our company's leadership, never mind my own two million airplane miles, that made it happen. I was the one who did the leg work. I was the one who spent months away from home. I was the one who spent endless hours wringing concessions from reluctant, and smart, partners who didn't want to go there. I was the one who brought this to the attention of the other major players in the industry. We had a lot to do with educating the buying public that there were unacceptable situations out there. At the end of the day, it was the shift in the marketplace that carried on the day. Increasingly, customers do not want to buy clothing, sneakers, or soccer balls made under conditions that are truly unjust or abusive. The tide turned when the moral imperative of human rights joined with the economic imperative of market demand and expectations. When the UN compact, introduced in 2001 by the UN secretary general, was drawn up, I was part of the team that pushed hard for the inclusion of the human rights provision and the prohibition against the use of child labor. There are now more than five hundred corporate signatories to the compact.

> *We can't even imagine*
> *What kind of parents*
> *What kind of parents*
> *Work their children*
> *Barbaric, disgusting*
> *Un-American*
> *To say the least*

To say the least, that oversimplifies things. None of this is tidy and neat and each choice and decision has a trade-off. Listen for a minute, just this once—try to have an open mind.

The relationships with our local manufacturing partners are not unique. While we do not own any of the factories, we are often the sole customer and, in fact, provide the capital to obtain the needed equipment and occasionally the financing to build the facility. In many deals with larger manufacturers, we are just one of a number of customers. The work conditions twenty years ago in these factories make the term *sweatshop* look benign. From the very beginning of the offshore manufacturing cycle, which really took off in the '70s, the American companies knew there were going to be problems. Every time the question of improving workplace conditions was raised, our partners would smile, and say, "If you want to pay the difference—do you want to pay the difference?" I would be hard pressed to say that our local partners had no sensitivity at all to these issues. It was, however, simply not a high priority for them and, unless one pushed, they somehow never got any attention. That's what we did—push and push.

> *Who are you kidding*
> *They don't care*
> *It's all about money*
> *Money money money*

No question the price competition in the footwear industry is brutal, and the cost of child labor is 20 percent less than the cost of adult labor. That I was a part of changing these ways of doing business is something I am proud of. Sometimes, like right now, I wonder.

> *No good deed goes unpunished*
> *If this was a good deed*
> *How do we even know*

The way you know is through compliance, and it is complicated and expensive. Other parts of the world have been really tough. Many factories in China still keep two sets of books, one for the inspectors and one that is real. It has forced us, along the way, to become more sophisticated, which is what we have done.

We'll believe it when
We see it
If you can't trust partners
Who can you trust

When *The New York Times* broke the news in January that soccer balls we labeled as "guaranteed not made with child labor," were in fact manufactured by young children, I was angry and frustrated. We had worked on the new protocols for more than two years. It was not easy to get the US industry to agree. I remember a tough meeting in Chicago with all the major players when the vote was only four to three to establish what became a partnership that included the manufacturers, the Sialkot chamber of commerce, the International Labour Organization, UNICEF, and ultimately Save the Children.

I had inspected those very factories just six months ago. The issues are broader than child labor and include air quality, harassment, and safety. The managers had agreed to abide by the terms and reassured me that they would remain in compliance, especially with the use of underage labor.

You should have known
If you did your job
You should have known
Right is right wrong is wrong
And what kind of parent
Lives off the sweat of children
You do not really care
It's all about money market share

It is always about market share, but you guys are still wrong on all counts. This is not the first time I have been caught in the paradox of the child-labor issue. In many cultures, including this one, children are part of the work force at a very early age. Rules that prevent children from earning money hit many very poor families hard. Thus, the end run around these rules was not so surprising; it was the scale of what really was a conspiracy that was outrageous.

> *Disgusting*
> *Have they no values*
> *No love for their children*
> *All for money*

That's the point, it is not just money, there are cultural norms that have an even bigger influence. These may be poor people, but they are also wise. What is the point of educating children if there are no jobs for them? Why raise expectations when they will never be realized? There is an added concern about girls. Some families worry that an educated girl may have problems with her life, even to the extent of finding a husband. This has been the reality in many parts of the world, and it is a huge obstacle to those societies, never mind to our business. The promulgation by UNICEF and others of universal primary education for all children is slowly changing those attitudes. Meanwhile, the practical obstacles are huge. There are fifty million school-age children who are not in school in India alone. This region of Pakistan has similar numbers.

> *You act like that is right*
> *Or fair to those girls*
> *Ignorance breeds ignorance*
> *Where is your moral center*
> *Are you gutless*

One's moral center has to be seen through the eyes of an indigenous culture. The line between these cultural norms and a family's economic need for income is hard to separate, especially in the harsh light of limited educational opportunities for children. I agree that when you add in the profit motive, you have quite a mix of things with which to deal. And I still have a major public relations and marketing disaster on my hands. It turned out to be even worse than an accidental violation. The work in question was being done at home by kids and on a regular basis. This was a true conspiracy with multiple factory managers involved. There may even have been some kickbacks. It was a mess.

> *You intrude*
> *Raise expectations*
> *Are they better off*
> *Bread on the table*

All true but for us, certain things remain nonnegotiable. We will only do business based on human rights and fair labor protocols that are finally really becoming normative.

The question was what to do. When I met with the managers and representatives of the workers, almost all of them parents, about what makes sense, about what incentive was strong enough to keep the integrity of the system whole, there was really only one. It was not enough to make rules—right, wrong, or indifferent. The ethical issues notwithstanding, if the children couldn't work, then they had to go to school. That is where Save the Children came into the picture. They were already in discussion with the Atlantic Partnership to develop several schools in the area. I did not want to wait around for that to happen, and we decided to immediately commit $1 million to build and support the one school. We made the commitment from the company's charitable foundation, and it had no relevance to the soccer ball–line's profitability. It was simply the right thing to do. The school is now up and running and, even though it is only one school and many more are needed, its very existence seems to have become a positive metaphor for change and, I think, hope. So, until next time, things have settled down somewhat. But I don't kid myself, there will be a next time.

Did we get the news of the new school on the front page of *The New York Times*? Of course not, but this is an incremental business and so maybe we have learned something.

> *We are still not convinced*
> *You have learned anything*
> *Anything worthwhile*
> *For a change*
> *Try staying home*

I think it's time for that scotch and water, far away from the annoying choruses that seem to haunt the airways.

Reset: The New Name of the Game

"There will not be an economic 'recovery,' everything is going to be 'reset.'"

This comment from a very smart TPI client, spoken three weeks ago, was the first time I had heard the term *reset*. Since then, that word, and others like *fundamental* and *transformational*, are being used by economists, business leaders, commentators, and government leaders to indicate that "what is going on" is a huge disruption of business as usual for the American, and the global, economy. *Disruption* is the term used when entrepreneurs introduce their innovations and, in the process, disrupt/destroy existing business models/industries. This disruption, however, was not of any entrepreneurial vision or design, but has been thrust upon us with astonishing vengeance.

President Obama's chief of staff, Rahm Emanuel, was quoted as saying, "You never want a serious crisis to go to waste. And what I mean by that [is] it's an opportunity to do things that you think you could not do before."[3] The question, then, is whether we can use this crisis as a kind of jujitsu that lands us as a society in a better place.

Philanthropy is contingent on the ebb and flow of individual, family, and corporate wealth, and the nonprofit sector is dependent on philanthropy, government resources, and earned income. What will a major reset of philanthropy's fundamentals look like, and what should the actors in this massive third sector—more than 8 percent of GNP—do to turn it in ways that are positive?

In 2002, in *The Atlantic*, Jonathan Rauch wrote an article entitled "Seeing Around Corners." The article dealt with how "we might learn to anticipate the kinds of events that lie ahead, and where to look for interventions that might work."[4] In my interview with John Abele, the cofounder of Boston Scientific, for my book *The World We Want*, John talks about the experience of using "parallel tracks" to overcome the "body of gods"[5] that fiercely resisted the introduction of less-invasive surgery into the medical care system, which today seems almost incomprehensible when those procedures have become normative. I think some of the answers lie in exactly these ideas—seeing around corners, running parallel tracks—and overcoming the resident body of gods. And perhaps even more relevant, as Peter Senge wrote, "We have no idea the power we have to create the world anew."[6]

So far, the chorus of concern emanating from the field has had some predictable themes. Nationwide, foundations and other major donors, with assets declined 20 percent to 40 percent, are struggling with how to 1) do no harm, 2) stand up and be counted at a time when it is important to do so, and 3) be responsible to their fiduciary responsibilities. Nonprofit institutions and organizations, reeling under the impact of reduced income from all sources, are trying to figure out how to maintain mission-critical programs and services with less. While difficult, and painful, these steps don't go far enough.

A plan for a nonprofit based on the assumption that revenue will recover from the same funding sources to precrisis levels is very different from a plan that acknowledges there may never be such a recovery. A plan that is based on a foundation's assets returning to previous levels is very different to one that assumes what we have today is what we have. A plan that only makes adjustments, even big ones, to the status quo, and does not transform how one goes about doing the work, is one of diminishing returns.

What else could be done now? Here are the elements on my short list:

- Deal with and acknowledge fear—the deer-in-the-headlights kind of fear that freezes intelligent response. Talk about it, stare it down.

- Create a clean slate. Sweep everything that you do now off the table. Take a deep breath and step way back, and assume nothing exists except a blurry vision. In essence, it is as though you are starting from scratch. Reinvent the way you pay for and do the work.

- Look around the corner. Exercise your moral imagination. Make wild scenarios. Do complete end runs around the prevailing best practices—create multiple parallel tracks. As Barry Dym, the founder of the Institute for Nonprofit Management and Leadership put it, "Shift the paradigm from loss to gain, from preservation to creation."

- Reassess your resources, especially those you have not valued enough. Think networks, contacts, the power of convening and access that you, your colleagues, and your board have. Make those calls you haven't made in years, pull out all the stops—be shameless in the use of your cache to further the work.

- Forget about going it alone. Subsume your ego. Collaborate and cost share on a scale that was previously unimaginable. Cross domains, tear down silos between what you do and others with whom you had never imagined sharing services, and jointly serve the needs of your community of interest.

- Put endowment capital to work. Make mission-based investing integral to program. Think hard about whether spending down is actually a capital investment in renewed sustainability.

- Recruit new talent. Leap on the sea-change shift in attitude the financial meltdown is having on young people. The best and the brightest are no longer looking to Wall Street. This could be the biggest opportunity the nonprofit field has ever had to add great human resources.

- Realize that the most influential "body of gods" that need to be overcome, in addition to funders and government policy makers may be the best practices within the field itself, or within your board, the staff, and even within you! Resist to your core the thoughts that "that won't work here" and "we tried that before" and "we never do that."

- Grit your teeth. This is going to be hard. Thousands of marginal nonprofit organizations will not exist eighteen months from now. Funders need to be objective, honest, and caring. Nonprofit boards need to be the same.

- Renew your vows. The passion you feel, or once felt, for the work that you do, is central to the exercise of creative moral imagination. The centrality of philanthropy to the making of a better world is the heart and soul of why you are an actor on this stage. Make a poem of it.

Will the above better prepare you for a "reset"? Will the field come through renewed and stronger? I think it is a fair beginning.

Parallel Tracks

Sometimes you have to find a way around a tricky intersection, just to avoid a collision en route to your destination. That's what John Abele did. Here is an email I got from him that shows something about his nature and leads us into his story.

> Last week in Newport we discussed how to make the Institute vision a reality. Several strategies involve bringing together a small number of change agents, futurists, publishers, producers, and experts for a conference I'm sponsoring. I want to call it "Searching for the Butterfly" after the chaos effect. I'd love to share these ideas with you since they mirror your own objectives.

John is someone with a whimsical, inquiring kind of mind, counterintuitive to the core. He also knows firsthand a lot about process, especially the process of change.

I first met John in the early '90s. We had dinner at the Concord Inn, an old New England–type place with wide, creaky floor boards and a smoky fireplace—an odd spot for a conversation about the future. (I came home and told my wife I had just had *My Dinner with Andre*, referencing the Louis Malle film with Wallace Shawn and Andre Gregory. Andre's ideas, shared over a dinner, are far-reaching for poor Wally, who is somewhat baffled, but mesmerized. I played Wally to John's Andre.) Since that first dinner I have had many such conversations with John who is, as he likes to say, someone "always trying to see around the corners."

He is the cofounder of Boston Scientific Corporation (BSC), a pioneer in the less-invasive medical device industry that has transformed medicine and surgical procedures, and a company that, twenty-five years later, has revenues of $10 billion.[7]

When I asked John that first evening what his role was at the company, he did not talk about his scientific or management contributions to the company's phenomenal growth, but gave a reply that has stayed with me: "I am the company ethicist, historian, and philosopher." So when John talks, I listen or, as an alternative, spend a day searching for butterflies.

John told me an interesting story about the challenges of the early days of developing and marketing of what ultimately became a whole new way to practice medicine.

> The problem was cultural and had to do with the prevailing medical view that the larger the hole the surgeon made in the body, the better it was because you could see what was going on. And here we were proposing you did not need a big hole at all and, in fact, could save a ton of money, and provide the patient with much less trauma and pain and significantly earlier recovery. All very good if we could actually deliver technically, which at that time few believed possible, but so foreign to the culture of organized institutional medicine that the resistance was huge. Now I admit it sounds like a *Saturday Night Live* skit. "A bigger hole is safer for the patient. The better you can see, the better the patient is. If something goes wrong, we can fix it more easily." I would argue that damage was a self-fulfilling prophecy, and you are left with this big hole that has to heal with all of that complication.
>
> But that was the culture, and we were marginalized, which is the natural response of any establishment to a

new idea. It is just like the human body when it takes a foreign object like shrapnel and immediately encapsulates it and pushes it to the side—that is what happens to you when you confront the power structure in any professional society or the powers that be in any culture.

What we did, what we had to do, was to go forward on parallel tracks outside of organized medicine. We started with individual doctors who were excited about the potential and independent and smart enough to ignore the conventional wisdom. It was at that time that Boston Scientific and others in the industry realized the imperative to develop highly sophisticated demonstrations, and teaching and conferencing methods that would be independent of the establishment. By design, those demonstrations and conferences were inclusive of a wide range of experts and especially included those who were highly critical—the early adopters.

Everything was on the table for analysis, and debate. The whole range of technical issues and quality of life and ethics issues were part of these discussions. Since technology does not spring whole out of a box and takes years of an iterative development, this open and transparent process was part of what built confidence. We listened carefully and we constantly integrated the feedback. As a result, credibility came not from Boston Scientific or the medical societies, but from leading physicians who had practical, hands-on experience and already had credibility with their peers, growing numbers of whom participated in this process. At a certain point, the number of physicians utilizing or demanding these amazing new technologies and procedures became greater than those who were not. It had become normative. As a result, what was a parallel track to the established order merged and became, over time, the established order. There were lots of bumps along the way with many dead ends and mistakes, but this strategy ultimately prevailed and the result for medicine and for patients was, and continues to be, truly transformational.

One can see why Abele calls Boston Scientific a "for-profit philanthropy" because, at the end of the day, the company's products reduce human suffering and reduce costs. Who can argue with that?

It is also why he believes that "social dilemmas need to be looked at through the lens of parallel tracks, especially if the goal is to transform and bring about change." There is always a protectionist culture that surrounds the conventional order composed of organizations, associations, and bureaucracies, most of whom have vested interests in maintaining that culture. While direct confrontation is a strategy, Abele believes "change agents have a better shot at success if they develop and organize constituencies from within those cultures that do not agree with the establishment."

John has applied his unconventional notions to other efforts as well. He is chair of FIRST, a nonprofit program that creates teams of high school students who design and build robots and compete with one another for prizes and scholarships. FIRST is an amazing undertaking for these students, and the work of building a robot is a very rich mix of math, physics, design, electrical engineering, manufacturing, and marketing, but it is even more a lesson in team building.

FIRST is not an Odyssey of the Mind–type experience, but instead very tactile and hands-on. It appeals to kids who learn best when they are working with concrete rather than abstract problems. FIRST has successfully defied conventional wisdom that says teams of weak students from very poor urban schools cannot compete with peers from expensive suburban schools (they do and often win), and that today's kids who live for MTV and instant gratification will not commit to such a demanding project—they not only commit and follow through, they love it!

The kids rise to the high expectations FIRST has, along with its high drama and showmanship. (If you ever get the chance, go and experience firsthand a FIRST competition; it will blow you away.) Students learn they are capable of amazing things, but that to achieve them they need to work with others. On one level, FIRST is a game and a competition, but to win big, participants must cooperate with those they are competing against.

> The social dynamic is phenomenal. One-third of participants are female, it's mixed-gender and multicultural, and who works with whom constantly shifts. It is an intensive experiential-learning activity. Mentors help with key elements like design management built around teams. In designing and building their robots, the teams do not compete one-on-one, but in alliance against alliance. Many times, alliances change and there is an incentive to know your competitors. It is a fascinating dynamic I call "coopetition."

FIRST does not rail against the prevailing youth culture in our society, which some see as negative and others defend, but instead offers a compelling alternative track, building on what is positive and potential-filled.

John Abele told me that his mother always took the other side, no matter what the discussion or argument, saying, "I must have picked up that trait by osmosis, because I am always drawn to the other side of a question. It is why I disagree with conventional approaches to social dilemmas that polarize, instead of bringing opposing forces and stakeholders together, even if that takes some doing."

At Kingbridge, his state-of-the-art conference center in Toronto, Abele is pushing the envelope on how advanced conferencing techniques can be adapted to other domains, including philanthropy.

"Too much philanthropy is polarizing," he said, "which just reinforces the status quo. We tend to live in our own silos, and unless we open things up, change is not possible. Deep learning only takes place when we are confronted with a mix of countervailing views."

He acknowledges that profitable dialogue has its challenges.

> There are often pontificators impossible to turn off and other people who speak entirely in innuendos and euphemisms. To cut through some of the puffery and bombast you have to be a benevolent despot, something wealth enables one to do.
>
> There are a lot of questions in regard to wealth. From a societal perspective, wealth aggregation, corporate and individual, is a tremendous asset because it distributes power. If the government turns you down, you still have a lot of options for your ideas. It is another kind of market and is part of what makes for an open-source society, one more likely to survive. But wealth, and being listed in *Forbes* magazine, is not what constitutes success. What you do with wealth is what defines you, and you never completely get there. The end goal is to provide value for society. That can happen in business, as I believe it happened at Boston Scientific, and it can happen in philanthropy.

Abele is on the board of Amherst College, and while he respects and loves this excellent school from which he graduated, he feels there is a moral dilemma when it costs $65,000 a year to educate a student. He said, "I think an Amherst owes society something in exchange for that kind of cost. Those who come out of such elite institutions run the risk of not being prepared for the real world. I don't mean Amherst should spend less, but I think the obligation is to do something that is visually productive for society." This belief has led him to fund an intensive community service program at the college that he hopes will be part of every undergraduate's experience.

When it works, Abele believes that philanthropy can be very effective in pushing against established authority and in bringing together those who would otherwise not talk. He said:

> I worry about any situation where there is a "body of gods" that makes rules by pronouncement. An awful lot of philanthropy, certainly well-intended, suffers from that problem. What is so unique about philanthropy is that it can act without some of the conventional restraints. Philanthropy can be a convener, an introducer, a bridge to common ground, and it can encourage others to expand the dialogue beyond the usual. There is no need for outside consultants to take this over. You have to own it.

At Kingbridge, he encourages the business groups, nonprofits, and state agencies that participate not to use "expert" facilitators, but instead to select one of their own to lead the session or process.

Openness, transparency, and seeing around corners is what Abele believes will lead to a better world, which makes him part of the open-source movement that is changing the way we interact.

Hope Within the Shithole

David Bergholz is one of the best people I have met in the field of philanthropy. For fourteen years, Dave produced high-impact results out of the Cleveland-based George Gund Foundation. Now retired, Dave works on a magnificent garden, and hones his talent as a photographer. When I asked how he was doing, this was his response:

> Garden is great, showing and even selling some photos and our kids are good. The world is a shithole but I don't know what to do about that. Glad you are well and say hi to Marty.
>
> Best,
> David

Well as usual Bergholz is on to something. First of all, he is hardly alone in not knowing what to do about things. So, in these days where the focus in philanthropy is on professed intentionality, it is good to be reminded of the limits and modesty of true wisdom.

As to the world being a "shithole," it is hard to argue with that for more reasons than there is time to list, even if we seldom use such trashy words in polite company. But maybe we should—witness these verses from the poet A. R. Ammons:

> but then it is a wastebasket and I
> put it out to the use of the world:
> it collects trash of the thoughty:

> others (the litter litterers) give
> theirs to the wind, the chance and
> random boys: but I don't think
> there's much distinction between
> saved and spent trash: trash is what
> you make of it: . . . and there is
> no way, of course, finally to
> throw anything away.

Bergholz is a man of fewer words but Ammons and he have very similar views. What goes around comes around, and only those "random boys"—those too sure they know the answers—profess otherwise. In philanthropic terms, Ammons reinforces the wisdom that "social change is incremental at best," which, while true, is also tough to deal with. We want solutions, answers, scale, and not half-baked measures, and patience is hardly an entrepreneurial characteristic.

Ammons goes on to give us a strange, almost liberating perspective.

> considering mutability and muck,
> decompositions, ups and downs, comings
> and goings, you have passed
> from a thousand orifices, some
> beneath you and the evolutionary
> scale: visibly moved, the gentleman
> got some roll-on ban deodorant
> and tried to rub off (or out)
> shit sticks: its fragrance in the old
> days confirmed the caveman he was coming
> home: a man's shit (or tribe's) reflects
> (nasally) the physical makeup of the man
> and the physiologies of those others
> present, plus what they have gathered

> from the environment
> to pass through themselves
>
> and the odor of shit is like language,
> tone, flavor, accent hard to fake:
> everything is more nearly incredible
> than you thought at first

What these lines say is that "we own it"! You can't sweet-talk or perfume away the catalogue of the world's problems that emanate from man—through man.

So how do we get our "shit" together and dig ourselves out of the hole? In the face of how incredibly difficult everything we want to do or fix is, how do we find hope?

The twentieth-century mystic Howard Thurman wrote:

> A farmer plants a seed in the ground and the seed sprouts and grows. The weather, the winds, the elements, cannot be controlled by the farmer. The result is never a sure thing. So what does the farmer do? He plants. Always he plants. Again and again he works at it—the ultimate confidence and assurance that even though his seed does not grow to fruition, seeds do grow and they do come to fruition.[8]

In these terms, hope is based on our conviction, our certainty, our instinct that something makes sense even if the evidence is not apparent except in ways mysterious. This does not diminish the importance of those things we can control—in the case of the farmer, the water, the fertilizer, the sweat of brow, all of which enhance the probability of fruition. In the case of philanthropy—smart process, including research, data, strategy, and evaluation—are all important elements that contribute to success. Yet even the most disciplined and best-intentioned donors, and the most high-performing organizations, often hit a wall. In the same way a long-distance runner needs to run through the wall, actors within philanthropy need the same resolve. That resolve is not sustainable without hope.

Wallace Stevens wrote that the nobility of poetry "is a violence from within that protects us from a violence without." Seamus Heaney adds, "It is the imagination pressing back against the pressure of reality."[9]

My translation/adaptation of these lines is visceral: the nobility of philanthropy emanates from our passion within—yes, sometimes violent—and our moral imagination pressing back against the real world in all of its disruptiveness.

How powerful is moral imagination? To answer this question, I return to Shelley, in *A Defence of Poetry*:

> For the mind in creation is as a fading coal, which some invisible influence, like an inconstant wind, awakens to transitory brightness: this power arises from within, like the colour of a flower which fades and which changes as it is developed . . . Could this influence be durable in its original purity and force, it is impossible to predict the greatness of the results.[10]

I think Shelley has lifted us out of the shithole.

It is still a given that we "don't know what to do." But a philanthropy unbound unlocks a legion of untouched capacities and "it is impossible to predict the greatness of the results."[11]

The Imagined Community
(the Crime of Not Listening)

There is where we live and with whom we live, beginning with those we love, and extending to our neighbors, and our colleagues at work. That is the inner circle. There is the broader community, a city, a society, a nation, and the world beyond. That is the outer circle that is called the commons. There is the community of interest where the aim is to come together to act for a common purpose. That is the circle that does the work of the commons. There is the community of the mind, and of the spirit. *That is the imagined community, about which we dream.*

What I am especially interested in are the unlikely connections that are yet to be made between our inner and outer life, our public and private persona, between community as it is broadly defined and in the way we feel, think, and live our individual, family, professional, and public lives. That we often do not find those connections is part of an unfinished journey.

And I do believe that life flows as a journey that is a kind of paradox of instincts. On the one hand, we cherish our private lives, and on the other we are drawn, sometimes reluctantly, to public ones. The same thing that motivates us, that propels us down the path to community, is also what holds us back, what cautions us to not proceed at all. This dichotomy is what makes it so hard to build and sustain communities, and why motivated leadership is so important. It is these twin themes, self and the broader world, as they weave in and out of our life that endlessly fascinate, challenge, and satisfy.

We all have a dream of a better world, a better city, for example, and even though we are busy in our lives, very busy, there are things that each of us could do to make things better. Not in some vague and abstract way, but in quite precise ways that might touch just one person, but in the aggregate would affect the quality of life and the happiness of all. And we are drawn to have that dream.

We are drawn to be in the company of others because of instinctive forces within us that make it clear we cannot live without them. It was Aristotle who held that human beings are basically social animals and thus the welfare of the many and the welfare of the individual are inextricably linked. Put another way, many species of animals sing to each other, but only humans sing together.

Community

What is your first memory of something that looked and smelled like community in a broader sense? Mine you will never guess! It was in 1952 when Rocky Marciano became heavyweight champion of the world and, since he grew up in my town, the whole community came out to Main Street to celebrate. We gathered around the newspaper office, listening to loudspeakers broadcasting the blow-by-blow of the fight. It was thrilling, especially for a young boy, to see all kinds of people from every part of the city mad with excitement and joy, and I felt very much a part. We love these kinds of experiences. Think of First Night in Boston and in other cities, with one million people celebrating, being nice to each other, the streets suddenly safe, or the phenomenal experience of walking in Barcelona on any Saturday evening in Las Ramblas amidst the throngs of citizens of all ages enjoying the spirit and joy of that beautiful city. Community experiences like these make life rich and full.

All of this background music is fine but it is not enough, we need something more, more than company, something that strikes a nerve and springs back out of ourselves. What we need is community in a broader public sense, what Peter Senge calls "a field of shared meaning."[12]

We have that sense sitting in a congregation where the liturgy, the prayer and the song, provide meaning. We have those feelings at a Bruce Springsteen concert when the singer's passion for social justice becomes animate within the music. We have that yearning when being alone is not an option, as it was not after September 11.

We struggle with aloneness and loneliness all of our lives. Alone we face internal reflections, ruminations, speculations, anticipations, hesitations, doubts, and fears. Faith in God and spirituality is one kind of resolution. So is humanism and so is love and so is community, which in many ways is the container for all of these things. All of these words are part of the same flow and while their source is mysterious, their power is undeniable.

Pico Iyer recently wrote of the fast-moving mobile contemporary life where a "new kind of soul is being born out of a new kind of life" asking, "What are the issues that we would die for? What are the passions we would live for?"[13]

Those are hard questions. Most Americans are not faced with such questions, but others around the world are. Here is what Amy Goldman, a trustee of the Better Way Foundation, wrote after a visit to Uganda:

> When we first started considering making grants to orphans in Africa, I frequently heard, "The problem is too big, we can't solve it, so why try?" I am now convinced this is a classic American response to the inconvenience of international aid, and perhaps also to the emotionally wrenching experience of trying to humanize the "numbers." It also is striking that people (Americans) delude themselves into believing that they do not have a connection to the orphan in Uganda, the grieving mother in Zambia, the devastated village in Banda Aceh. Or, that they are somehow more human. In my travels, I have come to believe that we Americans can be less human

than the poor and suffering around the globe. The mother who loses her child to HIV/AIDS in Uganda has lost everything! There is no solace, few distractions from the grief. The strength to carry on in the face of such grief, to physically toil each day to feed oneself and one's remaining family members, is astounding. Truly heroic! I don't think I could do what so many millions must in our world—to live with grief, poverty, and fear every day. Mother Teresa lamented the spiritual poverty in the United States. That is truly the trap we must all fight against.

You cannot answer the question of spiritual poverty alone. You need to find others who have similar values and goals and who, like Amy, are willing to commit, are willing to act. You cannot answer such questions simply as a passive observer. You have to become an actor. You have to act with others. You have to become part of a community of interest. It is the moment when you stand up and are counted.

It is why we have dreams about a "city on the hill." Imagine a new wave of communities of solidarity as a powerful life force. Imagine a citizenry galvanized, and organized, around critical social issues. Imagine if passion, commitment, and engagement were normative in the nurturing and advocacy of good works. It would be virtually unstoppable.

Home

I am luckier than most Americans and have lived in the same house for thirty-nine years. My sense of place is rich in memory and experience. It runs very deep, this sense of neighborhood. For many years, as an early-in-the-office person, I would drive through the streets at 6 a.m., and notice who had a light on and who did not, who was stirring and who had their shades drawn. I am also a walker and, like all walkers, conduct careful, if uninvited, inspections, noticing the incremental changes in houses and yards as they pass through various stages of repair, and disrepair. I know many of my neighbors but even those I have not met I know in these other ways—what kind of car they drive, the way they take care of it, the way their kids dress and act, whether they seem happy or sad. I once remarked to my wife that I probably know more about people we have never met than some of our relatives. I am conditioned and responsive, as anyone would be after thirty-nine years, to the goings-on of my neighborhood. It in turn provides me with a sense of place in a world where that is hard to find.

These connections nurture, inform, and define each other and, in the process, satisfy a need within us. This neighborhood, which I love, serves up a kind of background music to my life, comfortable and familiar, and is sometimes a place where I can even be silly. For example, there is Halloween.

I love Halloween. Not just because we have been giving popcorn and cider for more than thirty years to an ever-increasing—this year exceeding an astounding five hundred—number of neighborhood children and presumptive adults, some of whom masquerade as parents. I love it for what I get, which is far more than what I give.

One special favorite of mine is a certain kind of *jeune fille* still young enough to get all costumed up, radiant, freshly shampooed, positively electric with sparks flying in all directions. These are the girls who at age twelve or thirteen travel in packs, and are in love with many things but especially the word *so*. "This is *so* cool, this popcorn is *so* good, this is *so* much fun, you guys are *so* nice to do this," they say as they *ooh* and *ah* at the big popcorn machine, laugh at my silly jokes, and, without skipping a beat, scramble down the porch on their mad dash to enchant the next set of hearts.

So, it doesn't get much better than that, for me at least. It brings back all the memories of our own daughters at that brief intersection between innocence and what comes next, when the house was alive and kicking with a life force that, to this distant day, sustains us.

Every year, there is at least one moment when it looks like our little distribution system will crash. Perhaps there are more than forty-plus "customers" on the porch and all the way out to the street, clamoring for their popcorn/cider fix. A mob is a mob no matter how well-intentioned. We labor mightily and thus far have always made it through. What satisfaction we feel! It takes at least two weeks before the strong smell of popcorn oil leaves the house, so the taste of the whole thing literally lingers on. What a glow, what a kick we get from such a silly thing!

We are known as the "popcorn house," and all year long are congratulated for our generosity, for making a scene that has become part of the neighborhood, what one looks forward to, and as the years go by, what one looks back at. *So* my gratitude is boundless. I couldn't be more pleased with myself if I had won the lottery.

What a strange way to become a destination, what a good way. If you are around, come by next year. We will be glad to welcome you.

Connections

Tribe, gang, friends, teammates, colleagues, the infinite multitude of circles circling, real and imagined. The way we move in and out of these experiences is like those metal rings that magicians use, one moment locked in place and the next separate, unconnected.

Think about the many connections that are part of your life—colleagues at work, your basketball team, your son's Little League, your alumni association, your band, the group you ride the bus with each morning, your bridge friends, your reading club, your church or temple, and maybe a chat room or two. Some of these we choose, others are there by chance, and others go with the territory (i.e., your daughter wants to play soccer, so soccer league it is).

Most of these are small, passing-through, walk-by experiences, what Richard Florida calls "weak ties," but some become communities that fully engage and interest us.[14] Over time, these layered strands of life create the cozy feeling of what a small and interconnected world this is, one that instantly turns strangers into people with whom we feel a connection.

However, as good as these experiences are, as satisfying and as important as they are to instilling a love of place, they do not become true solidarities of common interest until they are at risk, until they are threatened by change, and there is always change.

Change

Some handle the challenge of change with great generosity of spirit. I am reminded of Webster, my friend and neighbor.

Webster lived in an old Victorian house, painted pale yellow, the smell of linseed oil on the front porch and plumbing from the turn of the century, with a very shy person by the name of Mae who took care of him. When we met, he was in his early eighties, and he remained feisty and fully engaged in life until his death at ninety-eight. Webster's big adventure occurred when he was a young engineer working for the telephone company during the construction of the Panama Canal. To say the least, his life experience had quite a reach back—two world wars, the Great Depression, and everything in between. He loved to fuss but somehow remained open to newness, to young people. He simply loved the energy and action of change.

I was part of a church investment committee in those years and we would meet occasionally for supper at Webster's—the living room piled high with church records going back sixty years, and the same bottle of B&B with the cork floating in it on the dining room table. We were apparently the only customers. Mae would call to Webster who would come clattering down the stairs with two canes, flying like a skier on stilts. Those were wonderful evenings, more about Webster than about the church's modest investments.

Every time, Webster would tell me we sold something he thought we shouldn't have or bought some stock he was convinced would go down the rat hole. In the same visit, I would hear about the good old days that he was glad were past, and whether or not the new people who were moving into the neighborhood amounted to a hill of beans, and he would ask who was this person and that. "Have you met the lovely new family from Guatemala who just joined the church? Why did the president do something so stupid? At least FDR was smart," he'd say. (Except he never agreed with FDR.) "Isn't life fascinating?" he'd ask, offering history, current events, and social commentary at its best. He was something else. I still marvel at how Webster, after almost a century of living, was fresh and receptive, and able not only to accommodate change but also to enjoy it. His generosity of spirit was rare.

Change often comes at us as a challenge to our privacy, our sense of what is right, and it often is in the form of something happening literally next door.

One of the participants in those long-ago evenings at Webster's house was Fred, a prominent lawyer with a big downtown law firm who made a ton of money in the bankruptcy business. Fred came to the rescue of a controversial project, and at the time he seemed an unlikely savior. The project was a halfway house for what in the '70s were being described as "alienated youth," and we had purchased a property in a prime residential neighborhood. The idea had been conceived in a high school classroom, and was student led and run at a time when that was unusual and, to the neighbors who abutted the property, highly suspect. After several public hearings, endless community meetings, local press having a heyday, and the city split between those who supported and those who opposed, a license was granted to open the facility. A well-credentialed executive director "house couple" was hired, and the first cohort of clients were selected and about to move in when the neighbors slapped a lawsuit on both the city and the project, claiming the project violated zoning regulations and the city should never have allowed it to happen.

I will never forget that first meeting in Fred's office when the student leaders, one other adult board member, and I, hats in hand, asked for help. Fred knew that if he was "in for a nickel" he was in "for a dollar" but

THE IMAGINED COMMUNITY (THE CRIME OF NOT LISTENING) 135

offered to help without hesitation. I think he was somewhat bemused by the situation, but also troubled that a good idea from a group of smart, passionate, and caring young people was unfairly being attacked. So he rolled up his sleeves and, with a team of litigators, conducted a first-rate legal defense all the way up to the state supreme court, where he won! The cost had to be staggering, and it was all done as a pro bono gift.

If Webster was an example of someone with an unusually generous spirit, Fred was someone who was generous with the whole nine yards—spirit, time, and money. He was also rare.

About the same time there was an even bigger "not in my backyard" (NIMBY) event in town that did not have a successful conclusion. The plan was to build five-hundred units of low- and moderate-income housing. The organizers had selected ten sites, most of them in the poorer parts of the city. All of the sites required zoning variances of one kind or another. This noble effort was led by a city resident who was a successful senior marketing executive from a large company. The case for more housing seemed self-evident. There was very little low-cost housing in the city, and prices were continuing to increase beyond the means of many citizens, especially the elderly, who were on fixed incomes, teachers, and other municipal workers. Armed with beautiful charts and graphics that illustrated why this was the "right idea" and "good" for the whole city, we began a campaign to persuade the mayor, the city council, and the community. None of us who were promoting this effort lived in the neighborhoods that would be directly affected, and none of us were income eligible for the proposed housing. We were simply citizens who cared about housing and had decided to do something about it.

The big plan was announced in the local newspaper and a series of hearings and community meetings were held. I acted as moderator for some of these meetings. One I remember in particular was held in the auditorium of my children's junior high school. The room was jam-packed with three hundred people. Any illusion about an orderly facilitation fell apart from the very beginning; the objections were loud and vociferous. They ranged from direct abutters to the sites who didn't want the traffic and density, to those who were angry that the poorer parts of the community were getting most of the units, to those who felt that some of the sites were marginal at best for the planned use.

Some had done their homework and argued that the laws around the financing for low-income housing precluded a community from restricting it only to residents of the city. Thus, there was no guarantee that the city's police, teachers, and elderly would ultimately live in these units. Simmering just below the surface, and clear from many of the comments made, was fear that the project would attract a bunch of outsiders, poor people (read Black), into the community. Lastly, there was anger that the whole scheme had been planned from the top-down, having been cooked up by a bunch of do-gooders and self-appointed elites acting for the benefit of the unenlightened. I was frustrated and angry for not being able to hold the meeting together. It was also clear that we had been naïve, missed the mark, not anticipated how people would react, and had not done our own homework. I will never forget when, at the end of the meeting, two men I did not know came up to me and said, "We know all about you, where you live, and what you do. Just wanted to let you know that!" This was one of the first, but not the last, experiences when I realized that, in fact, "no good deed goes unpunished."

In this story, no different than many such efforts, NIMBY-ism is real, racism is real, and it makes no difference whether you are a for-profit or nonprofit real estate developer doing what you perceive to be the Lord's work—resistance is the norm. At the same time, what went wrong had as much to do with bad selling, with hubris, and with patronizing behavior on our part. We broke the first rule of good community organizing—and every such effort is fundamentally just that—which is to involve, as participants in the process, those who are most affected. We didn't do that or we didn't do it well enough, and it was enough to kill the deal except for one project of fifty units that managed to survive and be built. It was a shame. Since that time, real estate prices have risen even more dramatically and the city's opportunity to build much more affordable housing has passed.

What we should have done is gone back to the rules about community organizing that the great labor organizer Saul Alinksy first developed in the '50s. Alinsky wrote that to be a good community organizer you need curiosity, irreverence, imagination, a sense of humor, a bit of a blurred vision for a better world, an organized personality, a free and open mind, and political relativity.[15] I think that today's community organizer would add the ingredient of being a listener, especially to unheard voices. These characteristics sound like a great profile for life from any perspective, and I wish we had more of them when we were doing this work.

Community organizing is a process that starts with clear goals, defining what the community is and identifying the key stakeholders, recruiting a team or board, gaining knowledge about the issue, analyzing what the constraints are, creating an action plan, and gathering people empowered to act.

Central to the process is that the community is both listened to and informed, creating a relationship of trust through which credibility is built and allowing key stakeholders to participate and feel ownership.

The organizing process helps to refine the goals and increase understanding of the issue and the impact on the community. It also helps later on when creative strategies to achieve the goals are developed and a work plan/business plan is put in place.

The object is to strengthen the community's capacity to carry out the action plan, as well as to monitor the progress, solve problems, troubleshoot, advise, and mediate.

Appropriate evaluation, measurement, and analysis of impact and results are key, and feedback to the stakeholder community and others who wish to learn is critical. Documentation and sharing of results are also important in keeping the community invested.[16]

In some situations, there might need to be a scale-up of the vision and project. If so, there needs to be a consensus built and a plan that marshals support.[17]

This is a good blueprint as well for those involved in philanthropy on any level. Substitute the word *community* with NGO, nonprofit organization, project, program, concept, social change theory, big new idea, etc., and it still works—the principles are the same.

These two experiences, the halfway house and the low-income housing effort, occurred in the early '70s. They were part of the formation of my own "certain slant" on how complicated it is to assume things in a community setting, on how "good" intentions are often held suspect, and on the reality that there are many voices and many perspectives and that they all want a hearing. The other major lesson was the realization that new ideas, to prevail, need to successfully bridge the old. There is a need to be careful and to tread softly, otherwise the unintended results can be dire. Here is a story from that same era that supports that admonition.

Tread Softly

My friend Fred, the lawyer, was also the moderator of a Unitarian society that I belonged to, and in the early '70s we found ourselves in the middle of a classic church fight: a congregation divided into two opposing communities of interest. In the aftermath of the death of Dr. Martin Luther King Jr. in 1968, many religious groups, including the Unitarians, long recognized for their interest in social justice issues, were approached to invest endowment funds in Black economic development schemes. Our church was solicited to do just that by purchasing bonds that were to be invested in minority-owned businesses.

The request struck deep into ongoing divisions within the congregation that had been festering for some time. The long-term older members, who provided the vast majority of money to run the church, had for some time been increasingly uncomfortable with the large number of new, young, and more radical congregants who had little money

THE IMAGINED COMMUNITY (THE CRIME OF NOT LISTENING) 139

but a lot to say. They were outraged with the idea that an endowment fund left to the church by caring parishioners might be put at risk in untested investments in the inner city. To them, it was an affront to both legacy and the prudent stewardship of funds. The whole idea only reaffirmed their suspicion that the new church members were in for a free ride and were irresponsible as well.

The newer members, backed and led by a young and passionate minister, were equally committed in their belief that making this investment was the right thing to do. They became even more convinced then that the older members of the church were basically reactionary, and racist to boot. The irony, of course, was that those older members who were being accused were, in their own day, considered by themselves and their peers to be great liberals. Both sides were using this issue to reaffirm their worst fears about each other. All the ingredients were in place for a classic church fight.

This kind of struggle has played out countless times, not only in churches but also within many other kinds of organizations where cultures of young and old, newcomers and old hands, liberal and conservative, affluent and otherwise, meet head on. Both sides organized for battle by soliciting support for a big meeting at which the church would take a vote. I will never forget that night. The vestry hall was packed. In amazement, I noticed a number of people in wheelchairs and realized some elderly members of the congregation living in nursing homes had been convinced to take an ambulance to the church so that they could register their vote! This was serious business, and there was Fred as moderator—presumptively assisted by me as a member of the investment committee—in the role of explainer of what these nonrated, noninvestment-quality, by any definition, bonds were all about.

How fragile small organizations—and even larger institutions—are; how easily they can be destroyed when polarization runs rampant and there isn't enough trust, enough goodwill or good process, to bring it back on course. In this story, the minister, who could have been a bridge-builder, made the decision to throw everything he had on one side of the issue. He did so based on his own beliefs, but it was a disaster for the community called the church. The big vote was a nonevent—a modest commitment of $20,000 that satisfied no one was made to purchase the bonds (which in this case were never invested and ultimately returned to the church). Many of the older members ultimately resigned from the church, and sadly that included Fred, who loved the church. Most of the more ardent younger members drifted off and, as you could assume, the minister left in both frustration and disgrace. It took years, and a very different kind of ministry, to rebuild the congregation. Many organizations that suffer a similar experience never recover.

This story illustrates the challenge of creating, nourishing, supporting, and sustaining communities of solidarity, and cautions anyone who advocates for what they believe in. The first rule of life is to do no harm. Yet I can also hear the echo of another piece of kitchen-table wisdom, "In order to make an omelet you have to break some eggs." And therein lies the art of crossing the bridge from a "community of one" to a "community of many." It is part of the paradox of the commons and our relationship to it.

No one thirty years ago in that church wanted to hurt and destroy the institution, yet that is what almost happened. If there is a common challenge to the work within the public space, it is how to mediate different points of view while retaining your beliefs, and still accomplish the end goal.

Unintended Consequences

If the first rule in life is to do no harm, there is another related rule, that of unintended consequences, and they are sometimes dire.

The best of intentions had dramatic unintended consequences at a time in the '80s when I was president of the state association for mental health, which had long led the fight for community-based care and treatment of the mentally ill. For more than a century, mentally ill people had been warehoused in the back wards of large state-run hospitals. The situation was awful on every level for these patients. The institutional facilities were run down, the staffing and treatment were inadequate, and patients' rights, as we know them today, did not exist. I had first seen those back wards while in college in the late '50s, and will never forget how depressing and desperate they were.

The cure sold to the state legislature was the notion of community-based treatment for all but the most seriously mentally ill. Several factors made the timing right. One was the increasingly effective use of pharmacology in the treatment of mental illness, which in many cases reduced the necessity for hospitalization. Another was the growing belief that more humane and effective treatment was possible in local community settings rather than dehumanizing, ostracizing hospitals. It was also argued the state was better off not being in the direct-care business, and that privatizing such services would result in better care and treatment. The final argument, which won the day, was that community care would cost far less.

Many of these arguments were sound, while others, including the wisdom and efficacy of privatizing services heretofore the province of government, are still being debated. The last assumption, however, that community care would cost less, was a complete fabrication. No one really knew how much a community-based care system would cost, but to make the case that it would cost less was pure political expediency.

In reality, the implementation of an effective community-based delivery system proved to be much more difficult than originally thought. Finding residential sites for halfway houses and other facilities was a big challenge, and remains so as most neighborhoods strongly resist having these populations of patients and clients literally next door. The hoped-for cost savings from closing the old state institutions did not materialize for many years, as many of the most ill patients continued to be cared for in these rapidly decaying facilities, and the plan to sell those large tracts of land in a timely manner did not happen. Many of those same properties are still owned by the state more than thirty years later.

One of the most troubling results of this policy change was the creation of a new and undercapitalized system of human service providers. Many of these providers were originally local mental advocacy organizations and only became direct service providers at the behest of the state. These nonprofit organizations, still among the most fragile within the sector, are constantly buffeted by the vagaries of state funding and, in the main, have not been successful at raising resources from private philanthropy. This phenomenon is part of a larger trend toward a two-tier nonprofit system, with one tier made up of wealthy institutions like universities, major cultural organizations, and hospitals, and another tier made up of small community-based organizations struggling to survive under weak economic models. In the human services and mental health fields, the net result is systemic organizational and human resources problems that limit the capacity of these groups to provide good service to clients.

An even more troubling and unanticipated result of the deinstitutionalization of state mental health hospitals has been the creation of a large, permanent, homeless population of mentally ill people. Chronic homelessness is tied to the larger crises in low-income housing that have escalated during this same twenty-five-year period, but it is especially inhumane and poignant when mental illness is a contributing factor. There has been encouraging but slow progress made in the development of supportive housing for those with mental health problems, but it is not enough.

No one would propose a return to the dismal back wards of the state institutions. Nonetheless, it was irresponsible public policy for all the actors involved—including advocates (of which I was one), the Department of Mental Health, and the state legislature—to neglect the risk analysis and planning that would have led to better understanding of the implications of emptying those wards. There was far more attention paid to the theory of change than to the implementation of that change, which is something that occurs over and over again. In retrospect, it is clear that *we* took a walk away from the public's responsibility for those who are among the most vulnerable in the society. It would have been far better had we acknowledged and acted on the central truth that social change is incremental at best.

There is a homeless man who wanders the downtown block near my office. He has long, straggly hair, and walks with his face down, muttering in his delusions. I often give him money and have learned that he is too disruptive to be welcome in the shelters. He could be a prospect for supportive housing with professional staff to deal with his needs, but there are no supported housing slots available in our city. Every time I see him, and it is at least once a week, I think of what was done for good and proper reasons, and I regret that we did not do a better job.

On Right and Wrong

Whether one is doing good or doing harm is often in the eye of the beholder.

Take William, who is at the epicenter of the movement to provide Americans with a choice to educate their children. He and his colleagues are passionate in their view that the public schools are a monopoly, the only such monopoly in our society, and that the only solution is competition. Vouchers, charter schools, or any idea that tinkers with the existing system doesn't go far enough. This man wants a total revamping of what he views as unacceptable and un-American control over a parent's choice of where a child goes to school. He argues that the public school system as we know it is a failure that has been corrupted by the self-interests of teachers' unions and administrators. He also argues that public schools are a far cry from what Thomas Jefferson meant when he made the case for an educated citizenry.

William and other like-minded activists have organized a social-marketing campaign of unprecedented scale. *Social marketing* is the term used to describe the adaptation of Madison Avenue advertising and public relations techniques to influence public opinion and behavior. It is expected to cost more than $200 million to achieve the objective: to convince twenty million American parents that the public school system, as we know it, must be dismantled or radically restructured. However, ask William what will take its place and his answer is this: "I do not know, and would not presume to suggest. I am not an education expert. But this is America, and once the door is open for real competition, the market will take over and create the solutions."

I asked William about breaking the rule to "do no harm." I asked, "What if the results are disastrous and a whole generation of American children fall through the cracks?" William thought for a moment and said, "I do not think it really is a risk, but if so, it is one worth taking." Is that so? William has a libertarian perspective and is "peddling" change on a radical scale. My guess, and my hope, is that he will not prevail, partly because he has no discernible plan or end game, and partly because his idea is so extreme, but mostly because I think his approach is not good social policy.

The concern about "doing harm" does hold some people back. I once asked a wealthy friend, whose charitable giving is only a fraction of what is within his capacity to give, what prevented him from giving more. He said, "It would bother me enormously if I made large gifts and they did not work out. It would devastate me if the gifts actually hurt those I wanted to help, and when I look at the things that interest me the most, I am just not sure enough." My friend is wise to consider carefully his actions.

If philanthropy has a shadow side, it is in the nuance, in the subtlety, and it is centered in what might be called the "messiness" of real-life situations. That is not to suggest that taking risks—even big ones—is unwise or that innovation and change are not needed, sometimes critically, but at the same time, new ideas are not necessarily better ideas. It is very difficult to take ideas, even good ones, and make them happen. Disruption and even revolution are sometimes exactly the right and good things. But only the foolish amateur, muddleheaded philosopher, constipated bureaucratic arrogant know-it-all, starry-eyed social planner, or romantic advocate pays no attention to the possible scenarios that could result from one's best intentions. Or commits the crime of not listening.

Section 3 Reflection

Bridges to Reconciliation: An Incantation

Here are some of the bridges that lead to reconciliation between our private and public personas, between the self and the larger world.

Internal Bridges

From	ambition	to	acceptance
From	ego	to	sharing
From	fear	to	love
From	pragmatic	to	poetic
From	materiality	to	spirituality
From	obsession	to	perspective
From	hyperaction	to	contemplation
From	passive	to	active
From	dominance	to	yielding
From	being alone	to	belonging

External Bridges

From	self	to	community
From	community	to	community
From	haves	to	have-nots
From	one race	to	another
From	one religion	to	another
From	prejudice	to	tolerance

From	confrontation	to	reconciliation
From	violence	to	peace
From	ignorance	to	knowledge

Ask yourself these questions:

1. What bridges have I built internally? Externally?
2. What bridges would I like to build?
3. What three next actions might start the building?
4. What do I need to do to become a more skilled bridge builder?

SECTION 4:

JUSTICE

*Justice is
love distributed.*

JOSEPH FLETCHER[1]

Peter had a long history, starting in the 1960s, of engagement in social justice issues. His work trying to rally the business community to launch a fund to support development in Boston's African American communities yielded important, and sometimes painful, lessons that appear in ruefully self-deprecating anecdotes strewn through his writings. His depiction of himself as a kind of young, earnest Don Quixote with his heart on his sleeve, pressing forward, sometimes obscures the wisdom he attained through deep engagement.

In the last decade of his life, Peter's commitment to issues of justice and his calls to action became more urgent as he observed growing inequities in wealth and political polarization.

Peter believed, as he often said, that "justice is love distributed,"[2] and the injustices he saw were, for him, a failure of both love and imagination. This was a personal matter as well as an institutional one for him. "Sometimes the sounds of silence can be deafening," he says in "Standing Up," an essay in which he reserves, as he always did, his harshest interrogations about moral obligation for himself. Starting with the personal failure to act, to stand up against a wrong at a dinner party, he describes a silence that, left unbroken, threatens our very social fabric.

Peter ends that essay with a lament and a question: "And we, where are we, where are you, where am I?" This is his call to us to locate ourselves, to stand up, to take a stand.

In "The Redress of Philanthropy," Peter begins to define a key role of philanthropy in helping to take such stands by "tilting the scale of reality toward some transcendent equilibrium—which brings a reconciliation." He paraphrases the poet Seamus Heaney, saying: "I believe that the nobility of philanthropy is our moral imagination pressing back against the pressure of reality."[3]

Peter was never one to shrink from "the pressure of reality," and he was haunted by those who do. In "Sleepwalkers," he speculates about what might make them—or us—wake up and engage more directly. "It is not a matter of knowing what to do" or having the resources, he concludes, but perhaps more a paralysis of not knowing what is right, and a general loss of the "we," the commons that connects us.

"The Sociology of Wealth" was one of Peter's last pieces—written just prior to the 2016 election—and is one of his clearest calls to the wealthy to do more to right past injustices.

In his essay "In an Era of Scarcity," Peter poses this question: "What gives us the right to 'intervene'" in complex social problems? He concludes that to not act is to deepen the wrong.

As always, he is generous and empathetic toward those he is criticizing, expressing his own struggle to find the right path and to know what justice is.

> Confusion is not what one expects from experience. Experience is supposed to teach how the world works and lead to greater clarity about how to live one's life. I thought that with age and experience more peace of mind would come, instead of less. I expected something

> different, a kind of resolution, a weaving together of the strands of living.
>
> The truth is I am less optimistic, less confident, and less sure about what to believe.

Still, he kept pressing forward, searching for "the untapped potential of spirit and action" that can be expressed through giving. He abhorred the emphasis on tax benefits as a rationale for giving more, saying, "Tax deductibility is simply an enhancement. Yet we trumpet and market that enhancement as though it were the real deal."

What Peter, the self-described "peddler," wanted to sell instead was philanthropy, was a way of community-finding, a path to the "'we' that represents a broad and open public purpose." In "The Speech I Have Always Wanted to Give," he makes the case for that quest and, in the piece that closes this section, "Movement Builders," he talks about finding—and becoming—the leaders who will create redress for injustice, a quest "you cannot you dare not abdicate."

Standing Up

Because a wink and a nod in the face of injustice have become a habit of mind for us.
ALICE McDERMOTT[4]

A continuous parallel between contemporaneity and antiquity.
T. S. ELIOT[5]

Sometimes the only audience is you. Alone with your soul, and your God if you have one.

Aristotle believed that the defining characteristic of humankind is our ability to understand the difference between the just and the unjust. The Alice McDermott quote above assumes so—otherwise the "wink and nod" line would not work, and it does. There is a natural instinct to lie low, to mind one's own business, to be polite in polite company, to defer to authority, and to stay out of the line of fire. Sometimes we cannot. Sometimes we find ourselves in the belly of the beast.

Imagine you are in a business meeting, and an important client tells a nasty anti-Semitic story. Your colleagues know you are Jewish even though you don't look it. Or perhaps you are at a dinner party, and someone makes a crude joke about lesbians. Only your hostess knows your eldest daughter is a lesbian, and that you consider her twenty-year partner a daughter, if not in law then in fact.

Let's make it less dramatic.

You are present in the meeting and at the dinner party and are neither a Jew nor the father of a lesbian, but you are embarrassed and bothered by what you have heard. Either way, you have arrived at a line in the sand of life, a moment of truth.

What do you say or do? What do you not say or not do? There are risks and there are rewards, no matter what you do. Let's explore some potential actions you could take.

You cause a scene, make a passionate speech, and stomp out of the room in righteous anger.
The potential risks here are that you might anger the client and lose the business; you could make a fool of yourself in everyone's eyes, including your own; you could embarrass your colleagues or your hostess who will never want to lay eyes on you again; you could be accused of overreacting—making a mountain out of a molehill; you could lose an opportunity to change the way someone thinks or, even worse, you could reaffirm the speakers' hostile attitudes toward Jews and lesbians.

The potential rewards are that you feel better, having spoken your mind; or that you are considered a hero by others in the room, and the speakers feel awkward and guilty about their comments and less inclined to make them again.

You remain cool, polite but firm, and attempt to engage the speakers in a dialogue.
The potential risks here are that they still get upset and an argument occurs, resulting in awkwardness all around; or that, despite your good intentions, you lose self-control (similar to the above); or that, it turns out, others in the room agree with the speakers' comments, which results in even more social drama.

The potential rewards are that a reasonable and maybe even illuminating discussion occurs, and that the speakers apologize and compliment your courage and tact; the relationship with the client is strengthened; and the hostess is thrilled with her memorable dinner party.

You dodge the bullet, laugh nervously, and try to lightly change the subject.
The potential risks with this behavior are that the awkward subjects come up a second and third time, as though silence was tacit encouragement; your

relationship with the client is changed forever; you never want to see the hostess again; and you hate yourself afterward for being a coward.

The potential rewards are as follows: the business meeting goes according to plan, as does the dinner party, and your colleagues and hostess breathe a sigh of relief and appreciate that you did not make a scene.

How many of you have been in a similar kind of situation? Quite a few is my guess, and since I fit these profiles and am both a Jew and a father of a lesbian, I have had variations of these experiences and, alas, have responded at different times in all three ways.

So I know how much time one spends after the fact rewriting those responses because, in the heat of the moment, clear thinking and eloquence are often in short supply. Of the three scenarios above, it is the third—the one of silence—that I find most troubling. The opportunity to be silent is ever present.

Sometimes the sounds of silence can be deafening.

———

I am with a friend, a very wealthy man with a large foundation, and we are discussing his deep concern about the rise of anti-Semitism in Europe. In his view, the Israeli-Palestinian conflict is being used as fuel for the resurgence of right-wing political activities, for renewal of ancient hatreds that lie just below the surface of too many cultures. My friend is not alone in these views, and as we were discussing what his foundation could do about it, he made this comment:

> Do you think, in the '30s, there were people in Europe like us, gathered around some table worrying about the growing danger of Nazism? Why didn't they act? How could they have been silent? I don't want to be like that, sit on the sidelines, and be responsible for history repeating itself.

As this man understands, T. S. Eliot's "continuous parallel" is not just between today and antiquity, it is between today and yesterday, and tomorrow.[6] His fears and nightmares are about quislings, Schindler's list, desperate partisans in the mountains, the stomp of boots in the middle of the night, and silence.

Worlds apart, far from speculations, are those who live in the midst of the nightmare of poverty, injustice, war, and terror, and still find the courage to stand up and act. Below, I celebrate some of these people and their accomplishments, as each was a recipient of the 2003 Reebok Human Rights Award.[7]

Pedro Anaya is a twenty-four-year-old Mexican American who chose as his hero Cesar Chavez, the great labor leader who symbolizes the immigrant labor movement's struggle for justice and fair wages. Pedro formed an organization that fights bias, bigotry, and racism, and works on behalf of very poor people for access to housing and education. "What inspires me is this amazing opportunity to make people's lives better. It is a blessing," he said.

Ernest Guevarra is a twenty-four-year-old physician from the Philippines who has devoted himself to the disadvantaged, and volunteers at a clinic to treat victims of human rights violations. After protesting government torturing of Muslims, Guevarra was jailed. Despite threats of violence, he continues to work as physician to thousands of displaced villagers in the midst of a war zone. Ernest is motivated to work "with people who have risen up to control their lives and chart a better future—that is my happiness."

Oona Chatterjee is a Yale Law graduate who works in Bushwick, a desperately poor section of Brooklyn, helping victimized garment workers receive fair wages from illegal sweatshop owners and organize for a better life for themselves and their children. Oona struggles with the "stark contradictions in this country between extreme wealth and . . .

serious human rights violations in the conditions people work under. Making the world make sense out of those contradictions—that's what moves me."

Mohamed Pa-Momo Fofanah, from Sierra Leone, is a thirty-year-old lawyer who devotes his life to protecting the rights of children caught in poverty and civil chaos. To Mohamed, the sight of seven-year-olds carrying guns was the final image that motivated him to become an advocate for children who live in extreme risk. "Dealing with poverty, cruelty, and death can be depressing, but children have values and virtues suppressed by war and, given the opportunity, they do wonders," he said. "In children there is hope and to see them smile . . ."

Christian Mukosa, a twenty-eight-year-old lawyer from Congo, where a decade-long civil war has created the worst kind of chaos and anarchy, represents impoverished victims of torture and human rights abuse. He does this at great personal risk. "In my country, people go to jail because they have no lawyer," he says. "For me to help them, it gives me great pleasure. And besides, if I don't do it, who will?"

And we, where are we, where are you, where am I?

The Redress of Philanthropy

Redress—noun
A relief from distress. Means or possibility of seeking a remedy. Compensation for wrong or loss. An act or instance of redressing. Retribution, correction.

Redress—verb
To set right, remedy. To make up for, compensate. To remove the cause of (a grievance or complaint). To exact reparation for, avenge. To requite (a person) for a wrong or loss. Heal.[8]

In his book *The Redress of Poetry*, Seamus Heaney calls poetry "the imagination pressing back against the pressure of reality."[9] Heaney concludes by saying:

> The redress of poetry is in its being instrumental, in adjusting and correcting imbalances in the world, poetry as an intended intervention into the goings-on of society.
>
> To be a source of truth, and at the same time a vehicle of harmony . . . These poets feel with a special force a need to be true to the negative nature of the evidence and at the same time to show an affirming flame, the need to be socially responsible and creatively free.[10]

This pushing and pressure are echoed by Wallace Stevens who said: "The nobility of poetry is a violence from within that protects us from a violence without."

Likewise, I believe that the nobility of philanthropy is our moral imagination pressing back against the pressure of reality. That imagination, when it is urgent, creates the kind of "violence from within" that Stevens names.

As Simone Weil put it:

> If we know in what way society is unbalanced, we must do what we can to add weight to the lighter scale . . . We must have formed a conception of equilibrium and be ever ready to change sides like justice, "that fugitive from the camp of conquerors."[11]

The whole essence of philanthropy is, as Heaney said of Weil's work, "informed by the idea of counterweighting, of balancing out the forces of redress—tilting the scales of reality toward some transcendent equilibrium"[12]—which brings a reconciliation

- between wealth (individual, family, and corporate) and responsibility to society;
- between the challenge of new ideas and change with the old order;
- between the art and the science, between passion, feelings, and intuitiveness on the one hand, and data and measurable effectiveness on the other;
- between "infinite need" and "limited resources";
- between the power of the donor and the dependency of the recipient;

- between urgency and the realization that change is slow and incremental at best; and

- between the idea and the plan, and outside forces over which the plan has limited or no control.

To do that, to be both a source of truth and a vehicle of harmony, requires hope as defined by Václav Havel:

> [Hope is] a state of mind, not a state of the world. Either we have hope within us or we don't; it is a dimension of the soul, and it's not essentially dependent on some particular observation of the world or estimate of the situation. . . . It is an orientation of the spirit, an orientation of the heart: it transcends the world that is immediately experienced, and is anchored somewhere beyond its horizons. I don't think you can explain it as a mere derivative of something here, of some movement, or some favorable signs in the world. I feel its deepest roots are the transcendental, just as the roots of human responsibility are. . . . It is not the conviction that something will turn out well, but the certainty that something makes sense, regardless of how it turns out.[13]

The untapped potential of spirit and action, fueled by hope, is the potential of philanthropy.

Sleepwalkers

> *To appraise a society, examine its ability to be self-correcting. When grievous wrongs are done or endemic suffering exposed, when justice is denied, watch the institutions of government and business and charity.*[14]
>
> DAVID K. SHIPLER

Prelude

I am confused, and the older I get the greater the confusion. While the confusion of which I speak is personal, it emanates from the troubles, or what might be called *disconnects*, within the society in which I live, and it affects the decisions I must make. It also affects my work, which happens to be philanthropy. Like an actor who cannot remember his lines, it makes one's stomach churn. Confusion is not a good thing, especially if the confusion is over fundamental moral questions. At what point, for example, does something constitute a grievous wrong, endemic suffering, or justice denied? When, for example, does an issue like systemic poverty become material to the moral health of the nation? If the numbers of the very poor were to increase by one million, ten million, twenty million, would that constitute more of a crisis of conscience than the one that we face today? None of this makes sense to me. It is part of my confusion.

Confusion is not what one expects from experience. Experience is supposed to teach how the world works and lead to greater clarity about how to live one's life. I thought that with age and experience more peace of mind would come, instead of less. I expected something different, a kind of resolution, a weaving together of the strands of living.

The truth is I am less optimistic, less confident, and less sure about what to believe. Even when I think the answer to a question is clear, I do not know what action to take that will be meaningful or what, if anything, will make a difference. Sometimes I am not even always sure what is right and what is wrong, but what confuses me the most is why, in the face of what seems to me to be overwhelming evidence, so many people, including those who are our leaders, continue to act as though nothing is wrong.

Do they? You may ask. Perhaps things are not as bad as I *feel* they are. I hope so, because this sense of helplessness induces a kind of alienation, angst, and, inexorably, a fear.[15] I don't like these feelings of anxiety at all—they seem self-indulgent—but I know I am not alone in this kind of complaint about the human condition. It is hardly new. If in doubt, look at the literature for those caught in equilibrium, those who are sleepwalking.

The Sleepwalkers

In the novel *The Sleepwalkers*, the monumental trilogy written by the Austrian writer Hermann Broch in the late 1920s and early 1930s, the protagonist of the first volume suffers from an existential malaise. He is disconnected from reality and unable to cope with the society in which he lives and dreams, and about which he feels a great sense of futility. And what, in his predicament, reminds me of my own is that action eludes him. In the same way, or so it seems, that action eludes our society as a whole.[16]

Two more recent novels that reflect the troubles of our own times also come to mind. The protagonist of Don DeLillo's novel *Underworld* drifts aimlessly through fear and denial of the threat of nuclear war while the society around him seems oblivious, and is obsessed with growing corporate materialism. And Jay Cantor's remarkable novel *Great Neck* takes us deep into the turbulent '60s when radical and self-destructive action took on a violent life of its own. For those caught up in that time of passion and idealism amidst powerful forces of race and class, the sleepwalker woke up and, for some, the dream became a nightmare.

Whenever we read books such as these, with the substance, symbolism, and beauty of great narrative, we understand better what it takes to face our own personal demons. We understand more vividly the dilemma of a society that has diminished capacity to be self-correcting.

But life is not literature and none of us are characters in a book. Instead, most of us would agree with the poet Jane Cooper when she wrote: "I am trying to learn to live a decent life and not want to be a great person, and at the same time know what I have the human right to draw the line at."[17] That is, in essence, what most of us want. But what does living a decent life mean for you, or for me, when a society has lost its soul, when the community in which we live has lost its way? What does it mean? What do you do? Knowing what is right, and having the right to "draw the line" is one thing, exercising it is another.

Action is hard in a society where trust is in short supply and cynicism is pervasive, where too many people are overwhelmed by cultural norms that are offensive to them. Action is hard if one feels powerless in the face of extremism, which is a kind of false faith. The result is what one contemporary writer describes as a "decreasing sense of relationship to the whole."[18] It is what many writers have written about from very different perspectives.[19] When that relationship is lost across an entire society, especially a democratic society dependent on citizen engagement, we give up a lot. We give up too much. Too many citizens are not participating, are not actors on the stage of life.

Scott Harshbarger, the former president of Common Cause, and a two-term Massachusetts attorney general, cites the central role of citizen mobilization in making democracy really work. Harshbarger believes it is all about the need to reeducate people about what it means to engage in democracy, what it means to be citizens. If too many citizens are sleepwalkers, which I believe is the case in the United States, that task is made hugely more complicated.

On Caritas—the American Social Contract

What I resist believing with all of my being is that we as a society do not care, or do not care enough. Caritas, caring for others, community, generosity, charity—and its American invention, philanthropy—has been at the center of the social contract that binds this society together. A social contract can be founded on a belief in God or on a belief in justice, values, or even prejudice and preference. It cannot rest on tax policy and tax exemptions, even though one might get the idea that those are the central elements.[20] At its heart, a social contract is about reciprocity, about sharing—sharing power and wealth.

The American "deal" between society and its citizens has been a blend of opportunity, personal responsibility, and benevolence within a context of democratic and free-market principles. Those principles are inextricably linked. Concepts like fairness, equality, access, a level playing field, community, and communities of interest—terminology that speaks to a kind of public stewardship—have been balanced with the energy and individualism of the entrepreneur and the competitive reality of the market economy. It has never been a simple, even-handed balance. And in many instances, it has been a difficult struggle, but in the United States that combination has produced remarkable results regarding both quality of life and equity for the vast majority of Americans.

Most remarkable has been the interrelationship and mutual dependency of government and citizen action—what we now call "civil society." The world has never seen this level of democratization before. Yet something may be eroding our civil society. It is the concentration of power of both ideas and capital, and the decline in both benevolence and equal opportunity. What I do not see is a self-correcting response that kicks in, even when we have crossed the line. What I see is less sharing.

While there are a number of indicators of this phenomenon, it is the growing gap between the very wealthy and the very poor that is the most striking evidence of the collapse of the American social contract.

Rich and Poor

In 2001, the top 1 percent of the US population held 38 percent of all wealth, double that of twenty years before—a concentration of wealth that is remarkable and troubling. For comparison, in 1989, the top 1 percent of the population held less wealth than the bottom 90 percent of the population. By 2001, the top 1 percent held $2 trillion more wealth than the bottom 90 percent.[21]

The United States is the wealthiest country in the history of the world, and yet, some thirty-eight million people, 12.4 percent of the population, a percentage that has increased every year in the last ten, live below the poverty line, with an additional six million classified as the "working poor."[22] For the working poor, the American dream is an illusion.

Families living in poverty grew from 6.6 million in 2001 to 7 million in 2002 and the number of children living in poverty is now 12.2 million.[23] This population has less mobility than ever; only a third of the poorest families have some kind of housing subsidy or financial assistance, and housing costs are at an all-time high.[24]

Hunger is an everyday issue for more than thirteen million children in America![25] (Can this actually be true? The answer is yes.) Overall, there are more than thirty million inadequately fed Americans.[26]

This is not new data to me, and it may not be to you. I have known about these statistics for a long time, and poor people are hardly invisible. The data is before our eyes, on the street corner, on paper, and in the Congressional Record, but somehow as a society we sleepwalk by it all. When I hear of an economist who is *not* troubled by this data because it is immaterial to the economic health of the nation, I wonder what I am missing. It is part of my confusion.

If the imbalance between the rich and the poor in the United States is troubling, it is more dramatically so elsewhere in the world. The disparity between the rich nations of the North, especially the United States, and the poor nations of the South is extraordinary. While much has been made of the destabilizing effect of desperately poor populations and how those conditions become breeding grounds for civil unrest and terrorism, it is the broader moral issue of massive human suffering that haunts my own dreams. And it awakens my own personal Greek chorus.

> I will consume less, and become part of a movement, urge my neighbors and friends to sharply reduce our absurdly high American standard of living.
>
> *Be my guest, that's a guilt trip for God's sake. Your individual action won't affect anything. Plus, if you and others were really successful, the United States would nosedive into a huge recession and take the rest of the world with us.*
>
> I will change my foundation's giving priorities and no longer support my local theater or arts organization in favor of poverty alleviation, even though I love the arts.
>
> *Great, you are going to turn your back on the one thing that you believe brings perspective, not to mention beauty, into the life of this arid society.*
>
> I will join the chorus of voices that argue for more responsible codes of conduct for multinational corporations and a reassessment of the forces of globalization.

> *Good luck! These guys have got it wired between the power and the greed of the market economy. They are not going to be influenced by do-gooders like you.*

I will advocate for the things that I believe in, make the politicians listen, and organize my community to lobby for a broader public interest.

> *Who do you think you are—Saul Alinsky? All you will do is get your name in the paper and on more lists.*

I will work my butt off to get rid of this president—he is the problem.

> *It would be political suicide for any elected official really to take up the cause of the poor. Bottom line—too many people don't give a damn.*

I do not know how to answer these questions.

> *That's right, and neither does anyone else.*

Is that true? Are there really no answers? I think the answer is yes and no.

It is not a matter of financial capacity. In fact, the cost to deal with much of the inequity is remarkably modest, well within the capacity of this nation and the wealthy nations of the world collectively. For example, it would take $5 billion a year to end hunger in America—today largely spent in updating the food stamp program.[27] Five billion dollars is not a large amount in a $10 trillion economy. Looked at differently, it is a fraction of what we spend annually on cigarettes, beer, or cosmetics.

It is not a matter of knowing what to do. There are solutions and there are strategies that work. There is much that can be done to enable people to lift themselves out of poverty.[28]

Then Why?

Perhaps the focus on the poor is the wrong one to test the thesis that our society has a decreasing sense of relationship to the whole. For example, the US middle class is caught on the dark side of globalization, outsourcing, and increased productivity. For many currently well-paid Americans, there are a decreasing number of postindustrial and information-age jobs. These jobs are moving offshore as multinational corporations follow, in a heartbeat, the inevitable flow of economics. For the first time in US history, economic growth is not directly linked to the creation of new jobs. This new dynamic is a tough economic and social problem that has the potential to lead, at least in the short-term, to a serious decline in the economic well-being of the American middle class. It certainly contributes to the resistance of most Americans to even the idea of raising taxes, and it certainly has its own moral dimension of something unfair, even if it does not sink to the same level of fundamental inequity as does the plight of the very poor.[29]

If we as a society can sleepwalk past the most vulnerable among us, it is highly unlikely we will respond to anything else. And that includes the other major ultimatums[30] of our time on this earth: weapons of mass destruction and environmental degradation.

Is it a surprise I am confused? The confusion is in the air. We stare each evening, courtesy of the TV news, into the face of an interconnected social malaise. The message overwhelms, numbs, desensitizes, and neuters our sense of what is possible. It dilutes our innate sense of justice. It feeds and contributes to the loss of trust. Asking whether we as a society care may be the wrong question. Whether we are able to feel is perhaps a better question.

Is there a root cause, something that can explain, or at least shed light on, why we do not respond? Perhaps there is.

A House Divided[31]

American society is deeply divided along several fault lines. To begin with, we are politically divided right down the middle. Many of America's divisions are ideological, some are economic, and some are based on class and race.

There are big and complicated lines of disagreement, where the argument has become increasingly strident, and even vicious. Mistrust is high at all levels. Say the word "liberal," or "evangelical," or "environmental," say any number of words, and the knee-jerk reaction is almost visceral. The American polyarchy, its inherent pluralism, has worked historically, but it is increasingly lopsided, and it is difficult to see how it can continue to work.[32]

And herein lies the greater risk. If we destroy, or have destroyed, the deeply democratic American capacity for civility, for consensus, for generosity of spirit that has been integral to the success of the society, we will grow more polarized, less able to deal with critical issues, and more lacking in political will. In fact, it may be completely wrong to say that Americans do not care because, in some instances, it may be that they care too much. We have gotten entangled in a kind of social war that begins with a loud argument about how to approach problems and then makes the *approach* the issue, drowning out and missing the substance of the problem. It is then, argues Jane Jacobs, the noted American-Canadian urban sociologist, that the gaps become unbridgeable.

Certainly, the ideological divide is not in every instance so clearly defined. Many Americans are concerned to see a society increasingly committed to the pursuit of pleasure and explicit sexuality, a society dependent on an all-consuming consumer-driven materialism, a country determined to become a bully economically and diplomatically and growing increasingly isolated in the process. It worries some Americans that we have become a society where priorities are warped, values are diluted, fundamental morality on some very basic level is lost, with a "beat the law" mentality that ranges from corporate fraud and greed to pervasive underage drinking on college campuses, where the law has become a joke. There certainly is no ideological divide on the problem of the working poor, for it is one of America's cherished assumptions that anyone who works full time should be able to make enough money to live on.[33]

Are these Republican or Democratic issues, liberal or conservative issues? I think they are everyone's. Are they troublesome to those who are religious and go to church or temple, as well as to those who are not churchgoers? I think they deeply trouble both. It is not delusionary to make the case that there are many spaces within the sometimes-contentious public debate over major policy and social issues where we agree far more than the rhetoric suggests. Perhaps that is why most Americans are in the ambivalent middle, and why most analysts conclude the country is not ready for a pitched battle on these issues and, if anything, has become more progressive and accepting.[34] And it is the middle that is most afflicted with alienation, and most unengaged. It is the middle that sleepwalks.

At the same time, huge differences of opinion and belief exist on matters that relate to the role and size of government, its involvement in citizens' lives, and governmental regulation—especially in regard to the environment and energy consumption. The struggle over values and the relationship of church to state is real. And globally, the relentless march of globalization, beyond raising domestic concerns about outsourcing, pits the unbridled expansion of the market economy and increased development against the wishes of Indigenous populations and major environmental concerns. These issues cannot be sugarcoated, nor solved through rhetoric or a mechanical process of conflict resolution.

The Commons

Jane Cooper is right, we are entitled to "know what I have the human right to draw the line at."[35] But are there other lines we are not entitled to draw, or to say, "It ends here!"? The truth is what is outrageous to one person is acceptable to another. We need to respect others as much as we respect ourselves. When I demean the beliefs and perspectives of others, and attack their lifestyles and perspectives, I have crossed the line of commonweal. When my passionate advocacy goes "over the top," when my private individual action "privatizes" the public space, I have abused the privilege of individual action. I have violated another's human right. I do not want the public space—the commons—to limit the diversity at the table. When it does, I cannot win, we cannot win, and there is too much anger and fear generated, too much mistrust. The truth is one cannot "win" without yielding. It is in the nature of all things, of any successful relationship between parties. It is true in our personal relationships (witness the critical ingredients of accommodation and compromise in marriage) and just as true in every other relationship. One cannot make a successful deal—be it business, political, community, local, national, or global—unless it fundamentally works for all sides.

Perhaps we need to read again Walt Whitman's lines from the poem "Song of Myself."

> I celebrate myself, and sing myself,
> And what I assume you shall assume,
> For every atom belonging to me as good belongs to you.[36]

Except for those few who believe entirely in their right to unbridled individualism, in essence to be pathologically selfish, I think this works. And for those, there are other answers.

One Has a Choice

Does the suggestion that advocacy can be carried to an extreme diminish the need to stand up for what one believes, or the need for communities of interest to argue their case? Or does it mute the differentiation between right and wrong, or good and evil?

In my view, it does just the opposite. It makes the practical imperative for strong countervailing voices even more important, especially in the face of extremism. It makes the case for an informed citizenry that takes an active part in the democratic process more essential. Rather than undermine the case, it bolsters the case for a robust multi-voiced and pluralistic advocacy. It is "a plurality of voices, a plurality of visions," that is the balance to extremism.[37] In the rising up of more voices is the answer to the question of which lines can be crossed and which lines should not be crossed. It ultimately leads to the heart of how democracy works and the answer of what makes people accountable, and to whom.[38]

It is those who sleepwalk who have the choice. As dazed or disturbed or turned-off as they might be by all the white noise from the inequities and great issues of our time, or by the strident and self-centered voices of the extremists, they have a choice. People can choose, even though it is hard to sort it all out, what they believe in and advocate for it. And I believe that is what they must do.

Response

Since I work in the field of philanthropy, these personal confusions affect me professionally. While government has by far the greatest responsibility to the social contract—as well as infinitely greater capacity to respond to major social problems—citizenship and voluntary individual action in a democratic society have the ultimate influence on government action. Philanthropy is an important articulation of citizen voice; it is uniquely positioned to encourage more inclusion, as well as to give form and clarity to the issues that engender this confusion. Philanthropy at its best is also nimble and creative.

My colleagues and I see the impact of these questions on foundations and donors of all stripes every day. The wealthy family confronting a decision on the allocation of wealth between family members and charitable gifts is influencing, on a personal level, the issue of rich and poor, and the redistribution of wealth. There will be millions of such decisions made by individuals and families in the years to come. The vast volume of the intergenerational transfer of wealth makes those decisions a material factor in the well-being of society. The donor moved by inequity—perhaps it is poverty, perhaps it is something else—who decides to act makes one statement. The donor who decides to play it safe and limit gifts to elite institutions that primarily cater to the wealthy makes another.

I admire the pluralism of American philanthropy, which is part charity, part preservation, part social venture, part system change, part social marketing, and part advocacy. I respect the importance of religion to so many Americans and understand why so much charitable giving goes to support religion.[39] I acknowledge the loyalty alumni have to their universities and colleges, and know how well-funded institutional fundraising efforts pay off. I know that recognition, social pressure and influence, and ego are huge factors in why people give money to charity. I know social relationships and business obligations are real and influence-giving. I know it is complicated to figure out how to tackle tough social problems, that it takes a lot of work to invest philanthropic resources thoughtfully, and that many donors do not know how to go about that work. I also know that many people simply do not have the time or interest to work hard at making a difference, and that a few do not care at all.

Despite all that, it is confusing to me that more wealthy individuals and families have not heard the wake-up call, do not see themselves as stewards of wealth, or do not have an instinctive sense of give-back. I do not understand why responsibility to the broader society, to the community where one lives and works, to the world itself, is not more pervasive. I do not understand the absence of stewardship, especially when one looks at the stunning role models that exist on every level.

I know, without knowing the specifics, there are thousands of stories of donor leaders. My confusion is why there are not tens of thousands. My confusion is why such behavior is not normative. My confusion is why so much wealth remains in the woodwork and not in philanthropic play, why there are so many with so many advantages who sleepwalk through their lives.

We and Me

Part of the problem is in the way we go about the business of philanthropy. For example, why do we put such a big emphasis on tax exemption as it relates to philanthropy and charitable organizations? If taxes were eliminated, would that eliminate the social compact connecting philanthropy with social good? Does moral obligation decline as tax rates decline, along with the value of the exemption?

Arguing for philanthropy from the perspective of tax benefits puts charitable giving in the box of a tax scam for the rich. It weakens and makes diffuse the basic moral rationale for philanthropy, which is that we act out of concern for the human condition. Overselling the tax benefits exacerbates the crisis in trust that impacts philanthropy and charitable organizations. Tax deductibility is simply an enhancement. Yet we trumpet and market that enhancement as though it were the real deal. Tax incentives have become inextricably tied to making gifts by the pitches of fundraisers and tax advisors who talk the tax talk. We have educated a generation of donors to think a certain way and, in the process, have become captive to a self-fulfilling prophecy. The common assumption is that tax deductibility is a huge swing factor in the level of charitable giving. Shame on us if that is really true.

Coda

This essay has come to a point that cries out for some kind of resolution, recommendation, ideas, anything that might begin to unlock and resolve the logjam of confusion. But all I can offer is the hope that clarion calls can sometimes move people to action. All I can suggest is that leaders and leadership are in demand.

And I do know what I want:

- A society that has enough common sense to understand (and bravery to admit) that good will and building bridges are neither naïve nor dangerous.

- A "we" that represents a broad and open public purpose and supports a citizen-driven process that inhabits the public commons and that has the humility to fund the structures of an open society.[40]

- Philanthropy dedicated to the promotion of citizenship and civic values, and to the education of society, especially the young.[41]

- Philanthropy that invests in social entrepreneurs and nurtures and incubates civic leadership.[42]

- A philanthropic sector willing to roll up its sleeves and seriously address the critical issues in America and around the world—especially poverty, but others as well. How about an adaptation of "tithing" where foundations and individuals commit at least 10 percent of their giving to issues that are truly in the public interest?

I see all of these things as possible. Do you? But the sleepwalker needs to awaken in order to make it happen—perhaps that is my job; perhaps it is yours as well.

ADMONITION

Tell me stories of kinship
Of tropes of caritas effortless
Across a world stage
Tell me what you want to hear

In the face of fury
Moderation is a great fiction
A rhetorical stance subject to guile
Too much is at stake

What good are voices of good will
Sleepwalkers haunt my dreams
The cascade of moments has begun
This macrocosm this heart will break

Sometimes you are the only actor
Alone in the audience of your soul
Or your God if you admit to one
You cannot you dare not abdicate

The Sociology of Wealth

The wealthy are caught in the high-beam headlights of toxic rhetoric around equity, inequality, greed, power, excessive affluence, and influence of the wealthiest 1 percent, and the anger that has generated, especially in the American society. That this has become a hot issue in the political circus we are currently in is an understatement, and it will persist long after the presidential election has been decided.

On the one hand, this is hardly new. The love–hate relationship with wealth in the history of the United States has ebbed and flowed forever. But perhaps not since the era of Andrew Carnegie and John D. Rockefeller, when these two men, the wealthiest in the country, were vilified for what was perceived as, and often was, cruel and ruthless action in the monopolistic creation of vast wealth, has the heat been so high. In fact, when Mr. Rockefeller approached Congress with the idea of establishing a federally licensed philanthropic foundation, the level of vilification and distrust was so strong that Congress refused. It is ironic that it led to the formation of the Rockefeller Foundation as a private foundation and charted the course for the way American philanthropy developed. Had Congress acted otherwise, the influence of government in private philanthropy would have been very different. It is even more ironic that both Carnegie and Rockefeller went on to establish a remarkable philanthropic legacy that continues to be a model of transformation, positive social impact, and how private wealth can, in fact, be invested for the common good. Whether the still-relevant "The Gospel of Wealth" and the multiple good philanthropic works that these two men accomplished led to redemption is still open for debate.

This is the messy democratic stew that in 2016 is reaching a fever pitch. Today, the names that have become metaphors for the power and influence of vast wealth are the Koch brothers on the right; George Soros on the left; Wall Street, the biggest excess-maker and most corrupt culprit of all; and, close behind, powerful global corporations who have no moral center and no allegiance to country, who follow the lure of lower taxes and less regulation and who, now, courtesy of the Supreme Court, are able to finance—on an unlimited scale—political and lobbying campaigns, often without any disclosure at all.

Somewhere in the messy stew is "big box" philanthropy led by Bill Gates, Melinda French Gates, and Warren Buffett, whose huge and, arguably, magnificent foundation is accused of being the "gorilla in the room" that suffers from arrogance, lack of transparency, and the "who elected you" syndrome. The Gates Foundation is not alone, and this week in *The New York Times* the Broad Foundation was accused of undue influence in San Francisco's public and charter school controversy, one of the many criticisms leveled at foundations aggressively pushing the charter-school agenda. Frank Karel, who brilliantly led communications for both the Robert Wood Johnson Foundation and the Rockefeller Foundation, famously said, "Philanthropy does not rest easily on the bosom of the American society." And it does not.

The "why" of all this is hugely complex but rooted in the dramatically increased division between rich and poor, both in the United States and globally. The astonishing data that places control of 60 percent of US wealth in the hands of literally a handful of the super wealthy underscores a rising tide that has not lifted all boats. The middle class especially has been losing—not gaining—ground. The real median wage earned for men in the United States is lower than it was in 1969. Median household income, adjusted for inflation, is lower now than it was in 1999.[43] It simply is harder today for many to make a living in the United States and support a family than ever before. Persistent poverty has shown modest improvement but remains pernicious for 11 percent of Americans.

Many books, including Thomas Piketty's best-selling *Capital in the Twenty-First Century* (published in 2013), which describes how those who begin with wealth have an insurmountable advantage over those without wealth, have attempted to define the concept of equity and income inequality. Other studies have traced the huge advantage that children of well-educated upper-income families have in the society. Both old media and new social media continue to add data that fuels the growing anger toward, and mistrust of, wealth.

If the above is a limited, and discouraging, context for the problem, it raises the question of what are realistic responses for those with wealth, the families and individuals who are in the 1 percent, even if their wealth is nowhere on the scale of the very wealthiest. The average wealth of the top 1 percent in the US is $14 million—a lot of money but nowhere near the level of the megawealthy who are the names most mentioned.

The actions of any one family would not influence what is such a complicated economic and political issue but, collectively, positive action by those with wealth could, over time, be a great positive influence. I would make the case that the wealthy should not be in denial of the implications of the issue. There are many practical reasons: Increased taxes for the upper income levels are almost, at this point, a given. More regulation, reductions in charitable giving limits, increased payout requirements for foundations (which could lead to eventual sunsetting of all foundations), and payout requirements for donor-advised funds have been on the legislative agenda for several years.

Many of these proposed changes are not unreasonable and may even be overdue, but the conventional response from wealth-industry advocates and lobbyists on any of these changes has been to fight them. The same response, perhaps even more vigorous, has come from major nonprofit groups like Independent Sector and the Council on Foundations, as well as new and influential foundation-advocacy groups. My read of this conventional response is that it is dead wrong and that it will only exacerbate the debate and increase the negative feeling toward wealth—even "good wealth." It will further make suspect and, therefore, reduce the potential for, some of the exciting new social innovation and entrepreneurship tools, including new hybrid corporate forms. A much better response is to get out in front of these proposals and use the opportunity for substantive dialogue on the moral dimension potential for wealth in our society.

More important to families than these financial and tactical concerns are qualitative issues. No one likes to be put on the defensive in the communities where one lives. No one wants a diminution of family self-worth, increased fear, unwanted exposure, or to be forced to live an ultraprivate life or constrained in speaking out or leading on important social issues about which one feels passionate. All these things lead to withdrawal and less, not more, investment of a family's human and financial resources at a time when the societal need and opportunity are greater than ever before.

Here are my suggestions, based on my experiences at TPI of more than a quarter-century of working with hundreds of families of wealth and their advisors, for some practical questions that could become the basis of discussion and action:

1. What is our family's definition of "wealth with responsibility"? How do our passions and values drive that definition? What guiding principles would help us be true to ourselves?

2. What public persona do we have today, and what do we wish to present to the outside world in the future? Being anonymous and invisible is not an option in our web-based environment where information is easily accessed, so how do we become more intentional in communicating that public persona?

3. How do we, as a family and as individuals, truly engage in the broader world? What does engagement mean regarding time, talent, experience, contact, networks, and financial resources?

4. What are the bridges between our isolation, our privilege, and others who do not have those resources? Consider the questions below.

    a. Philanthropy has been for many families a very successful bridge. What role does strategic philanthropy play for us, and how do we develop the competence and governance for a great philanthropy?

    b. A family's investment philosophy and policy can also be a bridge. How do we integrate our values and principles into a comprehensive investment philosophy and policy?

    c. How expansive a role does social and impact investing play? Where are the lines between social investing and traditional philanthropy?

    d. How can we engage the rising generations in developing our family's guiding principles about wealth and social responsibility?

5. How do we prepare and educate family members around these questions? How do we manage the so-called guilt syndrome or the feeling of being somehow different, and the fear of being a target?

6. How do we measure and evaluate whether we are successful in these objectives?

Many financial and philanthropic advisors to the wealthy address some of the above questions, and we would urge a deeper dive into those discussions such that they are made part of the ethos and culture of the relationship between advisor and client.

Could this become a movement? There are existing efforts like the Giving Pledge, which encourages billionaires to commit half or more of their wealth to society. There are high-profile models of individuals—Pierre and Pam Omidyar (Pierre founded eBay); Steve and Jean Case (Steve cofounded AOL); and, most recently, Priscilla Chan and her husband, Mark Zuckerberg (Mark founded Facebook)—who have made major societal social commitments based on their own answers to these kinds of questions.

Why do this? For me the answer to the "why" question is that the leverage of passion, will, creativity, and wealth has the most untapped potential to make the world a better place. There is no higher aspiration for any generation.

In an Era of Scarcity

Thinking about the moral dimension of philanthropy began on an evening in 1967 when the vice president of the Boston NAACP threw a chair at me—so angry was he at the arrogance and the hubris that my well-meaning friends and I had displayed in our intervention into the life of the African American community of Boston.

Perhaps that is the first moral challenge that philanthropy and social action faces—the assumption, the presumption, that we are Good Samaritans, acting in good faith, and as donors are doing good, not harm. But how do we know? And what gives us the right to "intervene"—a word I truly do not like, and yet one central to many definitions of philanthropy—in someone else's life, in a community that is not our own? For forty years I have been aware of those questions, and I still am not sure of the answers.

What troubles me most is what I see going on in the world and what is not going on in philanthropy to address it—how most philanthropic response has an astonishing lack of urgency. It still seems like business as usual. When Jeff Skoll, the first president of eBay, announced a new foundation to deal with urgent threats, it seemed to me a distressingly original idea!

The financial sky is falling in such a way that the most vulnerable among us are being hurt the most. If philanthropy does not stand up and be counted in ways that are appropriate, who will? I heard a phrase the other day that has stuck with me about how a lot of giving before 2008 had been a kind of "tithing of affluence," that is, it was easy to give and cost many of us very little. We no longer feel we have that luxury. Where will we come out?

I think we too easily let ourselves and others off the hook. We nibble around the edges of the real problems and issues. The Independent Sector and the Foundation Center's data indicates that, in 2002, only 11 percent of philanthropy in the United States went to poverty or social justice issues, and the percentages are even less globally.[44] I think that we are much too nice, too polite, too accommodating. I wonder: *What would not-nice philanthropy look like?* Something is missing—and it may be that the first step is a heightened awareness of the moral dimension of the work that philanthropy aspires to do.

But before we get to philanthropy specifically, let's talk about what is *moral*—a word so ideologically hot that some have suggested using another word, like *ethical*, but I can't.

Moral dimensions are radical—radical in the sense of "of or relating to the origin, fundamental."[45]

The philosopher Allen Wheelis wrote: "Some things are not permitted . . . there are immanent standards of man's making, but not of man's design, that they are, therefore, to be discovered but not created, that though absolute, they change but slowly, that to live by them is what is meant by being human."[46] That last line, "meant by being human," makes me wonder. How do we know what that is?

Aristotle had one answer when he said: "It is the peculiarity of men [and women] that they share a sense of the just and the unjust and that their sharing a common understanding of justice makes a polis."[47]

The making and unmaking of a polis, a country, a community, the bonds of civic friendship, what we call a *civil society*, is underwritten by our individual and collective sense of the just and the unjust.

I think that is right—we may be getting there, getting closer to something truly radical, truly moral.

If John Rawls, author of the 1971 landmark book *A Theory of Justice*, were with us today, he would add, "A moral personality is characterized by two capacities, one a conception of the good, the other a conception of justice."[48]

How do we decide what is justice? We make rapid, snap, moral judgments all the time. We often cannot explain to ourselves why something feels wrong or right. We know—when we see a family that lost their home and now is living in a car—that it is wrong. We know—when we walk at dawn on Hendry's beach at low tide—that it is stunningly beautiful. Seeing and evaluating are linked and basically simultaneous even if one is concrete and the other is not.

David Brooks refers to the "social nature of moral intuition," a warmer view of human nature, where "we don't just care about our individual rights, or even the rights of individuals, we also care about loyalty, respect, and tradition. Feelings of awe, transcendence, patriotism, joy and self-sacrifice are central to most people's moral experiences."[49]

This is the yearning to be a good person we are all familiar with, a yearning to be a moral citizen of the world that is real.

And I believe it is real for the vast majority of Americans who expressly care about an issue, but do nothing. We care about community, we need community. Brooks ends his piece this way: "Most people struggle toward goodness, not as a means, but as an end in itself."[50]

It always comes back to the struggle, the philanthropic journey—personal and public. It is, at the end of the day, a moral journey. We are in the game—we are actors because, as Allen Wheelis said, "some things are not permitted."[51]

You see, we do care about legacy, and we know without being told that the legacy we leave is the life we have led.

Enter philanthropy, which is not the only articulation of legacy but an important one. Philanthropy presumes to be a "conception of good," and the word *philanthropy* itself is based on love (i.e., justice). Philanthropy is an articulation of moral imagination, and an end in itself. Peter Goldmark, former president of the Rockefeller Foundation, wrapped it this way: "Philanthropy is the practice of applying assets of knowledge, passion, and wealth to bring about constructive change."[52]

If these are the assumptions that underlie philanthropy, and they are, why even have a conversation about the moral dimension of philanthropy?

Let's consider a few of the reasons.

To begin with, we need the discussion. Ethical issues permeate the daily news. As they should. Foundations, nonprofit organizations, and NGOs are not immune from ethical lapses. Philanthropy is private action in public space, and operates at the very intersection of social dilemmas and thoughtful responses. These are the very challenges that often mean a chair is flying across the room aimed at you—more often in the heat of emotion and in words rather than in hard wood—but real nonetheless.

From a practical, defensive perspective, the whole world is watching—philanthropy has grown enormously in scale and influence, and with it has come much more media and governmental scrutiny. Philanthropy is a metaphor, a lever, an influencer. Foundations, especially, carry weight far beyond their apparent resources. This is certainly true for major foundations, as witnessed in the amazing celebrity of the Gates Foundation. This scenario also plays out in every other community across the country. Yet many private foundations resent the very idea of public scrutiny and demands for increased transparency, and have a very limited sense of their public persona.

The erosion of trust across every domain of society extends to philanthropy. Philanthropy is held to a higher standard and it should be.

Everything is being reset, and the tax benefits and freedom of action that private philanthropy enjoys—its very special place in American society—is just as much at risk as everything else. The proposal in the Obama budget, now dropped, to reduce the tax deduction on large gifts was not an isolated example—there will be a serious review of the whole range of tax advantages that impact the field.

Change is always hard, but I think this trend is good as it puts more discipline on all of us. It makes us rethink how the personal and family values and passions that drive our philanthropy can have even more leverage, more impact, across the communities of interest that we care most about. I like the idea that we are being asked to be clearer to others, as it makes the imperative to be clearer to ourselves about why we do what we do even more important. It also comes at the right time for another reason.

Over the past two decades, the field of philanthropy has been driven by a movement for greater accountability through measurement of impact and outcomes. TPI has been among the champions of this trend for more strategic philanthropy for those twenty years, and much has been gained by the introduction of management science and market economy principles in the practice of philanthropy. What has been lost, or what is out of balance, is the equally important engagement with increased reflection about the values and the meaning of what we do.

In essence, philanthropy has been totally focused on the keeping of accounts, not the giving of accounts. It is in the intersection of these two complementary quadrants that the opportunity lies to elevate the entire field.

What we need is a movement that creates an expectation for moral reflection as a core competency of philanthropy and social action.

The question of what that would look like includes some of the elements and the challenges inherent within, some of which may fall in the category of not being nice: integrity of purpose, integrity of process, integrity of philanthropy in the public space, and integrity of the inner journey.

Integrity of Purpose

Vision and mission drives everything else. There are many issues to consider.

Ambition, boldness, and passion—in essence, high expectations, which are a precondition to great philanthropy—must be present. The challenges are lack of imagination, playing it safe, not working hard enough, being too self-assured and comfortable with the status quo, and being too afraid of taking risks. There is another challenge that may be more of a surprise. Ten years ago, TPI conducted a survey of high-net-worth individuals—$50 million and up—and asked, among other questions, what would motivate them to increase their philanthropy. The first answer was "knowing the organization would use the money wisely," which was not a surprise. The second answer, almost as important as impact, was "finding a passion"!

It is not an easy matter at all to decide what passion determines a hierarchy of need—in essence, why you do one thing and not another, especially in economic crises of seismic proportions. The challenges are making tough choices between competing critical needs, knowing what to do and that it will make a difference, and, for many donors, overcoming the pressure of social demands, personal relationships, and community expectations so they are able to address the things they really care about. I remember vividly a TPI meeting in Detroit with a prominent family who was talking about what issues they cared about. The patriarch, a man famous for his generosity and many major gifts, said, "I just made a list of the issues and things I really care about and my big gifts—they don't match!"

Managing conflicts of interest and self-interest, including issues of ego and status within the community, and ethical issues is difficult. The biggest challenge is admitting they exist, and establishing a governance and oversight structure that is honest and rigorous.

Putting the best and highest use of all available resources toward the greatest impact means facing the challenges of putting your whole self in the game, including taking on the role of advocacy in a world that requires multisector solutions, and rethinking the use of endowment as mission investment capital.

Integrity of Process

This concerns how we go about the work.

The first challenge is that vision and mission statements are often filed away and forgotten in a bottom drawer, and bear little relationship to actual process. I remember a plaintiff's comment from a program officer of a New York foundation who said, "All these great noble ideas are in our mission statement; the problem is we get so wrapped up in the day-to-day work, they are irrelevant."

What is most relevant is how to "do no harm," which may seem simplistic. The challenges, however, are many, and include hubris, lack of humility, an inability to be a sensitive and deep listener, insufficient context and data about the issue being addressed, and being unprepared for unexpected consequences.

A fair, respectful partnership and relationship with recipients and the communities of interest being served is crucial. The challenges in doing so are the inherent power imbalance between donors and grantees, and managing the tension between appropriate influence and oversight by a donor and inappropriate intrusion into the operations of an organization. The same challenges and tensions exist between NGOs and the Indigenous communities they serve.

Being open and accessible is also needed. The challenges here include the reality that demand far exceeds resources, and that being responsive to requests with the goal of being proactive and strategic is tough. And there is the natural tendency for donors and staff to want to drive the process.

It's important to learn from experience without exaggerating about success or refusing to admit failure, which in philanthropy is rare. And there is the difficulty of evaluating both impact and ethical practice.

Integrity of Philanthropy in the Public Space

This is our social responsibility to the greater good.

Private action in public space is at the intersection of public need and public policy, but the challenges involve the democratic, pluralistic nature of private philanthropy based on donor intent and choice. Many foundation donors still consider their gifts to be "my money," while, at the same time, acknowledging and accepting a public persona that embraces a larger responsibility to society beyond the goals of a foundation or a nonprofit organization.

Transparency and accountability to the communities of interest being served is very important. But the challenges begin with the sense of privacy and control that many donors value, and, for some, the uncertainty about what a rigorous, outside critique of the work will produce, which of course is one of the reasons why transparency is so important.

Then there is the issue of tax-exempt endowments and if they should be considered immoral or even allowed to exist. The challenges in this arena are economic and political, especially when government is desperate for new revenue sources. There are concerns about the immense concentrations of wealth in private foundations and college and university endowments. Do such accumulations of power and wealth run counter to a true democratic process? Do they add enough societal value?

The civil society, philanthropy writ large, may be the most promising place for moral learning in a world that is bereft of moral leadership. It is what philanthropy could become, but the challenges are the fractious and undisciplined nature of civil society, and the lack of awareness of what its role as educator and moral leader could be.

Integrity of the Inner Journey

This requires the expansion of moral imagination.

Growing one's soul—what the Dalai Lama called the quest for secular ethics—is a growing phenomenon in a world where religion is in decline, and it is at play here. We need a new kind of spirituality of care, of civic vocation, which is exactly the experience that philanthropy and social action provide. It is what we learn when we touch someone else, when we reach out, when we give of ourselves. This transforms the human heart and releases the poetry of the citizen within.

The challenges are both internal and external. How should we nurture and support those who work in the field when social change is incremental at best, and burnout is common? And, at the same time, how should we promote the growth of moral imagination within individuals and across society?

I met with Sam Walton and his family in Fayetteville on a Saturday morning about nine months before Mr. Walton died. It was one of the first real conversations about philanthropy for the family. We had been meeting for about two hours, and Sam had just sat there and listened to his wife Helen and his four children. Then he finally spoke. "I made a mistake," he said. "The last few years I have been running around the country opening stores, rallying the troops, and looking over everyone's shoulder at the company. I should have paid more attention to this—to what to do with all this wealth, to giving back." Then he said this to his family: "Don't make that mistake." And I have wondered ever since what Sam Walton, one of the most innovative entrepreneurs in history, might have done had he worked his philanthropy with the same degree of imagination that he had worked his business.

What would be different if moral reflection becomes a core competency of philanthropy and social action? I think the following would be a good beginning:

Donors and nonprofit organizations would have a clearer moral and ethical frame of reference within which to make choices and, as a result, those actions will have increased potential to add value to the civic sector.

Those who care about philanthropy would have better tools to provide a thoughtful response to pressing challenges and will be better able to understand, promote, and rationalize the role of philanthropy in a changed world.

Philanthropists and foundations would be more sensitive to the relationship between their mission and their practice, and to the impact of grants within recipient communities.

Nonprofit organizations would operate within their communities of interest with greater clarity about ethics and their moral purpose.

The moral imagination of those who work in this field would expand, and their energy and commitment to do this important work would increase.

Philanthropy will be bolder, more present in the public space, and would have greater impact!

The Speech I Have Always Wanted to Give

This is the speech I have always wanted to give, the speech about compassion, and about community, and about giving back to a society that has been so good to me. This is the speech that is missing from the national dialogue on what kind of society we want to be. This is the speech that moves beyond the politics of the moment; it is the speech of reconciliation, the speech of redress, the speech of convergence. This is the speech that is within every one of you in this room, and every ally who is not in this room. This is the speech of community action driven by the voice of the communities we serve. And this is the speech about reinvention and social innovation and the potential for an expanded role for private philanthropy in the work of community action.

The federal government provides funding to Community Action Agencies (CAAs) through the Community Services Block Grant and other programs.[53] The scope of work is huge, but often under the radar. A community may be well aware of Head Start programs, or lunch programs for the elderly, but not know that they are run by a local Community Action Agency.

My line these days is "I have forgotten what I have forgotten!" But one of the things I have not forgotten was a deep dive in the early '60s in a very early-stage effort at community action. We were nine young, overly confident, suburban, and White professionals with lots of presumptions of how we could help the African American community in Roxbury, Massachusetts. Among the good things we did—as opposed to those things that were not so good—was to acquire real estate to attract important community services. One acquisition brought a new Roxbury

Community Multi-Service Center to the neighborhood, led by Hubie Jones, who was then a dynamic young leader and who is today a wise elder in Boston. Another good thing was the acquisition of the Shawmut Market building on Blue Hill Avenue that became home to the first Head Start program in Boston.

I remember incredibly long meetings as we bumbled our way through the complex requirements to operate the program, which included an ongoing struggle with the city of Boston to keep the facility up to acceptable building codes. That was a very long time ago, but the lessons I learned then vividly resonate today. You know those lessons. They begin with the imperative to listen to the voices of the community that one presumes to serve, and they end with the supposition that if it isn't good for the community, it isn't worth doing.

There is a saying in the foundation world that when you have seen one foundation, you have seen one foundation. My guess is that is also true in Community Action Agencies, those that are nonprofit organizations, those that are government agencies, and those that are hybrids. The diversity of programs and services they provide is huge. This diversity is part of what makes the field so vibrant, but also contributes to the difficulty of messaging at a time when community action is right in the heart of the fierce debate within our society over the role of government.

Steve Schroeder, former president of the Robert Wood Johnson Foundation, recently gave a speech entitled "Does the Moral Arc of the Universe Really Bend Toward Justice?" which was based on the famous phrase used by Dr. Martin Luther King Jr.

Schroeder posed this question: "Do you agree that these are discouraging times?" And goes on to say, "There have been so many occasions when I have cringed at current events and how they reflect on our nation's values." Consider just a few.

- "During a debate among presidential candidates, when a questioner asked Texas Governor Perry about his state's high rate of executing criminals, the audience cheered before Perry could even respond."

- "In another debate, when Congressman Paul, himself a physician, was asked whether persons who voluntarily went without health insurance should face the consequence of death if unable to pay for care, he said yes. That audience also applauded."

- "When consultation for palliative care was introduced as a benefit in the House version of the Affordable Care Act, it was falsely labeled as government-sanctioned death panels by people who knew better. And, to the shame of our profession, no organized group of physicians . . . stood up to argue the absurdity of that claim."

Schroeder says, "These are just some examples of why these times are so disturbing."[54] They are the fallout of major global social trends. I will outline a few.

- Declining trust in all existing institutions, including government (for example, Arab Spring), church, corporations, civil society and NGOs, and foundations. No one is immune from this, including local poverty organizations and community-development organizations—and philanthropy.

- Major demographic changes, including family size, education, the impact of migration of peoples and new Diaspora communities—and the loss of place.

- The concentration of wealth and increased division between rich and poor. The collapse of the social contract in the West, which is happening in Europe as we sit here today and under great pressure in the United States.

- And lastly, the one most relevant to continued federal funding for community action, a growing lack of moral, cultural, and political "convergence," leading to polarization.

Schroeder then quotes Bill Moyers, who "recently came to a dire conclusion when he said, 'The great American experiment in creating a different future together has come down to the worship of individual cunning in the pursuit of wealth and power, with both political parties cravenly subservient to Big Money. The result is an economy that no longer serves ordinary men and women and their families.'"[55]

Is that true? If so, it does not suffice. If there ever was a time to stand up and be counted, it is now. But counted for what?

A memorable comment during a TED meeting in 2008 has stuck in my mind. One of technology's founding gurus said, "The problem with technology is that it doesn't know what it wants to be." I believe that is the same problem social action in all forms has today. What does the field of community action want to be? What does philanthropy want to be?

What follows is a framing of the case statement for community action as practiced by antipoverty agencies today. It could also, I believe, be a case statement for philanthropy. That case statement has three themes: equity, effectiveness, and social innovation. Equity is a theme because, while it is at the heart of the American experience, the concepts of equity and fairness are today diminished in public and political discourse, and that is not the American way. Effectiveness is a theme because the precondition of all funding, government, private philanthropy, and corporate social responsibility is increasingly based on data, on impact, and on results, and evaluation of many core programs of community action do not measure up. Social innovation is a theme because the delivery systems on which community action is based are in too many cases old and tired, and cry out for renewal, and change.

The Case for Equity

Community action has always had the concept of equity at its core. Why is equity as a concept so hard? The issue of equity is the reconciliation between wealth—government, individual, family, and corporate—and responsibility to society writ large. It has played out in US society since our country's birth, and continues to be at the heart of the political debate we are deep within today.

The Annie E. Casey Foundation vision statement imagines "a world in which the resources and support system taken for granted by the middle class are available to all families and children."[56]

The Casey Foundation's vision statement is striking in at least two ways. One, it addresses the issue of social justice directly and, two, it is part of the 11 percent of US charitable giving that does so—a remarkably small percentage that, despite the efforts of many, has remained the same even in this period of economic crises.[57] The Casey Foundation's vision statement is based on a moral assumption that has deep roots in the American experience.

Harvard philosopher John Rawls argued that economic inequality is not the issue as long as "it is to everyone's advantage" and it results "in compensating benefits for everyone and in particular for the least advantaged members of society." It becomes untenable when compensating benefits do not exist, when the imbalance goes too far, and when the response is not equal to the situation. Rawls wrote, "A moral personality is characterized by two capacities, one a conception of the good, the other a conception of justice."[58]

The whole essence (of community action and philanthropy) is, as Seamus Heaney says, "informed by the idea of counterweighting, of balancing out the forces of redress—tilting the scale of reality toward some transcendent equilibrium."[59]

Do you think that is a moral imperative? I do. I like the idea that wealth with responsibility, philanthropy itself—the very themes that TPI has been so intensely involved with since it opened its doors in 1989—has, at its core, the challenge of imagination. The nobility of community action, and I would add that of philanthropy, is our "moral imagination pressing back against the pressure of reality."[60]

Get that right and we are on the way!

Effectiveness and Social Innovation

The first question for every field is this: To whom am I accountable and for what?

Community action is accountable to those populations within society that struggle to be economically self-sufficient because of prejudice, circumstance, lack of education and training, or limitation of language skills, but who, with a smart investment of resources, can become successful as people, as families, and as contributors to their communities. Community action is accountable to those caught in a reiterative cycle of poverty, to children who do not have the preparation to succeed in school, to workers whose jobs no longer exist and who may never again earn what they once earned, to elderly people who need help getting through the day, and to companies that, given the right resources, can grow and stimulate economic development. These are the constituencies of community action.

What does community action owe its constituents? A kind of restlessness, a constant striving toward increased effectiveness, a willingness to unflinchingly look at the data that will drive continuous improvement—these are characteristics of effective organizations, and funders who focus on human services should be looking for that kind of restlessness in their leadership.

To move society toward equity and justice, Community Action Agencies must focus on effectiveness and assiduously pursue social innovation. At their highest realization, Community Action organizations are a platform for creative work in the resolution of our most troubling social dilemmas. Do they view themselves that way, or frame themselves as service providers? At the national meeting of the StriveTogether Cradle to Career Network Convening last month, someone made this comment: "If an organization has had the same mission for thirty years and the same problems are there from when the organization was formed, then the strategies are not effective."

Community action as a field came out of great social movements of the '60s on civil rights and poverty. The field today needs some of the invigorating energy of social movements.

How might that happen? There are three interrelated skills needed: The first is to be creative and to be able to imagine the possibilities and consequences of our actions. Disengage and step back, and become more deeply aware of one's situation. Imagine new possibilities. Think anew in ways that might be totally different than what you had previously envisioned.

The second skill is discernment—the ability to evaluate the impact of those actions both in the original context and within the new possibilities one has envisioned, and the possible moral conflicts or dilemmas that might be the outcome.

The third skill that leads to moral imagination—the one where President Obama excels—is to translate that into a story that others can understand and respond to.

This is precisely a time in human history when people seek deeper understanding and meaning and are willing—even driven—to plunge beneath superficialities to find essences. Creating a moral compass has never been more important.

Can any of this actually save the day for you and your colleagues? Yes, I think it can, but there are some major preconditions. To earn trust means that every nonprofit organization needs to walk the walk and talk the talk with integrity of purpose and integrity of process, and treat those they serve with dignity and respect. And every private foundation needs to deeply listen to the community, and acknowledge its responsibility to the larger society. Fred Miller, an experienced consultant for twenty-five years to nonprofit organizations, believes "when trust is lost what is at risk is the potential loss of an organization's franchise to operate." That is not an acceptable risk for philanthropy to run, especially when the resources needed to address the critical needs of society are escalating.

For my short list of how organizations can gain public trust, please see "Reset: The New Name of the Game" in Section 3. And here is a poem about the critical ingredient that can make it so—it is called "Will."

WILL

It's a matter of will
This game of life
Is inner rather than outer

Conception is nice
But doesn't express will
While execution oh yes

No prescription here
Yet focus drives
Closure

Organizations are built
Survive and prosper
Based on will one or multiple

Governments fail from lack
Fortunes rise and fall
And great art is made by force of

You won't find will in resumes
It isn't always noisy
And often lies deep

Obsession while not will
Is part of the intensity
Which is a precondition

The ah ha components are
Passion and huge ambition
All over a good idea

Will unromanticized
Along with love
It is our most powerful force.

Movement Builders

Are you a funder who wants to support social movements? Look for leaders who are movement builders as defined by Dr. Martin Luther King Jr.'s concept of a Beloved community. Movement builders

- understand that suffering and oppression are not enough to create a movement; a movement begins when the oppressed begin seeing themselves not just as victims but also as pioneers in creating a new, more humane society.

- are able to recognize the humanity in others, including their opponents, and therefore are able to see within them the possibility of change.

- are conscious of the need to go beyond slogans and to create programs that transform and empower participants.

- believe in the concept of two-sided transformation, both of our institutions and ourselves.

- are intergenerational, involving children, youth, and adults.

- can accept contradictions that develop in the course of a struggle; great movements create great hopes but they can also lead to great disappointments.

- choose boldness over timidity.

- call forth a vision that is larger than the issue at hand, distinguishing between social reform and social transformation.

- strike a balance between control and autonomy, recognizing the importance of allowing people to make mistakes.

- recognize the possibility for historical moments in the convergence of time and events.[61]

Does this sound right? What else would you add?

I would add this: Movements, if they are to be sustained, need to renew and revitalize themselves.

Section 4 Reflection

Philanthropy as Counterweight

1. Do you agree with Peter that part of philanthropy's role is to act as a "counterweight," to redress inequities in society? What in your own giving addresses this?

2. What is your definition of "wealth with responsibility"? Does justice enter into it? How do your passions and values drive that definition?

3. How do you and your family engage in the broader world? Do you have opportunities to listen to the voices of those with less power and influence than you? If not, how could you create those opportunities?

4. What is the story behind your wealth? If it is self-made, who or what contributed to it? (This can be anything from a loan from a family member to tax deductions.) When you tell the story behind your wealth, do you acknowledge those contributors?

5. Who in society does not have the opportunity to benefit from such help? What, if any, are your obligations to them?

6. Peter says that "movements, if they are to be sustained, need to renew and revitalize themselves." How could your giving help renew and revitalize movements and their leaders?

7. Peter also calls us to "renew [our] vows" to philanthropy.

   The passion you feel, or once felt, for the work that you do, is central to the exercise of creative moral imagination. The centrality of philanthropy to the making of a better world is the heart and soul of why you are an actor on this stage. Make a poem of it.

8. What would "renewing your vows to philanthropy" mean? How could you make a poem (a work of deep and personal expression) of your giving?

VILLANELLE

FOR HENRY HAMPTON

The story is finished but it is not complete
We have listened, we have seen, we have been told,
Accolades, applause, are no mean feat

Nor celebration, nor awards. So why do we weep?
Weep for the archives, the untold metaphors of gold.
The series is finished but it is not complete.

In a great land, a country we so yearn to greet,
The comings, the goings of color, bright, black, unfold,
Accolades, applause, are no mean feat.

In life, in love, in passion, there is no retreat,
We go deep within our soul and pray it will hold.
The story is finished but it is not complete.

Was it today or yesterday the prize was sweet,
Pain and vision magnified a thousandfold,
Accolades, applause are temporal receipts.

Gentle spirit, castles in the air, these are concrete
Around us, surround us, told, untold and retold.
The story is finished but it is not complete.
Accolades, applause, are no mean feat.

SECTION 5:

COMING 'ROUND RIGHT

*The philanthropic struggle to understand,
to be sensitive and creative in response, and to ultimately take
a good and appropriate action is equally relentless.*

PETER KAROFF

In all his writing, his conversations, his restless middle-of-the-night hours, Peter—sometimes to the exasperation of his friends and colleagues—turned problems over and over, retracing his steps, viewing them from new angles. He believed deeply in the value of this practice. He loved the Shaker hymn "Simple Gifts" with its call to "come down where we ought to be."

> To turn, turn will be our delight,
> Till by turning, turning we come 'round right.[1]

And no one took more pleasure than Peter when a generous act or a thoughtful foundation came 'round right. He tirelessly promoted the good works of others, holding up their example to the field and to the light.

For Peter, one of the elements of coming 'round right was making sure that philanthropic resources added value to society and contributed to justice. In "A Teachable Moment," he calls us to "address the more fundamental issues that affect whether philanthropy deserves to be trusted by our society." He returns to his idea of the 360° mission, and poses "carrot and stick" questions that help donors interrogate their intent to determine whether their giving is trustworthy. Answering these questions about mission and motivation requires turning things over, unearthing our own motivations and biases as we pursue the work. This inner journey, for Peter, is crucial to coming 'round right.

In "Listen to the Voices," Peter argues that one of the conditions required for "inspired, creative, artful, and powerful philanthropy" is outward facing: deep listening, observation, and "subjugating one's ego." In "The Magic of Philanthropy," he describes what can happen when inner and outer work come together, when the right donor meets the right recipient, and a powerful exchange results. And in "Catechism for a Great Foundation," he outlines the practices and policies that make that magic more likely to appear in the institutions we build.

A Teachable Moment

One problem, among many, of the preoccupation by the field of philanthropy on proposed regulation, and the various troubling issues relating to governance that have been spotlighted recently, is that it sucks all the air out of the room. It diverts those who are responsible for charitable organizations from looking at issues that are far more important. "How could that be?" you might ask. What could be more important than stopping illegal and immoral exploitation of foundation and philanthropic resources, which is what the media has focused on and what new regulation purports to do? Here is my answer.

First of all, we already have laws and regulations on the books, and many of the irregularities that have surfaced in the press are, plainly and simply, illegal. Section 4958 of the tax code enacted in 1998 contains the "intermediate sanctions" that govern matters of compensation and conflicts of interest in 501(c)(3) organizations. Private foundations are exempt from these rules because they are subject to even more stringent rules and tax penalties on self-dealing. In my view, new regulations won't much change the likelihood or number of incidents of aberrant and illegal behavior. The concern that new regulations will only make life more complicated, and expensive, for foundations and NPOs to do business is justified.

The problem to me is that we are not taking advantage of this teachable moment to address the more fundamental issues that affect whether philanthropy deserves to be trusted by our society.

Better governance, transparency, and communication by foundations would improve trust, but these are not in themselves sufficient to restore, and keep, society's trust in philanthropy. Much more important are what foundations do with the money, and *how those resources add value to society*. And equally important is how, and with what attitude, the philanthropic process operates. These questions, which are fundamentally about mission and its execution, have the potential to turn what has been to date a defensive reaction by organized philanthropy to media and regulator criticism into an opportunity.

The mission of a philanthropic organization lays out the relationship between the destiny of the organization and the public space it inhabits. Mission drives everything, and I think we have to reinvent it to become a 360° mission.

A 360° mission would disaggregate organizational self-interest from the public interest. A 360° mission would have less emphasis on what "I"—the foundation, donor, or nonprofit organization—want to do, and more emphasis on the broadest possible interpretation of the issue from the perspective of the people being served, that is, what works for the individual, for the community, and for society. A 360° review of mission and operating procedures would reach beyond the traditional, especially into the gray areas of self-interest and conflicts of interest. Some of the questions foundation and charitable organizations should ask are the following:

- Have we carefully thought through the implications of our actions on others, including possible unintended consequences?

- Do we avoid simplistic solutions to complex problems, issues, and social systems?

- If there is resistance to what we want to do, is there merit in that resistance?

- Are we respectful and sensitive to cultures and beliefs that are different from our own?

- Are we sufficiently on guard against hubris and excessive personal and organizational ambition?

- Are we absolutely committed to integrity and to avoiding conflicts of interest, including between personal and family relationships of both board and staff?

- And perhaps overarching all else is this question: Is our mission the right one, and do our actions at all times live up to that mission?

Would a combination of commonly agreed-upon standards and an attitude that better respects those with whom we work and the public space help answer the issues facing philanthropy? Would they help build and maintain trust? I think so. Do you?

Some questions are the stick; they force us to think. Those who lead philanthropic organizations need the answers much more for themselves than for others. There are, however, other questions in philanthropy that are closer to the carrot, such as the following:

- What really makes philanthropy special? What draws us in, and what could draw others in?

- What does this incredibly rich and idiosyncratic field, this pluralistic philanthropic universe, this third sector, mean in today's world?

- We mess around and think creatively, but so what? Are we working around the edges of issues? Why are we not outraged more often?

- How do we turn powerful visions into practical strategies for leadership and even transformation?

- How do we learn to think beyond money, services, and programs, and instead think about convening and organizing communities of interest?

- How do we keep from falling in love with the rhetoric of our own importance? Or, put another way, how do we transcend personal ego?

- How do we believe more in ourselves? How do we resurrect the values of maturity and wisdom?

I think these are the issues that represent the true "teachable moment." These are the questions those who believe in philanthropy need to talk about, the ones that really matter.

Listen to the Voices

> *In each piece I play there lives a story created by all the lives that made this music happen. Of course, those included would be the life of the composer, lives of artists who have performed the work, as well as the lives of the listeners. I am a listener, too, as well as a player, and each time I listen I have an experience unique in its time and space, an experience distinct from that of other listeners. It is true that there are similar responses we all share, but no one has the exact same response. That is not to say I am a better listener: it simply means what one hears is the sole property of the individual.*
>
> VIOLINIST MIDORI GOTO[2]

I am one who views philanthropy as an art rather than a science, and agree with Midori that as the violinist is also a listener, so is the donor. I think that philanthropy as art is underrepresented and that few donors are practiced at listening. By *listening* I mean putting aside what might be called our "presumption of brilliance," and subjugating one's ego, one's preconceived conceptions and prejudices. In this way, listening becomes the bridge of learning between what we know, or think we know, and the knowledge we lack.

By *art* I mean intuition, instincts, passions, the heart, spirit, and soul within—those things that constitute judgement and wisdom. By *science* I mean the data, the analysis, the technical, and all the strategic tools that make up good process. That is not to say that art does not require science in order to practice its craft; it would be nothing without it and, in fact, the creative process is a mysterious blend of craft, intensely practiced, and inspiration. The issue is which is the servant and which is the master?

The artistic struggle to "make it new" is as relentless as the tide. The philanthropic struggle to understand, to be sensitive and creative in response, and to ultimately take a good and appropriate action is equally relentless.

Artists have especially acute powers of observation. What they see/hear/feel is the springboard to make the leap to something original, and occasionally to something sublime. To make it new means you must build on what has come before. The novelist closely reads (rereads) *Middlemarch*, the painter stares for hours at the *Mona Lisa*, the musician takes the score of the Jupiter Symphony apart note by note, and the filmmaker studies each frame of *Citizen Kane*. I remember a comment as to whether one could actually teach someone to write poetry. The answer given was "no," but it was said that you can teach someone to *read* poetry and that is the condition precedent for writing poems.

What are the conditions precedent for philanthropy, for inspired, creative, artful, and powerful philanthropy? The inspired listener, observer, reader is one, and attitude is another.

Much of life's experience is indirect and composed of images. Sometimes the images are very powerful, burned forever into our consciousness, such as the picture of JFK shot in that open car in Dallas or the second plane bursting into flames as it hit the World Trade Center. More often, they are the things we see each day on television, in movies, or that come into our minds from books or newspapers or simply from talking with friends. These are the fleeting images or ideas that float in and out of what might be called the "walk-by" part of our lives. The infinite collage of a world that is often hurting—a homeless person huddled in a doorway on a rainy night, a starving child with a bloated stomach in a Sudanese village—and often beautiful, like your children building sand castles on South Beach in late afternoon or Midori playing the violin.

These images synthesize with the "walk-in" part of our lives, the *experiential learning*, to borrow a term from education reform, that comes from family life, student life, work life, community life, and all the things we do that define what we are. Some of these are of our own making. We choose to go to graduate school or we do not, to get married or divorced or not, to enter the armed services, to travel, to live in a certain community, to go to church or not. Much is beyond our control, the accidents of birth, race, economics, talent, and chance, or what appears to be chance. When my eldest daughter traveled to China six years ago, and came home with our lovely granddaughter, I mentioned to a friend how amazing it was that this one little girl out of millions of little girls just happened into our lives. His response was startling—he said that the odds were really no different when one considers the millions of sperm cruising merrily along in search of an egg to fertilize. I rather like that image as it deflates what often is overeager purposefulness and zealousness.

Every one of us is conditioned in these multiple ways. It is what prepares us, makes us ready to receive and to respond, or not. This is the soil in which our values and passions grow, and out of which evolves what is, in most cases, a weak attempt at articulating a belief system. It is the beginning of wanting to become involved. Midori, of course, is right when she says of the concert audience: "It is true that there are similar responses, but no one has exactly the same response."[3]

Aristotle observed that the defining characteristic of humankind was our intrinsic ability to differentiate between the just and the unjust. I believe that is true but so are the poet Seamus Heaney's words: "Human beings suffer/they torture one another/they get hurt and get hard."[4] It is one thing to know right from wrong, it is another to decide to do something about it. Some remain receptive, open, and curious all through their lives. Others do not; they raise shields, turn off, and remain observers in the face of demonstrable need. Some people act automatically, naturally, and in the process grow, become more spiritual, more generous, more *something*, some word we do not know. Others do not. The point is we have a choice, and it is of our own making.

———

Who are the great listeners in the world? Here are a few of my favorites.

Studs Terkel who, for forty years, has been listening to workers of all stripes and sharing with us the on-the-ground sociology of our time and place. Alan Lomax who, in the '50s, took a tape recorder into remote rural communities, into prisons, into Grange Halls, and into more neighborhood bars than he could count, and in the process saved and documented a generation's indigenous music. I love the idea that one of those songs, "O Brother, Where Art Thou," sung in 1959 by an inmate of Camp B of the Mississippi Penitentiary, is now in a movie and that the Lomax family tracked this guy down to give him a big check.

Among the world-class listeners who come to mind is Dr. Robert Coles, who lived with and interviewed very poor African American families in the midst of their great migration from the South to the North, and then wrote as only a poet can write about them. And, of course, we all know people, some professionally trained and many, many more who are instinctively good listeners.

I was lucky because my father was one of those people who others simply sought out and confided in. I remember, as a kid, working afternoons in his hardware store, how customers, men and woman, many of them with accents touched with Polish and Lithuanian, would stay and talk and talk. I can still see my father's warm, pleasant face, leaning toward the person, nodding sympathetically about who knows what.

These are my role models. I have some learn-to-listen stories I've learned—the hard way.

The death of Dr. Martin Luther King Jr. had a powerful effect on our society and, among other things, it led to a bright spotlight on the long-neglected status of African Americans. Concepts like Black

Power became actualized in many cities, including my own. Among the responses were new organizations in both the Black and White communities dedicated to the support of economic and social development. All this led me, and others, on an unusual four-year odyssey into more than five hundred suburban homes. At highly energized 7 a.m. breakfasts, we engaged in a remarkable in-your-face dialogue about racism and the pursuit of social justice. It ended with a pitch for $1,000 and a day a week of time. We raised money, and some consciousness, but I learned how hard it is to talk about such issues in polite company, how ill-equipped we are to hear things that we would rather avoid or deny. How hard it is to change our thinking.

These experiences, for me, now long in the past—with their mix of naïveté, good intentions, youth, and inexperience, coupled with a healthy dose of guilt—raised a set of questions that I struggle with to this day. They are not principally questions of what impact or results we achieved, which were modest and not long-lasting. Nor is it about my own motivation and involvement that contains elements of both positive and negative ambiguities. They are simply part of life. The bigger questions are more around the immense difficulty in bridging different worlds. The sociology of those who live in newly remodeled kitchens in the suburbs juxtaposed with a family living day-to-day on the street is like Mars to Pluto, or even beyond. How we talk to one another, how we relate, how we listen as citizens may be the most important thing of all. If we do not get that right, what we do will not work. It is also what we take away from such experiences, to what extent we have learned anything. It comes back to whether we choose to "walk by" or "walk in."

These events were forty years ago, but the same kind of mistake is repeated, sometimes on a much larger scale. There is a neighborhood in Baltimore called Sandtown. In the early '90s, Sandtown was the site of a comprehensive neighborhood, community-development effort. Conceived by the Enterprise Foundation, and funded by a number of national foundations, especially the Annie E. Casey Foundation, it was very ambitious. Unlike our rump effort in the '60s, there were many sophisticated actors in the Sandtown story. After a lot of money, and several years of frustration, the project failed for essentially the same reasons ours had failed forty years before. It lacked the filter, the lens of the community, and the voices of those most involved. Not to say that it is easy to define what the "community" is and isn't. Perhaps that is the very first step in tackling any serious philanthropic or social change work.

Here is a poem about a different kind of community.

EACH DAY

At a certain point when tide is dead low and about to turn,
Witness a feeding frenzy—Sanderling, Willet, Marbled Kowtit
Work furiously within inches of each other. Choreography
Synchronized—each wave's deposit of fresh, rich nutrients,
Irresistible to the invisible, seething, life forms just below
The surface of the sand, tiny clams, crabs, beetles, worms,
Bait rises to bait to feed or be met by sharp piercing thrusts,
Birds and beaks bred for this work, as we are bred for ours.

Moments of high drama pass quickly, the actors scatter,
Work alone, recongregate around the cliff, down the beach,
And then in a blink the birds are gone as though never there.
Tidal flats, tidal pools, slowly fill, secret denizens of the sand
Burrow down, waiting until called again as we wait to be called.

In my poem, the actors are the sea, the birds, and the "denizens of the sand." The listening is for a particular sound made by the waves as they move slowly up the beach, or for a certain stirring below the surface of the sand that the birds somehow sense. For Midori, the actors are those who have come before, the composers, the performing artists, and the listeners. In philanthropy, the relevant voices are determined by the "nature and terms of the engagement" between the parties at interest. How they relate to one another is governed by what I referred to earlier as "attitude."

Some donors have figured out how to operate close enough to the ground that they seem part of the ecosystem they are serving. They succeed by building relationships of trust; I know a charitable trust that has been successfully operating a program in Nepal that builds low-head hydro dams. The reason it works is because both the villages and the government want and need the competency that the trust has, and it is made available only when invited in.

Dan funds a scholarship program, one with a surprise ending, and we are interviewing a prospective student. She is a tall, angular, young, African American woman who wants to go to an Ivy League college, but has only marginal SATs and grades. She will be the first person in her family to go to college and that she survived her circumstances in a very tough neighborhood to this point is a miracle. She is nervous, maybe highly strung. Dan has a very direct manner, and asks, "Why are your SATs so lousy? And why Brown—why not UMass?" The girl's response is bold. "My SATs are lousy because I don't test well and freaked out during the test itself, but I know I can do Brown, and I know if I go my world will open up in ways that would not happen at UMass."

"Ah ha," says Dan. "It really will, if you can do it." I watch as these two people, one a wealthy, seventy-year-old real estate man and the other a lovely, eighteen-year-old kid from the poorest part of the city, converse. It is the girl who is talking, and Dan who is listening—his eyes really start to sparkle. The room is filled with a kind of hum, and what you feel is Dan's love for this person, and how she rises to his high appreciation of who and what she could be. At the end of the interview, Dan shakes her hand and says, as he always says when it goes well, "I feel lucky and proud to know you, and I'd like to help you." It doesn't get any more concise than that. The surprise in Dan's special scholarship program is that if the student graduates successfully, all student loans will be paid off, but the students do not know that.

How would you describe the relationship in that room between the two? Perhaps tough but supportive and nurturing with a kind of positive tension based on high expectations. It was also one that left both parties feeling just right. It is hard to get that relationship right.

Let's try something.

Midori is conducting a master class, and the student is a tall young man who towers over the amazingly petite personage of the internationally acclaimed concert violinist. The student plays pieces of Dvořák's Violin Concerto with great passion and fluidity. He is excellent, and Midori says so, and compliments him on his obvious love of the piece and of playing the violin. She cautions that he is playing too much for himself and not projecting enough out to the audience, and demonstrates what she means. She then spends almost an hour on the nuance of individual themes, and has him repeat the same parts several times. The student responds, and the two of them enter into a kind of dance, with Midori literally singing along in a lovely clear voice as he plays. Her body is weaving to the music, her voice is conducting his playing as it grows more interpretive with a wider range of mood, especially in the cadenza, which is pushing him to go where he wanted to go, but had not known how, or perhaps had not dared.

How would you describe the relationship between master and pupil? Perhaps deep but analytical, respectful but demanding, supportive but not satisfied. It was as excellent as it could be.

With Midori and her student, and with Dan and his, the listening process is quite straightforward and the voices self-evident. Both Midori and Dan know exactly what they are looking for. That it is an art is also clear. In Midori's case, she has spent twenty years developing her world-class ear. In Dan's case, he has spent a lifetime "kicking the brick," intuitively sizing up whether this is a deal he wants to do or a person with whom he wants to do business. His criteria for what constitutes a good grant is internal to his life experience—he knows it when he sees it, and he can tell if this person is someone he wants to support. Is he interested in the young woman's grades, scores, and home environment? Yes, because he doesn't want her to fail. He also wants to know her well enough to provide the kind of mentoring and support she will need to succeed. What he is most interested in, however, is a certain spark within her—it is more important than anything else.

You don't know Dan, but it would not surprise you that he likes to meet face-to-face, and is not interested in funding what he refers to as "bullshit," which has no real definition but has something to do with too much process. If you put an intermediary between Dan and the direct experience of meeting the young student, it would not work. If the same student's profile were presented to him on paper, he would not be able to *listen*. Would he do more of these scholarships? Without a doubt, the amount of money by Dan's standards is small, even though it is huge to the students. But the very hands-on experience required imposes serious limitations. It takes Dan and his advisors an immense amount of time to discover, meet with, and then nurture these students. In his book, he is getting far more out of the deal than the student does. His is a lovely story but it is his, in Midori's words, "sole property."[5]

It is also not everyone's cup of tea. Many donors are unable or unwilling to put in that much time. Many would be uncomfortable, and even afraid, to sit in that room the way Dan is able to. And many more do not know how to make the connection. Their world is too far away from these other worlds. I remember a friend saying to me once, "I would like to give some money in the Bronx, but I really don't know where it is and would be afraid to go there anyway." This comment came from an active philanthropist who is a lifelong resident of the New York City area. My guess is the same words are said, or thought, about Watts, the South Side of Chicago, the *bairros* of Rio, or any other very poor neighborhoods in the world. The gated communities that have become a common phenomenon—even in parts of the country where it is unclear where and what the threat is—are a reflection of the even more widespread gated communities in our minds, and in the way we live. Fisher Island may be separated by a seven-minute ferry ride from Miami Beach, but the symbolism and reality of that distancing is one and the same. This is a hard place to listen from.

As lovely as Dan's story is, it also illustrates what might be called the "beauty contest syndrome." Donors are drawn to the attractive kid; the smooth, articulate, social entrepreneur; the great proposal writer; the better salesman; and are turned off, or even frightened, by the sounds and smells of the messy, the difficult, those who mumble, offend, or are radical. This is true even if they are the very ones who are deserving, or who can make a difference. I remember a visit to an organization that worked with street gangs. We were seated in a circle and I was the only "suit" in that circle. These were tough, aggressive kids and I was on their turf. They were not an easy group to like. I think that most philanthropy is drawn to fund "poster child" people and organizations who, in their own worlds, may be the equivalent of "suits."

At the same time, what every donor wants is the same sense of engagement and satisfaction that Dan got. What every potential donee wants is the same listening and respect that the young student got. It is a donor–donee relationship that is perfectly balanced. New terms have entered the vocabulary to describe this relationship, like *partnership*, *collaboration*, and a *two-way learning experience*. The power imbalance between the supply side and the demand side is intrinsic, but attitude is not, and these terms are reflective of a very changed attitude. The optimum relationship is not a vertical one, from the donor down to the donee, or the reverse; it is more horizontal, or lateral.

The degrees of separation, however, are real. Rather than a two-way conversation between donor and donee, the voices in one's ear are typically once or twice removed from the ground. It might be an ask from the development staff of an institution or organization, or from a board member, or from an intermediary like United Way, Community

Foundation or Federation, or even from your golf partner. The terms of the engagement change when the donor is relying on someone else to filter, interpret, analyze, and evaluate the deal. They change when the primary information is in the form of written proposals, when outside advisory committees or reviewers are involved, and when the inevitable creep of bureaucracy has entered the room. In large foundations, professional staff has the direct contact and thus board members are much removed from the client, the project, and the direct action. Boards struggle with this all the time, and worry that the staff is running away with the foundation. And frustrated staff just as frequently ask, "How can we get the board's attention and get them more involved?"

The nature and terms of the engagement depend on the philanthropic goals. If the objective is to advocate for more services for the mentally ill, then the parties at interest should include legislators, health-policy experts, patients, providers, and even governors, as well as those directly affected. If the objective is systemic change within any issue area, then public policy, and increasingly market forces, are considerations that need to be assessed through research and evaluation of public opinion and political will. Determining who the parties at interest are, which voices among them need to be heard, and how to interpret them is indeed an art.

It is often a cacophony of voices and often a moving target—as reflected in my poem "Each Day" where I write: "actors scatter / Work alone, recongregate around the cliff, down the beach / And then in a blink the birds are gone as though never there."

That poem came from time spent in Santa Barbara. To get down to the beach, we would navigate steep wooden stairs that had 144 steps, counted very precisely by my granddaughter. Each day, at the foot of the stairs, it was always different. Some days you could step easily onto the beach, and on other days the sea had been at work and a jumble of rocks and small boulders made the last step difficult, a small climb or jump. The tide is huge there, and the waves rolling across the Pacific carry tremendous force. Even so, it was a bit of a surprise to see this daily rearrangement of a tiny speck of earth. The sea is relentless; it keeps track of time differently than we do, counting its victories in infinitely patient ways, and rewriting over and over again. That is what it takes.

Listen:

We are at a conference of public-school educators, all of whom have successfully competed for a multiyear grant to bring about systemic change in their schools. This is the third year of the program, and the group, numbering about one hundred, has become a closely-knit network that has supported and learned from each other. At one time, the sponsors of the program hired experts to consult with the schools; now they hire participant teachers and principals who work with their peers on the very same issues they have successfully overcome. Someone says what has been said before, "These conferences, and the chance to be with others who have the same challenges as I do, are worth more than the money."

Listen:

The L Fund supports grassroots organizations with small grants, and each year brings them together for an "institute" where they attend workshops on fundraising, back-office issues, and contracting. It is immensely useful to the participants; they meet others, often for the first time even though they may work in the same part of the city. Connections are made, visits are arranged, help is offered and accepted. A network has been formed where before there was none.

Listen:

M Charitable Trust, which focuses on homelessness, has funded and regularly convened advocates and other major stakeholders for more than ten years. In the process, the strength of the statewide movement to deal systemically with the issues of chronic homelessness along with state and private funding has grown exponentially.

The results from such horizontal listening can be almost magical; it contributes to a sense of self-worth, often lacking in the nonprofit field, and it contributes to the formation of communities of interest. I have commented before on the essential loneliness of being, on how peace of mind is so elusive. There is an organizational analog to that feeling. It is the little-understood cultural phenomenon that faces nonprofits, which I would describe as "aloneness." Each teacher is alone in her classroom. Each tub is on its own bottom and, if the tub is small, it is very difficult to do all the things that one must do to function well, ranging from program development and execution to financial and administrative issues. It leads to lots of competition for limited resources, and a lack of synchronization of services. If businesses suffer from too much convening, nonprofits suffer from the reverse.

Sometimes you can listen to voices by putting yourself in someone else's shoes, or at least trying to.

I am with a group of senior executives of a major investment company. They are a committee of eight, representing thirty-five of their colleagues who have collectively put $2 million into a pot to give away. This "giving circle" is just getting going, and the idea on the table is to do something with families and kids. One member has proposed that they "adopt" an elementary school class and promise scholarships to those who ultimately graduate from high school. The committee agrees to do a role-play on how the $2 million should be directed, based on what the characters in three different scenarios most need, and most want. The first scenario involves a mother on welfare with two young children. The second concerns a mother who is working and making a modest living, but whose youngest child has severe asthma. The third concerns a couple living on minimum wage with three teenage children who live in a gang-infested part of town. The committee members have a small *aha* moment and realize they had been thinking too narrowly, and not holistically enough about the needs of families and children. From this learning experience comes the criteria for an RFP for proposals from organizations that work with families and kids. Four of these groups are ultimately funded. Three years later, the members of the committee still talk about the role-play.

I have made the point that we are all players and listeners at the same time, and that the voices we need to hear are often not the ones we listen to. There are many kinds of voices, and infinite ways to listen. I started out as a door-to-door salesman, and you learn a lot going door-to-door. If you are one of five hundred thousand people in the middle of First Night, where families with kids are running around and celebrating, you learn a lot by listening to that crowd. It is perhaps my bias that the further away you get from that kind of experience, the more you miss. Simulating that kind of immediacy, however, is not always practical or possible. The examples I have given of alternative ways of listening have the common thread of an attitude that is open to learning.

In addition, this essay doesn't even begin to reference so many other footprints of experience where one learns from listening, such as being in the middle of the deep woods or climbing a mountain or listening to the earth or the sound of falling water. Or if you are in the middle of the bay, with the sails stretched against the spreaders in a following sea, listening to the wind and the slap of the waves against the hull of the boat.

For me, the unanswered questions continue to hover just out of reach in that part of my own portfolio of unresolved ideas that, to date, I have simply "walked by." At the same time, I have learned that when faced with certain kinds of stimuli, certain images, I, like so many, respond in the same way as the sand creatures, and rise to meet the flow of tide.

Tidal flats, tidal pools, slowly fill, secret denizens of the sand
Burrow down, waiting until called again as we wait to be called.

The inevitability of that call has never seemed more present.

Who Is My Stranger?

There is a theory of writing poetry that one should keep the personal life of the poet out of the poem. That a poem needs to stand on its own, and anything biographical or based on personal beliefs works against that possibility. Under this theory, a true poem is a work of the imagination. What comes to mind are the poems "The Bridge" by Hart Crane, which includes a transformation of the Brooklyn Bridge into a metaphysical journey, and "The Home Burial" by Robert Frost, which offers a portrait of unrelenting grief and anger resulting from the death of a child.

As a poet, I aspire to write those kinds of poems but consistently fail. My personal limitations, my loves, my hates, my prejudices, and my angst keep coming out. I have great difficulty rising above the domestic, above the ordinary turn of mind and turn of phrase. Sometimes, however, within these personal tropes, there is a glimmer of something deeper, a turning to language that is more figurative, more metaphorical, to ideas that transcend the literal. When that happens, I sense there is a poem embedded within the poem that wants to come out. That is why there are so many false starts in the writing of things; the real beginning may be halfway down the page and the writer, at first, hasn't a clue. This is true not only in writing, but in the experience and doing of almost anything. It is a critical moment. Will the poem be transformed from a walk around the backyard to a walk through the looking glass? If successful, the result has the potential to become what is called *art*.

I have the same struggle in how I live my life, how I balance my private and my public self. It is the ongoing and never fully resolved tension between those interests, desires, and ambitions that are self-serving, many of which are reasonable and a few that are absurd; and, on the other hand, what I give back to friends and to the community, however I define that community; and finally to the larger society, which allows me to live that personal life. It is the balance between what Aristotle called "meanness," which involves an excessive, self-indulgent concern with one's own things, and the desire to ease suffering and make people's lives better, which is the prima facie source of common good. It is the fundamental struggle between the "I" and the "we," and it is hardly new.

Hillel wrote, "If I am not for me, who will be for me, but if I am for me alone, who am I?"[6]

How do you answer those questions in a society like our own, which is rooted in proud individualism, is materialistic and consumer-driven to the core, and is deeply divided ideologically and politically? How do you answer them in a world so fractious that many people turn off, and tune out, for no other reason than self-protection from the heavy metal *rat-a-ta-ta-tat* of the evening news? I think the answer is "not very well," and that we are terribly adrift in our society as to the relationship we have to each other.

There is a serious "missing person" syndrome; too many people, too many citizens are not actors within the commons, and are not on the public stage. Citizenship is almost anachronistic to a whole generation.

Too many of us are "sleepwalkers" who do not feel connected to others. Mixed in with the incredible busyness, the poverty of time of our lives, there is something else, a poverty of spirit, of connectedness. We are not getting along.

While these issues sound abstract, they are more real than the most real reality show. They may be the biggest questions we've got and, in their answer, we define ourselves and the world in which we live.

Yet, like the poet and the poem, something lies embedded within us, something that wants to come out. As much as I wish to be left alone, as much as I want to curl up in a corner of my own making, as much as I want to leave behind the chaos, the violence, and the risk that we may have botched things so badly that even the planet may be at risk, I cannot.

I think that what wants to come out is the instinctive human yearning to turn, as in the old Shaker hymn that says, "To turn, turn will be our delight, / Till by turning, turning we come 'round right."[7]

If the poem, when it moves into the realm of imagination, becomes art, then the person who successfully "turns" becomes whole.

Often, we do not know what "coming 'round right" means until it happens upon us.

My daughter, son-in-law, and grandchildren live in Madison, Wisconsin. Next door is an elderly woman in failing health. My kids, despite leading very busy lives of their own, have assumed a caretaker role, mowing her lawn, shoveling her walk, and just keeping an eye on things every day. There is always a "Verna story." They are neighbors, not kin. What do you call that? Certainly kind, but not a big purposeful act of humanitarianism or philanthropy. There is no rhetoric, but I know my two grandchildren, ages eight and twelve, have absorbed into their precious selves that this is simply what one does. For them, Verna is not a stranger.

In the remarkable book *The Gift Relationship*, the author Richard Titmuss asks the question, "Who is my stranger?"[8] It seems to me to be the absolutely right question. The universal "stranger" he refers to is the unknown recipient who the donor of blood will never know.

The gift in *The Gift Relationship* is blood, and the book documents, in some detail, the differences in social policy between the UK system of voluntarily giving of blood and the US system where blood has become a commodity. It turns out to be hugely important that a blood donor is a volunteer instead of paid. In all ways, a voluntary system costs less and works better, but the larger issue is the impact on society, and the individual's role within it. Turning blood into a market transaction, and privatizing its distribution, creates its own set of dilemmas. The book, however, is really about something else: the place of altruism in human affairs. Titmuss makes the case that altruism is both morally sound and economically efficient and, even more important, essential to the human experience, essential to becoming "whole."[9]

Perhaps Walt Whitman was being more than metaphorical when he wrote about this in "Song of Myself."

> I celebrate myself, and sing myself,
> And what I assume you shall assume,
> For every atom belonging to me as good belongs to you.[10]

Titmuss's claim is that there is a biological need within us to help others. Biology teaches us that every species, including our own, has certain things that are essential to live together well and flourish. From this perspective, altruism is indispensable and moves the religious, political, spiritual, philosophical, and societal reasons for generosity, of which there are many, into the realm of science.

A commoditized blood market raises issues of equity. It increases the separation between rich and poor. When blood is sold, most donors are poor, and the recipients are rich. This is regressive economic policy and creates an inequitable flow of the resource, a most vital resource. It is a variation of hiring someone else to fight in your place in a war, a concern that lingers today with America's volunteer army. But a commoditized blood market also denies us the experience of altruism.

One of the limitations of the economic cost–analysis approach to social policy is that it has no moral center. The market economy itself is based on the view that each person is out for themselves, and only the fittest will survive. The sale of blood, kidneys, eyes from an eye bank, or anything that makes money out of human suffering, raises moral questions that economists rarely address.

How we organize our social structures greatly affects, for good or bad, behavior in other spheres. Titmuss's conclusion is that the "commercialization of blood represses the expression of altruism, and erodes the sense of community."[11] Taking away the opportunity of the individual to make a gift of blood—a gift of life itself—is a restriction of freedom and contributes to the retreat of the individual from public life.

His summation is powerful: "A competitive, materialistic, acquisitive society based on hierarchies of power and privilege ignores at its peril the life-giving impulse toward altruism which is needed for welfare in the most fundamental sense."[12]

In other words, the fact that we are materialistic, acquisitive—all of those things—is exactly why we need the counterbalance of something opposite; without it we are at risk of losing something critical. Call it what you will, I would call it *humanity*.

Would you like those with great wealth to be voluntary blood donors? Do you wish that, while growing up, there was someone in their personal history like Verna? How would you hope they would answer the question of who their stranger is?

I was reminded of Titmuss's book by the strange, almost surrealistic article in *The New Yorker* entitled "The Gift."[13] It was a story about Zell Kravinsky, a successful real estate investor who first gave away his $45 million fortune to charity, and followed that with a gift of one of his kidneys to a "stranger." One got the sense that this man would give away his second kidney if allowed to. Kravinsky's extraordinary acts were driven by an acute, painful sense of his individual responsibility to others—in the case of his kidney, to someone who would have died without it. In some ways, this man is making a dramatic and poignant stand against the notion of impotence. He is shouting it to the rooftops!

Kravinsky's extremes are very extreme and the price he and his wife and friends paid were evident in the article. The man could be called crazy, but his moral instincts are stunning.

I have met many people of wealth who have given, or are planning to give, all or most of their money away. Some are motivated to do so based on altruism, others because of the "selfish" pleasure they get from giving back, and others by not wanting to leave "too much" money to children. In fact, perhaps half of the several hundred individuals with great wealth my colleagues and I have met over the years have come to those conclusions. Most intend to wait until after they have died.

Kravinsky is exceptional because he has defined for his own purposes the "universal stranger" in the most expansive way possible. He is a harbinger of a changing moral view, what Titmuss called "creative altruism."[14]

The concept of creative altruism does not call for a return of any kind, but makes the case that self is realized through the process of giving, sometimes with the help of anonymous others. These are some of the words shared by the givers of blood, regarding their experiences:

> "Knowing I might be saving someone's life . . ."
>
> "Anonymously, without financial reward to help others . . ."
>
> "You can't get blood from supermarkets and chain stores."
>
> "No man is an island."
>
> "I thought it just a small way to help people."
>
> "A small contribution to the welfare of humanity . . ."
>
> "Someone in my family may one day need blood."
>
> "Some unknown person gave blood that saved my wife's life."

"In order to help maintain the supply of blood so urgently needed at all times . . ."[15]

The blood donor never learns who the recipient is and the recipient never knows who the donor is. This is much the same way the medieval alms box worked, where the recipient was unobserved and quietly visited the church in the middle of the night. Maimonides was certainly not thinking about blood when he put anonymous gifts at the top of his scale of generosity. There are, however, variations on the notion of creative altruism that evolve around notions of kinship and community that are not anonymous.

In the *potlach* of the North American Indians or the *kula* of the Melanesians, gifts are made without any expectation of a personal reward or gain; the assumption is that the return is guaranteed by the virtue of the things passed on. In these cultures, the act of giving is a group process where interdependence is an assumption. It acknowledges that we are all in this together.

That has been part of the American experience, which is based on mutuality, community, barn raising, the Grange, the neighborhood, and overarching concepts of brotherhood, sisterhood, justice, access, and fairness.

———

A man I know was meeting with a group of homeless women who told their tough and sobering stories of how they came to be homeless. In almost every instance, it was a matter of not earning enough to support their children, and of bad luck, and from circumstances over which they had no control. His wife and children were with him at the meeting, and after listening for several hours to these strong, struggling women, he turned to his family and said, "This could have been us, we've always been lucky to be able to throw money at our problems."

This man had what could be called a small *r* revelation, and as a result changed the direction of his foundation.

When I was interviewing a person of great wealth about the influences that had made him philanthropic, he responded with this:

> It was certainly my family and their dedication to taking care of people. My mother feeding the hobos that came to our farm from the railroad that was close by comes to mind. They would chop some wood, and get a meal. There was respect on both sides. Another story that my mother told happened in 1929. The local priest came out and spent until two in the morning talking my father into a pledge of $2,000 for the new church, which he did not have. He had lost his farm in 1925, and so it was a great sacrifice. The thought of my father giving $2,000 at that time was a really great example for me.

People may be deeply affected by what they see around them, but often it takes a while to register, to become a wake-up call, to become an *aha* moment as it did for me forty years ago when I would regularly drive through Roxbury on the way to work and see great-looking kids from the projects playing on the street or in dangerous rubble while my own kids were living an idealized suburban life just a few miles away.

I realize much of what I have become goes back to images and realizations like these that stayed with me until I finally decided to do something about it. I know that most of you reading this essay have had similar experiences.

What we feel toward others is very complicated. The debate on welfare reform is around the differing views about where the line is drawn between individual responsibility and public responsibility. While those differences are substantial, they are more differences in strategy and vocabulary rather than differences in the essential agreement around need, opportunity, and access. Terms like *entitlement* and *compassionate conservatism* have taken on lightning-rod characteristics. The public-policy issue of what is the best way to help people in poverty escape poverty is caught in the cross fire.

What is missing is the lack of respect between these different views, or what might be called a *mean*, a common ground. My friend's mother, who readily agreed to give a meal to the hobo, had the expectation that he would "earn" that meal. It formed the basis for the mutual respect between the parties—the woman needed wood cut and the man who was hungry was not offended by the request to cut wood. It was the norm, the "policy," of the day. We do not have those norms today. We do not have the vocabulary.

Philanthropy is part of the problem. Creative altruism is in many ways the opposite of the prevailing philanthropic process, which increasingly is based on an economic model. Some of the same issues that were observed in the commoditization of blood surface when philanthropic gifts/investments become transactions. The donor "buys" his/her name on a building or onto the board of an organization. The donor dictates the terms of a gift, what the recipient will or will not do, or the donor's intent is cast in stone.

Obligatory philanthropy is a different kind of transaction. Obligations come in various ways. There is an old saying in fundraising that for every dollar you raise from your friends and contacts, be prepared to reciprocate with contributions to those charities that interest them. When your biggest customer is being "honored" by a nonprofit organization, the gift you make has far more to do with your business than a charitable interest. It's the gift to the land trust that just so happens to ensure that the view from your deck will forever be maintained.

To become a board member in good standing of a major cultural organization or university board carries a stated or assumed level of giving. It is a kind of quid pro quo. The same is true for being part of a church or temple or ethnic community where expected levels of giving are assiduously pursued. A friend once commented that too much of his giving was like a tax on life.

At least those gifts are going to the communities of interest that one chooses. However, why do we choose them?

Are you a member of the board of the symphony because you love music and want to help make it available to the community? Or are you on that board because of the status, the business contacts, and the parties? The answers to these types of questions are often quite mixed.

I got a phone call recently from a lawyer whose client wanted to know whether he could get a better "deal" on a major gift from X as opposed to Y University. Tax planning is still the primary focus for most advisors in their discussions with wealthy clients, and does not include an appropriate focus on philanthropic objectives.

To complicate the situation even further, the vocabulary that philanthropy uses has become increasingly economic. Terms like *strategic*, *investment*, *outcomes*, *impact*, and *metrics* are driving a new generation of donors as well as many established foundations. Lost in the shuffle is the moral vocabulary of *caring* and *kinship* and *love*.

―――

There are ways to test the quality of a generous act. The philosopher James Wallace uses the term *primary generosity*, which he defines as

- the agent gives because of direct concern and to benefit the recipient;

- the agent gives something with a market value that he values and wants to keep; and

- the agent gives more than normal for the situation than is expected.[16]

The "stretch gift" by my friend's father in 1929, when he made a $2,000 contribution to the church, meets those conditions. But most charitable gifts would not qualify as primary generosity. Pay-back gifts to colleges and universities, gifts made for tax purposes, gifts given because one is asked by someone one cannot refuse, and gifts given from guilt are clearly not expressions of primary generosity. And few give in the manner of Zell Kravinsky.

There are pragmatic as well as philosophical implications operating here. One view is that it does not matter how or why money is given, as long as it goes to a good cause. While true in the short run, I do not think it does not matter as it relates to the bigger picture. Something is not right under the prevailing mode of transactional philanthropy. Fundraising is too manipulative, too ego-driven, too unrelated to the good cause being promoted, and too often turns people off. Rather than making gift-giving an expansive experience, the process is a restrictive one. It plays to the "I" and not the "we."

Transactional philanthropy, in all of its forms, dilutes the moral center and erodes altruism just as surely as does making a market in blood. It does not have to be so. It is possible to be, or to become, an exceptional donor.

It is the exceptional donor who gives based on values and passions. When those elements are combined with a 360° mission that is sensitive to all of the stakeholders involved, the footprint for creative altruism has been laid. It is in the process of deep listening to the stories, the needs, and the dreams of others that the exceptional donor expands his or her horizon beyond the familiar and expected. It is then that the charitable gift can be like perfect pitch. It is then that philanthropy becomes an act of creative altruism.

One might start by asking this question: Who is my stranger?

In the Jewish tradition, a place of honor is made at the Sabbath table for Elijah, who is both a representative of God and the universal stranger. It is the exceptional person who welcomes that stranger. In ordinary times, that is.

Sometimes we rise to be exceptional because of great events. Otherwise, how do you explain the immense outpouring of generosity and need for community following the cataclysmic events on September 11? The explanation is in the desire to ease suffering and make people's lives easier in what Richard Titmuss called our biological need to be altruistic. When called upon, the humanist within rises. The challenge is how to awaken that gene, the one embedded within us. It is how to rouse ourselves, how to generate the missing vibration of connectivity and the realization that we are all in this together.

Who is my stranger? The answer is in our hearts and in our soul. My answer is this essay. What is yours?

Coda for the Individual

- When you feel impotent, handled, and obligated, the response is tentative and cynical. If you believe that each person has the power to make a difference in the destiny of our planet, the response is empowered.

- If you are engaged in an exciting social venture, the response is energized.

- If you are engaged in a spiritual quest, the response is liberating.

- If you have just emerged from a Bruce Springsteen concert, the world is alive with feelings of goodwill toward others.

- If you believe conflicts with each other can be mediated, not to agreement but to a position of mutual respect, the door to the stranger opens.

- If you set a place at your table for Elijah (or as my daughter and her husband in Madison, Wisconsin, have for Verna), the door to the stranger is wide open.

- If you believe the forces for good are stronger than those for evil, and that goodness can be taught and nurtured . . .

If you believe all of these things, then you are with me in believing that we can create a society where we do get along, we do respect one another, and altruism will become a way of life.

The Magic of Philanthropy

Magic: The pretended art of influencing the course of events by compelling the agency of spiritual beings.[17]

There has never been, to my knowledge, a true discussion, never mind a workshop, on philanthropy as magic. So together we are going to break new ground, but what do we mean by that? Are we talking about literal magic? Or are we using the word *magic* as metaphor for a certain kind of experience that transcends the ordinary? Or it is both? Well let's decide at the end of our time together.

For the next ninety minutes, this is the deal. I am the magician and each of you is either a believer or a nonbeliever. You may switch back and forth with impunity. However, you must declare yourself; go on record, so to speak.

First some context. There are all kinds of magic. There is *natural magic* that has nothing to do with spells and spirits, but comes about through the laws of physical causation. The sun comes up each day, the regeneration of all living things, the way a frozen pond awakens in the spring, the birth of a child—these all have elements of mystery, of magic. The natural order of things is all around us and while scientific explanation goes a long way, at a certain point we cross over into realms that we are not able to fully explain.

There is also the transforming magic of genius. Mozart, when he first performed at age eight, was a perfect example of what the English poet Spencer called a "magic-gifted hand."[18] Think of the magic of "The

Heavens Are Telling" chorus from Haydn's *The Creation*, or the chills you experience during the "Ode to Joy" from Beethoven's Ninth Symphony, or listening to Yo-Yo Ma perform Brahms's Double Concerto. The magic of genius is evident in all of the arts and in other domains as well.

From mathematics, the "magic square" is one divided into smaller squares, each with a number the sum of which from every angle adds up to the same total—for example, a square divided into four boxes with the number four that always adds up to sixteen.

Or in nuclear physics where a set of numbers becomes "doubly magic" when "an atomic nucleus exhibits a high degree of stability when either the proton or neutron count is equal to the number."[19]

Magic can be used as a verb—to transform, to make happen. One can "magic" something away, causing it to disappear.

I am going to mention some variations on this theme. *Tell me what comes to your mind.*

> A magic carpet—on which we travel to places of our dreams
>
> A magic marker—with which we highlight those things we think are important
>
> A magic lantern—with which we illuminate places we otherwise would not see or go to
>
> A magic curtain—behind which lies places of delight, terror, and knowledge
>
> A magic wand—with which we alter reality, making something or someone disappear or change
>
> A magic box—from which comes the seemingly inexplicable, as in radar, a radio receiver; even television was first called "the magic box"

Perhaps magic is a state of being, of mind—a highly intense, elevated state of being where you feel wonderful, lovely. Perhaps you are in love and the whole world is in your hands. Perhaps you just reached the top of a mountain after an exhilarating climb. Perhaps you just broke par for the first time. *Are these things magical?*

To be magical, does there have to be something serious going on? I promised my colleagues that I wouldn't admit in such a public place that I am a fan of *The X-Files*, but I am willing to say that I rather like the image of Mary Poppins flying over London's rooftops. I, and especially my nine-year-old grandson Jacob, like Harry Potter, who has brought the world of magic to an amazing level of interest for millions of people around the world. The Potter phenomenon is representative of how much hunger there is for transcendental storytelling. It is, on the one hand, fanciful and, on the other, a substantive story about heroes, heroines, and good and evil.

So—what is the magic of philanthropy, or is there magic in the experience of philanthropy?

From the outset, it is clear that you cannot "magic" away the critical problems facing the world. One of TPI's operating premises is that "social change is incremental at best." Thus the waving of wands doesn't do it. At the same time, we are looking for wonderful, lovely moments. We yearn for that time when things mesh, come together in a confluence that does, in fact, transcend what often seems insurmountable. When the existential, spiritual, and values-based propositions all converge and there is a kind of revelation—small *r* revelation.

Let me illustrate a few examples.

In 1968, following the death of Dr. Martin Luther King Jr., I was part of an organization called Fund for Urban Negro Development (FUND). Dr. King's death was the stimulus for widespread soul searching in this country. It was the first time the notion of Black Power made it onto the cover of *Time* magazine. It was a time of high emotion, of deep yearning to find ways to respond, and it was a time when people wanted to be together. On a Saturday, two months after Dr. King's murder, eight hundred people from all walks of life crammed into the ballroom of a Boston hotel to support an ambitious effort to promote economic development and social justice in the Black community. It was an inspirational meeting, the kind that is memorable, and I remember to this day the feeling of community and solidarity in that room. That meeting was the stimulus for highly energized effort that, for four years, raised money and consciousness in Greater Boston around the issues of racism in our society.

This experience was, for those of us involved, transformational. Do you think that qualifies as magical? If not, what is missing?

A few years ago, I was in New Orleans to give the keynote speech to the annual celebration and thank-you lunch given by the Freeport-McMoRan Foundation to the community. Invited were more than two hundred local, not-for-profit organizations that receive more than $8 million in annual grants from the company. Walking into the grand ballroom of the Sheraton Hotel, I was overwhelmed. The room was jammed with more than a thousand enthusiastic people representing a broad cross-section of the city's leadership and nonprofit sector. It was an impressive sight. The flamboyant CEO warmly welcomed everyone, and the "volunteer of the year" award was then presented to a lovely woman who told her story in lilting Cajun English. She spoke about the hospice she had helped to start in her neighborhood, the difficulties she had to overcome, and how comforting the hospice was to those whose lives have become sad and desperate. She was wonderfully eloquent and as she went on, she began to cry. Soon the whole huge room filled with the good people of the city of New Orleans were crying with her, me included. When she sat down, the applause was deafening.

It was very moving and, as I sat there, aware that my prepared remarks were weak and would not work at all, I had a strange vision. I saw, over in the far corner of the ballroom, sitting and listening even more intently than me, a solitary man facing half toward the podium and half out over the river. And I realized that man was Alexis de Tocqueville. He was literally and figuratively there, observing the amazing American phenomenon of philanthropy at work, of citizens joining in voluntary association with each other to make their community a better place. In fact, de Tocqueville had been in the New Orleans Parish in 1831, perhaps in that very spot on the riverbank, which was yet to be improved by an eighteen-story hotel.

It was a remarkable and emotional moment as I stood there on the podium. As I shared this vision with the audience, they began to look around the room to see if in fact a mysterious stranger was actually there. Of course, it was they who were there, all one hundred of them, living and breathing participants in the uniquely American story of community involvement. It was a moment somehow close to the heart of an America that I very badly want—an America we all want, one that often seems elusive.

This experience crossed over the line of fantasy and reality. Do you think that qualifies as magical? If not, what was missing? Has anyone here had a similar experience?

A TPI client is an artist and is interested in supporting art teachers in public schools. For the last three years, this donor has offered $5,000 renewal grants to art teachers in several counties in Massachusetts, Connecticut, and New York. The teachers have submitted proposals as to how they would use the funds to create curricula for their classrooms or work on their own art. The winners are invited to a conference in which they share their challenges, successes, and stories. All of the grantees have said that this recognition has been immensely important to them as professionals and as individuals.

This program, while modest, has been remarkable in building self-esteem, in promoting the importance of the arts in the schools, in creating a community. Would you use the word magical? If not, what is missing?

We work with an individual in Boston whose disdain for organizational bureaucracy, self-promotion, and rhetoric is ever present. When we first met him some years ago, he offered up one of the greatest lines: "I sometimes feel it would do just as much good to drive down to the poorest neighborhood in the city, open up the car window, throw the money out, and drive back home!"

For him, we created and ran the Boston Neighborhood Fellows program for twenty-one years. Each year, we found six unsung heroes in the city—the cop on the beat, the street worker, the nun who works with victims of domestic violence, the community organizer in a housing project—and gave them $30,000 with no strings attached! Our donor, who insisted he remain anonymous, sat in the audience each year at loud and enthusiastic awards ceremonies, beaming. The eloquence of the winners—who are people who never thought their work would be recognized—is always amazing. You leave that room with your heart singing. It is community at its best.

Is it magical? If it isn't, why not?

A family foundation has been struggling with how to get its act together. Everyone is on a different page. While the values are the same, the interests range from economic development to literacy to support of the local museum. In addition, the siblings are still stuck in arguments that have more to do with their adolescence than anything connected to the foundation. The patriarch, who is also the donor, has begun to think it may not work.

The family agrees to try to address one issue that interests some of the group, but not all. They choose microcredit and with our help they do some research on the successes, the challenges, and the opportunity for expansion. For some reason, the whole group wants more information and they invite Michael Chu, then-president of Accion International, to come to a meeting. He brings with him a colleague from Bolivia, a woman who had built a business that now employs twenty-five women from her village, all from a $150 loan. The family was enormously impressed and decided to make a capital investment in a new community bank in Bolivia. That one grant loosened up the logjam, and the energy and interest in the foundation changed overnight. Today, some six years later, the family foundation is functioning to everyone's satisfaction.

What was the magic in this situation? Was it good process, good chemistry, were they ripe for something to happen? Or was it not magic at all?

All of these stories are experiential. My view is that we become donors through our experiences, a lifetime of experiences that we carry around, sometimes for a long time before we do anything about it. Perhaps you have been reading about or thinking about or are sad about something. I had that experience in the '60s when I would drive through Roxbury and see beautiful, smart-looking kids playing in rubble. It seemed wrong to me and when FUND came along, I had an *aha* moment because I found a way to act.

Action comes when we have that revelation, that *aha* moment. Sometimes that *aha* is small. Maybe you meet a young person who needs help with tuition and you say, "Yes, I can do that." Sometimes that *aha* is big. When the family foundation realized they could make a real difference in the lives of literally thousands of very poor women, it was thrilling to them—enough so that they were able to leave behind the various domestic issues that had thus far hamstrung their efforts.

Is an *aha* magic? If not, why not?

Here are some lines from *The Cure at Troy* by Seamus Heaney:

> History says, don't hope
> On this side of the grave.
> But then, once in a lifetime
> The longed-for tidal wave
> Of justice can rise up,
> And hope and history rhyme.
>
> So hope for a great sea-change
> On the far side of revenge.

Believe that a further shore
Is reachable from here.
Believe in miracles
And cures and healing wells.

Call miracle self-healing:
The utter, self-revealing
Double-take of feeling.[20]

What do you think "Call miracle self-healing" means? I think it means that the miracle lies within each of us. If not, where does it lie?

Catechism for a Great Foundation

Great foundations begin with the extraordinary opportunity that has been bestowed on them to use their immense resources with compassion, and strategy, in the relentless pursuit of better and more equitable health, social, and educational outcomes for the world. But while faith and great expectations are all well and good, they need help and support—this is not a go-it-alone trajectory. There is much at stake and no hard and fast rules of engagement; there is a large and growing community of caring that can be tapped to leverage a better world.

Integrity of the philanthropic process begins when we become a listener, a learner, or a learning organization about others who are different, about the issues, about what works and what doesn't. Great foundations learn how to listen to the community, learn how to touch. In addition to building networks of organizations that can deliver measurable results, they build networks that are based on a culture of listening and touching. Perhaps every person of responsibility in a great foundation should spend part of every year immersed on the ground.

Great foundations believe that integrity of purpose for any social action is based on one simple condition: "If it isn't good for the community, and only good for the donor, it isn't worth doing."[21] Anyone who doesn't understand that runs the risk of having a chair thrown at them someday. Sometimes that chair is literal, and sometimes it is because you have broken the golden rule, which is to "do no harm."

Great foundations of the future will increasingly learn how to use their cachet and convening power to significantly increase communities of interest by expanding boundaries and intersections between ideas and people and sectors.

Leadership matters; it matters across cultures, it matters across time, and it matters greatly. Virtually all lasting significant social change comes from leaders working in intersecting networks of influence. Great foundations work hard at identifying and supporting leadership.[22]

Great foundations focus on more than problem-solving and investment return, and make the time—as hard as that is—for reflection and scenario-planning for the long-term reality of what will take, in most cases, decades to accomplish.

Great foundations, irrespective of size, resist—to their core—bureaucracy, remain nimble, and bring energy into a room, as opposed to taking it out.

Great foundations do more than ask the tough questions, they want—they really want—honest answers, even if those answers counter and disturb/disrupt the very assumptions the foundation holds.

Great foundations use data that drives and moves programs, but watch carefully that data expands thinking and does not narrow it, and that it increases the opportunity for risk-taking and not the reverse.

Proof of concept for a great foundation is nothing—scale is everything. Going to scale surfaces what is called the "giant spiders and medieval cathedral" dilemma[23] that makes the case that, as objects grow larger, they by necessity must change their design.

Great foundations acknowledge that innovation in social systems does have a scientific basis—but it requires a different paradigm. Technology and new products alone will not achieve large-scale lasting impact without creative systems innovation, and we don't understand how to do that well.

Great foundations work hard to develop a powerful public persona that is aligned with mission and is fundamentally accountable and transparent to its communities of interest.

Great foundations build heart into the fabric of the culture of the organization. In addition to research, data, advisory boards, and well-thought-out theories of change, other aspects of human interaction that bind us together also become part of the equation such as story, anecdote, and poetry. Great foundations, like the best of American philanthropy, combine the heart and mind in "the search for the best in people, their organizations, and the world around them."[24]

Great foundations find ways to harness the philanthropic instincts of the society, of the millions of Americans who care about the world we want. It helps lift those aspirations, and seeks to democratize philanthropy. What, for example, would be the result if the Gates Foundation issued a matching challenge to every American to support charitable organizations doing important work?

And lastly, the heart and soul of great philanthropy flows from those who work in this field, from you, and your colleagues, from all of us who do this work. In my book are these wise words from Shirley Strong, who has been working on the issue of racism in America for many years. She says, "One of the first questions that must be asked of leaders and participants in any movement is: 'Does everybody understand that we are coming to work on our own stuff?'"[25]

Section 5 Reflection

1. Peter talks about an integrity of purpose and action that is necessary if philanthropy is to be trustworthy and benefit society. Do you think your philanthropy is trustworthy and that it benefits society? Why or why not?

2. What have you learned about yourself and your values through giving?

3. What gifts have you received that have been transformative and generative?

4. When for you does giving feel energizing and liberating? When does it feel dutiful, disconnected?

5. Do you agree that deep listening is crucial to effective giving? How could you and/or your foundation develop better listening skills?

6. What stands between you and coming 'round right? Where is the magic in philanthropy for you?

SECTION 6:

THE WORLD WE LEAVE

*It is impossible to separate the legacy you want
to leave from the life you lead.*

PETER KAROFF

In the week I spent with Peter before he died, our conversations often turned to Peter's belief that being a more thoughtful giver would change you. In his clippings was an interview with the pianist Jonathan Biss about recording a cycle of Beethoven's thirty-two sonatas over nine years.[1] In the interview, Biss says, "In a sense, the pianist who finishes the project will not be the same one who started it." And Peter thought that would be true, too, for the giver who dives deep.

Peter liked the idea of titling the last section of this book "The World We Leave." It was, of course, a play on his earlier book *The World We Want*, which was thick with his generous and affectionate profiles of the people he thought were shaping that world. In his last weeks, he was very conscious of the world he was preparing to leave, the one that he loved so deeply, despite its many troubles.

In that vein, here are some of Peter's "Reflections on Legacy," which he terms "a very big deal," filled with ideas about how one might think about what they'd like to leave behind and how they'd like to be remembered.

And there is "Sitting by a Still Pond," one of the many gorgeous vignettes he wrote about the outdoors he loved so much, the places where he was "filled with a powerful yearning to be the best that [he] can be, to do the work it takes to turn, to 'come 'round right.'"[2] Those places and his people, his wife Marty, his beloved children, grandchildren, neighbors, and friends, and even the birds, are such vivid presences in his poems, his essays, these meditative pieces.

Of the many pieces of advice Peter offers in these pages, perhaps the most heartfelt is this exhortation: "The most important transformation is the transformation of the human heart. To get there means growing your soul. Work on it—"

"Work on it—" with that dash at the end, like the end of a line in an Emily Dickinson poem. That dash implies something unfinished, an abrupt departure, something that hangs in the air like a pause in a significant conversation or . . . the death of a beloved friend. I think he chose the dash carefully. He chose it because he knew that work he described—the transformation of the human heart—is never-ending, that it's worth a lifetime of exploration, of wonder. I think he chose to call us to that transformation of ourselves, to call us to imagine a better world. As he says at the very end: "Make it so!"

Reflections on Legacy

Legacy is a very big deal. If anything deserves our complete attention it is how we leave things. Legacy assumes the end game—it assumes we are not here and the only tea leaves left are up for interpretation by others. From one perspective, your legacy is the sum total of everything you have done, which means everything you have learned.

We leave two kinds of legacy, one that is personal and one that relates to the broader community, and both of these have a moral dimension. Moral in the sense that legacy is an articulation in word and in deed of what you believed, of what you felt was right and wrong, and of what you did, or did not do. The "moral" of the story in this case is, in fact, the journey that is my life, and your life—life that is multidimensional, sometimes overwhelmingly so.

There is our private persona, our ambitions, our fears, our dreams. There is our family, and family is, for most of us, the most important thing in our lives. There is community life, and we belong to more than one—we may identify strongly with the Jewish community, but we are also part of the Los Angeles community, and we are citizens of a nation. We also belong with varying degrees of commitment to other communities of interest, neighborhoods, professional organizations, nonprofit boards, social issues we are passionate about, and, for some, there are bridge, baseball, and golf.

The moral dimension may seem stronger when personal self-interests cross over into the yearning within us to make the world a better place, but the two are actually integral to each other.

This is dramatically reflected in this poem by Adrienne Rich.

IN THOSE YEARS

In those years, people will say, we lost track
of the meaning of we, of you
we found ourselves
reduced to I
and the whole thing became
silly, ironic, terrible:
we were trying to live a personal life
and yes, that was the only life
we could bear witness to

But the great dark birds of history screamed and plunged
into our personal weather
They were headed somewhere else but their beaks
and pinions drove
along the shore, through the rags of fog
where we stood, saying I

That clearly will not do. It is impossible to separate the legacy you want to leave from the life you lead. The two are inseparable. You cannot hide in your "personal weather" while you are alive and expect your legacy, on any level, to be one of wonderfulness.

Nowhere is that more true than with family, and with family there is no escape from truth and truth-telling. One of TPI's clients, the mother of three daughters, once remarked in a family meeting with a sigh, "You know there is no protection from a smart daughter." I bear witness to that statement! We don't fool our kids. Children are the messages we send to the future, and it is what we do, not what we say, that is our major influence on them.

Family legacy, however, often evolves in unanticipated ways.

We have four children and my wife Marty and I, like all of you, have thought about what we want most for our kids. To us, there are three interrelated things. The first and maybe the most important is that they have the self-confidence and the competence to deal with the vicissitudes of life, because one thing we know for sure is that they will be tested. One way or another, we are all tested. The second is that they are able to sustain long-term loving relationships because that may be the only way one can keep the essential loneliness of being at bay. So much of what we do in life, with our families, our work, and our ongoing search for place and community, love, and faith, is because we do not want to be lonely. The third thing is that they have good values and care about others, the community, and the world—that they stand up, and when needed, are counted.

In the main, our family has been very blessed; however, in the past few months a wild card hit. One of our twin daughters, who lives in Madison, Wisconsin, with her husband and two fantastic kids—Jacob and Sophie—discovered she has breast cancer. Rebecca is forty-seven and has a PhD in comparative literature, a great job with the university, and is a wonderful mother and wife. She has had surgery and is now undergoing intensive chemo, and we are optimistic, but of necessity, guardedly so. But something happened in this process that has been immensely moving to Marty and me. It is the way Rebecca's two sisters and brother have surrounded her with an outpouring of love and support. All kinds of trips from our far-flung diaspora of a family, back and forth from New York City and Santa Barbara to Madison, winter storms and all, phone calls, and emails have resulted in a renewed bonding of our adult children that we have not seen since they were very young. When our son, who is finishing his residency in internal medicine in New York City, shaved his head in solidarity and tribute to his sister's loss of hair, it made us cry.

What Marty and I realize is that the odds are looking good that our family will still be a family when we are not here to be the convener and glue. We talk a great deal about, and aspire to, the transfer of values from one generation to the next. To see it actually happen is thrilling.

Perhaps it is because I am a writer that I find the creative process in literature very similar to the life process necessary for a successful legacy.

When you write a book, or even a poem, you learn a great deal that you did not know before. If you don't learn much, then it means you have a failed book or poem. The whole endeavor of sitting down to develop an idea or story is to go deeper. To discover what is behind the curtain. To see around the corner of the space you inhabit and be visited with a new level of understanding or persuasion. This intense exploration of insight, emotion, and metaphor is what makes the creative process so demanding, and so compelling. The experience, one of experimentation and risk-taking, is the only route to making something new—perhaps the greatest aspiration an artist can have.

I think the successful making of legacy, the successful living of a life, is exactly the same kind of creative learning experience. If all we do is reaffirm what we already know, then we are not growing.

The Talmud tells us that "we see things not as they are but as we are."[3] In a similar vein are Mahatma Gandhi's famous words: "We but mirror the world."[4] To be able to mirror the world you need to be open to change, not just external but internal. You have to be willing to learn and learn to grow your soul. And that takes work, hard work. Otherwise we are empty vessels, and the legacy we leave will be empty as well.

Peter Drucker, the management guru, said that you should be able to get the essence of your life on the front of a T-shirt. Could you do that? What would it say? And would your beloved—that may be the person sitting next to you, by the way—find those words believable? I think it is very hard to compress the essence of the learning from life down to a few words. Or is it?

I have a T-shirt that says, "Citizen of the World," and when I wear it on my walks or going into a store people always comment: "Right on!" "Like your T-shirt!" "Good for you!" And it makes me preen a little even though it would be a huge stretch to say I fit that definition.

We can't seriously consider legacy without thinking about the world we want. In my book with that title, there is an assumption that form follows essence in this way: "To get to the world you want, first figure out what you want to do with your life and treat money as an extension of that. Then follow your destiny."[5] Does that sound like a route to legacy? It does to me. It starts with a vision, and ends with how close we come to realizing that vision. The book, framed as a journey, is a kind of a way station in my own journey. It asks these questions of an extraordinary group of people:

> What is your vision of a better world?
> What are the conditions needed to realize it?
> What are the obstacles?

Based on your experience, what parts of the vision are realistic, and what ideas, strategies, and plans can make it so? How would you answer those questions? It would be fascinating to spend some time doing just that with each of you. I know the answers would be revealing.

Among the reasons philanthropy is so appealing is that it is fundamentally an articulation of values and passions, and in addition, it puts the best possible perspective on money—"best" in the sense that it counters the acquisitive and materialistic aspect of wealth, and places it in a moral framework that adds to the greater good. "Best" in the sense that philanthropy can be a bridge between the rarefied exclusivity that wealth can create, with the gated community being only one metaphor, and the many social dilemmas that the world faces.

But there are all kinds of philanthropy. One of my friends in the book puts it this way: "A lot of philanthropy that turns people's crank is 'lousy' philanthropy based on personal satisfaction instead of whether it's good for others. My view is that if it isn't good for the community, it isn't worth doing."

Do you believe that is so? Does your philanthropy reflect that belief?

The creative process I referred to earlier is key to high-impact philanthropy, especially when you make an important gift. Important, by the way, does not necessarily mean large, but important because you care deeply about the results, important because you bring passion to the table. As a TPI client said, "You have to be on fire to do this work." If at the end of the gifting process you have not learned anything more about the organization, or the social issue and how to improve the chance of its resolution, then I would call the philanthropic process a failure. It means, perhaps, you were not serious—you did not go deep enough, you did not do your homework, due diligence, a considered analysis, or most importantly, you did not listen carefully to the voices at that table. It seems to me these elements and this way of thinking are at the heart of great philanthropy.

The dictionary definition of legacy begins with "a gift by will, especially of money or other personal property."[6] Yet most of the focus on wealth-planning is around preservation. The army of investment and financial advisors that we all attend to is primarily preoccupied with asset growth and tax planning. In fact, one of the biggest questions those with wealth struggle with is the allocation of wealth between children and society. "How much is enough?" and "How much is too much?" are both practical and existential questions. Some testamentary gifts have as much to do with wanting not to leave children too much money as they do with generosity.

We know that the things we want most for our children cannot be bought. What money can do is provide security, opportunity to live an expansive life with lots of career-choice flexibility, and generally make things easier. Wealth can also make things too easy, erode self-confidence, and work against the very values that enabled the wealth-creator to make the money in the first place. There is a famous saying, that is too often true, that many families go from shirtsleeves to shirtsleeves in three generations.

Legacy can happen during one's lifetime. A board on which I sit is making what the founder calls "Legacy Gifts." These are million-dollar-a-year gifts *in perpetuity* subject to two conditions, that the funds are used in ways that are innovative and transformational, and that the recipient continues to adhere to certain values, in this case Judeo/Christian values. The gifts to date have been to colleges and universities, but the board is now considering making commitments to other major issues like domestic and global adoption, and building bridges between the Muslim world and the West. This is a donor with a very clearly defined sense of legacy.

Are these gifts part of this person's legacy? Sure they are, but whether they are really transformational remains to be seen. Size and structure alone do not get you from good to great. One of the fascinating data points from Jim Collins's *Good to Great* team's research was that the most common characteristic of those CEOs and leaders of organizations that became great was not brilliance, charisma, managerial excellence, creativity, or any of the typical assumptions about great leaders. It was humility. Isn't that interesting? In fact, one of the more compelling stories in the book is of the Dallas police department chief who the mayor of that city referred to as "charismatically challenged."[7]

So it is not always the fancy dancer, but instead the close observer, the listener who has the best shot at making a difference. Are you a good listener? If you had to rank yourself on a scale of one to ten, with ten being the highest—where would you be?

Doing the math of legacy gifts to organizations you care deeply about usually is based on calculating the capital needed to sustain your annual gift today after you are gone. That is the endowment principle, but there is another principle, which is this: Do it now.

Statistics show us that estates over $25 million on average leave bequests that total four times the cumulative giving of the household's prior ten years. In other words, most people could be giving substantially more during their lifetimes.

We have seen this evidence in TPI's practice. Time and time again we encounter situations where the current annual giving is far below what it will be, based on the foundation funding at the donor's death.

One of my friends currently gives $4 to $5 million a year, but when he dies his foundation will be obligated to pay out $12 million a year.

It makes no sense, but he told me he holds back because he would be so upset if he made gifts that "did harm." Others hold back because they don't want the recognition. Some have not figured out what their passion is, or have not dug into an issue that might potentially become a passion. It's strange but true that finding a passion in a world in which we are inundated with needs and requests is not always easy. Another thing that holds people back is trust; trust is in short supply across society.

What holds you back? What would motivate you to give more?

At TPI, we have seen that learning leads to increased giving. The more you know and understand, the more comfortable you are that you can make the right decision. In that sense, strategic philanthropy increases the odds for results. And that is what every donor wants.

In the end, it comes down to the world you want. It comes down to what you want your personal legacy to be. It comes down to what you want your broader community legacy to be. And it raises this question: Why wait?

As I get older, I feel more and more the truth of these words: "Whatever happens here, happens to us all." If the Human Genome Project taught us anything, it is how intrinsically, how completely, we are biologically connected to each other. Science now shows us that there is a 99.9 percent commonality to all humanity if you get past the many cultural barriers we learn growing up. How can we not believe in life's connectedness? From that perspective, your legacy is like the pebble in the still water of the pond, rippling out in ever-widening circles that reach the far shore. Why wait? Why not make some ripples now?

Here's some advice to get you started:

- You can't get there from here—*there* being a better place—with the way things are. Something needs to change. New resources need to be brought into play, and new attitudes as well.

- Listen to the stories of others before you tell your own—serious listening yields big dividends.

- Acknowledge that people know what they need. Help individuals find their own power and take control of their own destiny.
- Seek out the assets that every community has, build on them, and celebrate. Make heroes of those who do this work.
- Find the alignment between self-interest and the common good. When there is none, push back and stand firm.
- Make bridges and go across them. Break down silos. Create common ground. When there is no firm ground, do the right thing.
- Go downstream—transformational and top-down change only work when they become concrete and align with individual and community needs and aspirations.
- Break out of the box. Use all available resources and innovation from every sector—business, citizen, government, nonprofit—to get the work done.
- Do whatever it takes—disruption, confrontation, jujitsu, logic, data, advocacy, and traveling the parallel tracks. The tactics and strategies are endless and absorbing.
- Abandon comfort. Raise the bar. Put your whole self in, and hold the moral conscience of your community dear.
- Open it up: open yourself up. Provide building blocks for others to make their own dreams come true.
- The most important transformation is the transformation of the human heart. To get there means growing your soul. Work on it—

Sitting by a Still Pond

Here I sit, on a rock by a still pond. It is early evening, the last rays of the setting sun filter through the tops of the trees. Too early for the loon but the cardinal calls out for its mate as the woods settle in, ready to transition to night.

Across the pond in a small cove, I can just make out a great blue heron balanced on one leg. I imagine the concentration, the analysis and observation of the pond's murky bottom.

I sink deep into this place, wet and primeval with almost infinite shades of gold and green, with moss and lichen that covers the ground and wraps around the base of trees. Water bugs scoot around the rock outcropping where I sit, moving rapidly in great number and variety and I sense the presence of bass and pickerel lurking lazily below.

It all seems like a gift and the words from an old Shaker hymn float into my head:

> 'Tis the gift to be simple,
> 'Tis the gift to be free

I have been given the gift of solitude tucked away in the deep woods, alone with mind and spirit and peace while the world in which I live and work in all of its tumult, energy, pain, and joy, seems far, far away.

> 'Tis the gift to be simple
> 'Tis the gift to be free
> 'Tis the gift to come down
> Where we ought to be

I sit on a rock by a still pond in the midst of a perfectly balanced natural system, one that is harsh and gentle, competitive and yielding, rigorous and forgiving, pragmatic and magical. A system so, so violent and still capable of producing serenity. You would not have the one, the beauty, without the struggle of the other. Nature is immensely complex, more complex than the most advanced technology and requires a multitude of collaborative and interdependent initiatives for its residents to survive and prosper. All of this happens intuitively without doubt or hesitation. What seems to underlie nature is an incredible amplitude and abundance as though the plan were overengineered, and unless man interferes, a remarkable regenerative capacity to carry on, and on, and on.

Nature is anything but neat with constant spillage and what seems like error and waste, but what wins out in the end is this magnificently generous system yielding one gift after another.

> And when we find ourselves
> In the place just right
> 'Twill be in the valley
> Of love and delight

Something startles the heron. It awkwardly gathers up those long, spindly legs, and hesitates for a moment as though reluctant to let go of the intrigue of the pond's muck and mud. The great bird lifts, huge wings cast a muted shadow on the water, and flying straight toward my rock gracefully swerves off to the right, disappearing among the tall pines along the shore.

These are gifts given to me, a still pond, a heron, Monadnock Mountain, tall marsh grass, dunes overlooking South Beach, the immense, undulating sea beyond—all, all valleys of delights.

> When true simplicity
> Is gained

> To bow and to bend
> We shan't be ashamed

On my rock by the still pond the water mirrors nature but so much of my own world is reflected here as well. My world has many of these same characteristics, sadness, suffering, despair, chaos, inequity, and certainly violence. It also has the same capacity for regeneration, for hope, for beauty, for joy, and even for peace and solace. But where the natural world knows what to do, and is driven, governed, and balanced solely by instinct, my world is not intuitively balanced at all and constantly demands other more elusive elements: courage, patience, and especially, will and love. Perhaps even more difficult, knowing what is right and good to do. Without will and love, without a sense of the just and the unjust, without confidence in ourselves, we are at risk, on the edge, ready to fall into a void or even worse spin completely out of control taking those we love with us.

> To turn, turn will be our delight
> Till by turning, turning
> We come 'round right[8]

My will is weak and tempered by what the philosopher[9] calls *natural shame* from within, and *moral shame* from those who know me. I am often afraid, wracked with self-doubt, and not sure what is right and good. I want to love but that requires much courage, and a giving of myself fully while risking rejection. You see, both will and love are acts of selflessness, of generosity.

> What do I seek, what do I yearn for?
> I seek a rock by a still pond.

The evening is rapidly becoming night and all around is a softening of sound, wood, and sky and I think of these lines about dusk, written for my grandson Jacob, who at age five asked me the question "What is the difference between dusk and evening?"

> There is evening and evening song
> sun goes down and takes the light along
>
> and at a certain moment difficult to define
> day or night light or dark is hard to find
>
> you see a milky misty shadowy fall
> softly sending goodnight kisses to us all.

    I sit on my rock by the still pond and dream of "goodnight kisses" sent to us all, of "valleys of love and delight," of finding oneness of mind, spirit, and self, of finding the will and the courage to love, to do the right thing, and I am filled with a powerful yearning to be the best that I can be, to do the work it takes to turn, to "come 'round right."

    As I sit on my rock by a still pond, how clear it becomes. We are all nurtured by this generous world and we must in turn make it so. We must make it so!

ONE WHO DID NOT GO GENTLE

FOR LENNY ZAKIM

This one did not go gentle,
He went out with a roar
And he lived; well he lived like a Columbus
Whose faith shook the world.

This one lived in a fortress of love,
A thousand voices added to his own,
The strong beat of syncopated sound,
The surround sound of justice and joy.

This one went to the very edge
And faced the dybbuk of intolerance down,
Drew a line of right in the sand
And in the end stood his ground.

This one made us a great amphitheater,
A magnetic for generosity, for hope.
I feel his pull here, deep in the Negev,
Sun rising in a clear, cold, dawn.

Be'er-Sheva
December 3, 1999

APPENDIX A

A BIOGRAPHY OF PETER KAROFF

Peter Karoff was a champion of civil rights and social justice, a published poet, and a pioneering leader in the field of strategic philanthropy and philanthropic advising. In 1989 he founded The Philanthropic Initiative, a nonprofit philanthropic advisory firm that designs transformative giving solutions at the local, national, and global levels. With his guidance, vision, and passionate leadership, TPI became a major influencer in the world of philanthropy.

Peter served not only as mentor and wise counsel to hundreds of donors and foundation leaders, but as a board member of more than thirty nonprofit organizations and foundations, including the Robina Foundation, the GHR Foundation, Ascent Private Capital Management, and Blackside Productions, producer of the PBS series *Eyes on the Prize*. He also taught classes on philanthropy and poetry at Tufts University, Boston University, and the University of California at Santa Barbara.

Other Karoff works include being the author of *The World We Want: New Dimensions in Philanthropy and Social Change* (AltaMira Press, 2007) and editor of *Just Money: A Critique of Contemporary American Philanthropy* (TPI Editions, 2004). He was an accomplished poet—his book of poems, *Parable*, was published by David Robert Books in early

2017. Among the many awards he received, he was named a MacDowell Fellow and a Purpose Prize Fellow.

Peter was born in Brockton, Massachusetts, and lived in the Boston area and then Santa Barbara, California. Prior to founding The Philanthropic Initiative (TPI), he worked in insurance and real estate for more than twenty-five years. He earned his degrees from Brandeis University and Columbia University, and received an honorary degree from Lesley University in 2002. Peter dearly loved his family, his home, his community, art, music, and sailing. Most of all, he loved his life with his soul mate of fifty-nine years, Martha.

APPENDIX B

PETER'S INSPIRATIONS

Peter was inspired by many books, poems, and songs not quoted in this book as he wrote these pieces and his own poems. Here is a selected list.

T. S. Eliot's poem "The Hollow Men"

The writings of Václav Havel, particularly his words on hope in *Disturbing the Peace: A Conversation with Karel Huizdala*

The poetry and essays of Seamus Heaney, particularly "The Cure of Troy" and *The Redress of Poetry*

Carl Rakosi's poem "Instructions to the Player"

Paul Simon's "The Boy in the Bubble" from *Graceland*

Wallace Stevens's poem "Final Soliloquy of the Interior Paramour"

ACKNOWLEDGMENTS

Peter Karoff believed deeply in the power of words, ideas, poetry, love—and of course, philanthropy—to inspire and bring out the best in people. And he truly did bring out the best in so many who were lucky enough to know him. He worked tirelessly to lead, inspire, mentor, and challenge all of us to envision a better world, and to find ways to make a difference. As Melinda Marble explains in her introduction to this book, Peter began to ponder in the last few weeks of his life whether his writings could continue to serve as an inspiration to donors, wealth advisors, and others in the field of philanthropy. He asked Melinda to help bring this idea to life, and we are indebted to her for her work in compiling his writings and capturing the essence of Peter so beautifully.

When Peter died, we invited those who knew and loved him to contribute to the Karoff Fund for Leadership in Philanthropy, set up at The Philanthropic Initiative (TPI) to honor Peter and his legacy. We are so grateful to John Abele, the Russell Berrie Foundation and Angelica Berrie, Amy Goldman and the GHR Foundation, Doreen Goldman and the Joyce and Irving Goldman Family Foundation, Beth and Seth Klarman, the Henry & Marilyn Taub Foundation, Peter's beloved family, and so many others who contributed to the Karoff Fund. Their support has been critical in turning the idea of this book into reality.

Thank you to all who understand and appreciate the power of Peter's voice to continue to serve as a calling to donors, dreamers, and doers. We are deeply indebted to Jay Hughes and the James E. Hughes Jr. Foundation for the invaluable support, encouragement, and partnership in helping to get Peter's inspirational words and ideas out to the field of wealth advisors. We also thank John A. Warnick, founder of the Purposeful Planning Institute, who played an instrumental role in connecting the dots; Phil Cubeta, whose brilliant development of the Chartered Advisors in Philanthropy curriculum has helped to keep Peter's legacy alive; and so many other kindred spirits who inspired Peter and countless others in such meaningful ways.

In his speeches and writings, Peter loved to incorporate quotes, poems, songs, and ideas from many different sources—which made the editing process quite interesting. Thank you to David Robert Books for giving us permission to include some of Peter's poems from *Parable: Poems by Peter Karoff*, and to all who agreed to be identified and quoted in the book. We are also so appreciative of the wonderful guidance and partnership with the team at Disruption Books, including Kris Pauls and Christina Pulles—and we thank Susan Solomont for introducing us to this unique publishing firm.

Last but certainly not least, we extend a special thank you to Peter's beloved children and grandchildren. Deb, Lorinda, Rebecca, and Tom were instrumental in helping us think through the formation of the Karoff Fund for Leadership in Philanthropy and supporting the creation of this book. While we well know that nothing can even begin to capture the magical, enchanting, extraordinary Peter Karoff, we hope the Karoff family will find great joy and warmth from *A Generous Life*.

Leslie Pine, Ellen Remmer, and the TPI Team

NOTES

Introduction

1. Peter Karoff, *The World We Want: New Dimensions in Philanthropy and Social Change* (AltaMira, 2008), 6, Kindle; Robert Frost, "The Figure of a Poem," in *Collected Poems of Robert Frost* (Halcyon House, 1939).
2. Peter Karoff, "Passion—Not Strategy—Drives Successful Giving," *The Chronoicle of Philanthropy*, September 20, 2001, https://www.ncfp.org/wp-content/uploads/2018/09/Passion-not-strategy-drives-successful-giving-TPI-2001-passion-not-strategy-drives-successful-giving.pdf.
3. Peter Karoff, "Reflections on Two Decades of the Poetry and Practice of Philanthropy," presented at the International Association of Advisors in Philanthropy Conference on Philanthropy, April 2011, https://giving.typepad.com/files/aip-presentation---april-2011-2.pdf.

Section 1: The Calling

1. Frederick Gates, letter to John D. Rockefeller (1906), quoted in Ron Chernow, *Titan: The Life of John D. Rockefeller, Sr.* (Vintage, 2004), 563.
2. Philip Larkin, "High Windows," Poetry Foundation, https://www.poetryfoundation.org/poems/48417/high-windows.
3. "Maimonides' Eight Levels of Charity," *The Rambam's Mishneh Torah*, Chabad.org, https://www.chabad.org/library/article_cdo/aid/45907/jewish/Eight-Levels-of-Charity.htm.
4. Peter cites *Giving USA: The Annual Report on Philanthropy for the Year 1991*, Giving USA Foundation, American Association of Fund-Raising Counsel, 1992.
5. Giving bequests by wealthy individuals accounted for 8 percent of all charitable gifts made in 2023. *Giving USA: The Annual Report on Philanthropy for the Year 2023*, Giving USA Foundation, 2024.

6. John Gardner, "Personal Renewal," *John Gardner: Uncommon American*, PBS, November 10, 1990, https://www.pbs.org/johngardner/sections/writings_speech_1.html.

7. Allen Wheelis, "When the Void Is Not a Void," *The New York Times*, August 25, 1973.

8. Emily Dickinson, "There's a certain Slant of light, (320)," Poetry Foundation, https://www.poetryfoundation.org/poems/45723/theres-a-certain-slant-of-light-320.

9. Andrew Carnegie, "The Gospel of Wealth" (Carnegie Corporation of New York, 2017), https://www.carnegie.org/publications/the-gospel-of-wealth/.

10. *Oxford English Dictionary*, "family," accessed December 12, 2024, https://www.oed.com/dictionary/family_n?tab=meaning_and_use/.

11. Peter C. Goldmark Jr., "The President's Letter," *Rockefeller Foundation Annual Report*, 1996, 5–8.

12. Baba Dioum, paper presented at the General Assembly of the International Union for the Conservation of Nature and Natural Resources, New Delhi, 1968.

13. William Butler Yeats, "A Prayer for Old Age," All Poetry, https://allpoetry.com/A-Prayer-For-Old-Age.

Section 2: Embarking

1. Stephen Colgate, "Sails and Wind" in *Colgate's Basic Sailing Theory* (Van Nostrand Reinhold Company, 1973).

2. Colgate, "Sails and Wind."

3. Colgate, "Sails and Wind."

4. Chadd M. Funk and Michael S. Gazzaniga, "The Functional Brain Architecture of Human Morality," *Current Opinion in Neurobiology* 19, no. 6 (2009): 678–681, doi: 10.1016/j.conb.2009.09.01.

5. Robert Wright, *The Evolution of God* (Little, Brown, 2009), 595. Overdrive.

6. David L. Cooperrider, Jacqueline M. Stavros, and Diana Whitney, *The Appreciative Inquiry Handbook: For Leaders of Change* (Berrett-Koehler Publishers, 2008), 3.

7. Walt Whitman, "One's-Self I Sing," Poetry Foundation, https://www.poetryfoundation.org/poems/48857/ones-self-i-sing.

8. *The 2023 Bank of America Study of Philanthropy: Charitable Giving by Affluent Households* (Lilly Family School of Philanthropy, Indiana University, 2023), https://agb.org/wp-content/uploads/2023/11/2023_Bank-of-America-Study-of-Philanthropy_Final_ADA_102023.pdf.

9. "Looking Good by Doing Good," *The Economist,* January 15, 2009, https://www.economist.com/finance-and-economics/2009/01/15/looking-good-by-doing-good.

10. According to the 2024 *Forbes* 400 list, the net worth of the list is $5.4 trillion, which means that if they gave away half their wealth, they would give away $2.7 trillion. "*Forbes* 400: The Definitive Ranking Of America's Richest People 2024," *Forbes*, September 2024, https://www.forbes.com/forbes-400/.

11. As of May 2024, there are 244 people who have signed The Giving Pledge across 30 countries. More than $500 billion has been pledged to charities. "Annual Gathering Connects Giving Pledge Community Through Learning and Action," The Giving Pledge, May 28, 2024, https://givingpledge.org/pressrelease?date=05.28.2024.

12. Famous advice from Mike Sviridoff, former vice president of the Ford Foundation and founder of the Local Initiatives Support Corporation (LISC).

13. *Highlights of Social Justice Grantmaking: A Report on Foundation Trends*, The Foundation Center, 2005, https://search.issuelab.org/resource/social-justice-grantmaking-a-report-on-foundation-trends.html.

14. "Global Food Crises, 2008 vs 2022: New Report Finds Disparities in Hunger and Funding," CARE, June 2023, https://www.care.org/media-and-press/global-food-crises-2008-vs-2022-new-report-finds-disparities-in-hunger-and-funding/.

15. Alan Broadbent, quoted in Peter Karoff, *The World We Want* (AltaMira Press, 2008), 67, Kindle.

16. Peter Senge, C. Otto Scharmer, Joseph Jaworski, and Betty Sue Flowers, *Presence: An Exploration of Profound Change in People, Organizations, and Society* (Crown, 2005), 26.

17. Karoff, *The World We Want*.

18. Lao Tzu, "Tao Te Ching," quoted in John Heider, *The Tao of Leadership: Lao Tzu's Tao Te Ching Adapted for a New Age* (Humanics New Age, 1985).

19. Robert Frost, "The Road Not Taken," Poetry Foundation, https://www.poetryfoundation.org/poems/44272/the-road-not-taken.

20. Leslie Gadman, "Knowledge Creation in Commitment-Based Value Networks in Multinational Organizations," in *Strategic Knowledge Management in Multinational Organizations*, ed. Kevin O'Sullivan (IGI Global, 2008).

21. Gadman, "Knowledge Creation in Commitment-Based Value Networks in Multinational Organizations."

22. Whitman, "One's-Self I Sing."

23. H. Richard Niebuhr, *The Responsible Self: An Essay in Christian Moral Philosophy* (Presbyterian Publishing Corporation, 1999), 60.

24. Joel L. Fleishman, *The Foundation: A Great American Secret; How Private Wealth Is Changing the World* (PublicAffairs, 2007), 59.

25. W. Brian Arthur, Jonathan Day, Joseph Jaworski, Michael Jung, Ikujiro Nonaka, C. Otto Scharmer, et. al., *Illuminating the Blind Spot: Leadership in the Context of Emerging Worlds* (McKinsey–Society for Organizational Learning, 2004), https://www.management.com.ua/ld/ld029.html.

26. *Merriam-Webster Dictionary*, "knowledge," accessed December 20, 2024, https://www.merriam-webster.com/dictionary/knowledge.

27. Percy Bysshe Shelley, "A Defence of Poetry," in *Essays, Letters from Abroad, Translations and Fragments* (Edward Moxon, 1840).

28. *Merriam-Webster Dictionary*, "art," accessed December 20, 2024, https://www.merriam-webster.com/dictionary/art.

29. W. Brian Arthur et. al., "Illuminating the Blind Spot."

30. Rainer Maria Rilke, *Letters to a Young Poet* (Shambhala, 2021), 13.

31. Donald Schon, *The Reflective Practitioner: How Professionals Think in Action* (Basic Books, 1983).

32. Joseph M. Hall and M. Eric Johnson, "When Should a Process Be Art, Not Science?" *Harvard Business Review*, March 1, 2009, https://hbr.org/2009/03/when-should-a-process-be-art-not-science.

33. Hall and Johnson, "When Should a Process Be Art, Not Science?"

34. Hall and Johnson, "When Should a Process Be Art, Not Science?"

35. Hall and Johnson, "When Should a Process Be Art, Not Science?"

36. Dennis Littky and Samantha Grabelle, "If We Love Our Children More Than We Love Our Schools, the System Must Change," *Educational Horizons* 82, no. 4 (2004): 284–289, https://files.eric.ed.gov/fulltext/EJ684846.pdf.

37. Martin Buber, *I and Thou* (Germany, 1923; repr., Free Press, 1970).

38. Harold Bloom, *The Anatomy of Influence: Literature as a Way of Life* (Yale University Press, 2011).

39. Bloom, *The Anatomy of Influence.*

40. Bloom, *The Anatomy of Influence.*

41. Parker J. Palmer, *Healing the Heart of Democracy: The Courage to Create a Politics Worthy of the Human Spirit* (Wiley, 2014), 6.

42. J. Courtney Bourns, "Do Nothing About Me Without Me" (Grantmakers for Effective Organizations, 2010).

43. Ronald Heifetz, Alexander Grashow, and Marty Linsky, *The Practice of Adaptive Leadership: Tools and Tactics for Changing Your Organization and the World* (Harvard Business Press, 2009).

44. Bourns, "Do Nothing About Me Without Me."

45. Dev Patnaik, *Wired to Care: How Companies Prosper When They Create Widespread Empathy* (Pearson Education India, 2008).

46. P. Catlin Fulwood, "Participatory Evaluation Research: An Overview," Girl's Best Friend, https://www.girlsbestfriend.org/downloads/per_overview_doc.

47. Peter J. Klein and Angelica Berrie, *A Passion for Giving: Tools and Inspiration for Creating a Charitable Foundation* (Wiley, 2012), 260.

48. C. Otto Scharmer, *Theory U: Leading from the Future as It Emerges* (Berrett-Koehler Publishers, 2009).

49. Hall and Johnson, "When Should a Process Be Art, Not Science?"

50. Fred Kiel and Doug Lennick, *Moral Intelligence: Enhancing Business Performance and Leadership Success* (Pearson Education, 2005).

51. Paul G. Schervish, "The Moral Biography of Wealth: Philosophical Reflections on the Foundation of Philanthropy," *Nonprofit and Volunteer Sector Quarterly* 35, no. 3 (2006): 477–492.

Section 3: Trouble

1. Associated Press, "Biggs Has Plans for Tyson," *Oroville Mercury-Register*, August 19, 1987.

2. Stanley Kunitz, "Graduation Speech," St. Mary's College, May 14, 1994.

3. Rahm Emanuel, "Rahm Emanuel on the Opportunities of Crisis," The Wall Street Journal CEO Council, November 19, 2008, posted November 19, 2008, by *The Wall Street Journal*, YouTube, https://www.youtube.com/watch?v=_mzcbXi1Tkk.

280 NOTES

4. Jonathan Rauch, "Seeing Around Corners," *The Atlantic*, April 2002, https://www.theatlantic.com/magazine/archive/2002/04/seeing-around-corners/302471/.

5. Karoff, *The World We Want*.

6. Peter Senge, "Creating the World Anew," The Systems Thinker, https://thesystemsthinker.com/creating-the-world-anew/.

7. In 2023, Boston Scientific Corporation's net sales were $14.24 billion. "Boston Scientific announces results for fourth quarter and full year 2023," Boston Scientific, January 31, 2024, https://news.bostonscientific.com/2024-01-31-Boston-Scientific-Announces-Results-for-Fourth-Quarter-and-Full-Year-2023.

8. Howard Thurman, *Disciplines of the Spirit* (Friends United Press, 1963), 62.

9. Seamus Heaney, *The Redress of Poetry* (Farrar, Straus and Giroux, 1996), 1.

10. Shelley, "A Defence of Poetry."

11. Shelley, "A Defence of Poetry."

12. Peter Senge, "On Schools as Learning Organizations," interview by John O'Neil, *ACSD* 52, no. 7, April 1, 1995, https://ascd.org/el/articles/on-schools-as-learning-organizations-a-conversation-with-peter-senge.

13. Pico Iyer and From Prospect, "Nowhere Man," *Utne Reader*, May 1, 1997, https://www.utne.com/politics/nowhere-man-transnational-tribe-pico-iyer/.

14. Richard Florida, *The Rise of the Creative Class: And How It's Transforming Work, Leisure, Community and Everyday Life*, updated edition (Basic Books, 2019), 284.

15. Saul Alinksy, *Rules for Radicals: A Pragmatic Primer for Realistic Radicals* (Knopf Doubleday, 1989), 72–79.

16. Alinsky, *Rules for Radicals*, 72–79.

17. Alinsky, *Rules for Radicals*, 72–79.

Section 4: Justice

1. Joseph Fletcher, *Moral Responsibility: Situation Ethics at Work* (Westminster Press, 1967), 17.

2. Fletcher, *Moral Responsibility*, 17.

3. Heaney, *The Redress of Poetry*, 1.

4. Alice McDermott, "Regis College Commencement Address," Regis College, May 2002.

5. T. S. Eliot, "*Ulysses*, Order, and Myth," *The Dial* 75, no. 9 (1923): 483.

6. Eliot, "*Ulysses*, Order, and Myth," 483.

7. Quotes below come from the winners of the Reebok Human Rights Award in 2003. Peter attended the ceremony.

8. *Merriam-Webster Dictionary*, "redress," accessed January 2, 2025, https://www.merriam-webster.com/dictionary/redress.

9. Heaney, *The Redress of Poetry*, 1.

10. Heaney, *The Redress of Poetry*, 193.

11. Simone Weil, *Gravity and Grace* (Routledge & Kegan Paul, 1952), quoted in Seamus Heaney, *The Redress of Poetry* (Farrar, Straus and Giroux, 1996), 3.

12. Heaney, *The Redress of Poetry*, 3.

13. Václav Havel, *Disturbing the Peace: A Conversation with Karel Hvíždala* (Knopf Doubleday Publishing Group, 1991), 181–182.

14. David K. Shipler, *The Working Poor: Invisible in America* (Alfred A. Knopf, 2008), 298.

15. For a further discussion on the relationship between helplessness, confusion, and fear, see Peter White, *Ecology of Being* (All In All Books, 2006).

16. Hermann Broch, *The Sleepwalkers*, rev. ed. (Knopf Doubleday, 2011).

17. Jane Cooper, "Nothing Has Been Used in the Manufacture of This Poetry That Could Have Been Used in the Manufacture of Bread," in *Scaffolding* (Anvil Press Poetry, 1984).

18. White, *Ecology of Being*, 51.

19. See the work of Robert Putnam and Richard Florida.

20. This idea is inspired by Phil Cubeta's comments on Peter's "Essay on the Issue of Trust," published on his blog "Wealth Bondage."

21. 2001 numbers from Reuben Romirowsky, "A Venture Worth Taking? Sustaining 21st Century Nonprofit Organizations Through Social Venture Philanthropy," *Journal of Jewish Communal Service* 82, nos. 1 and 2, 2007. In terms of more current numbers, Federal Reserve data indicates that as of Q4 2021, the top 1 percent of households in the United States held 30.9 percent of the country's wealth, while the bottom 50 percent held 2.6 percent. See "Distribution of Household Wealth in the U.S. since 1989," Federal Reserve, https://www.federalreserve.gov/releases/z1/dataviz/dfa/distribute/table/#quarter:129;series:Net%20worth;demographic:networth;population:all;units:shares.

282 NOTES

22. These numbers reflect the data in 2003. Peter notes that the 2003 federal poverty threshold for a family of four (two adults and two children) was $18,660, according to the US Census Bureau. The poverty rate has declined slightly in recent years, to 11.1 percent in 2023. Source: US Census Bureau. See Emily A. Shrider, "Poverty in the United States: 2023," United States Census Bureau, September 10, 2024, https://www.census.gov/library/publications/2024/demo/p60-283.html.

23. Original source: American Community Survey 2002, the US Census Bureau. In 2023, the Bureau estimates that 16 percent of all children in the United States—nearly 12 million kids total—were living in poverty. See Shrider, "Poverty in the United States: 2023."

24. Peter's original source: "Rental Housing for America's Poor Families in 2002: Farther Out of Reach Than Ever," National Low Income Coalition, August 2002.

25. Source for numbers from 2002: Doug O'Brien, Halley Torres Aldeen, Stephanie Uchima, and Erinn Staley, "Hunger in America: The Definitions, Scope, Causes, History and Status of the Problem of Hunger in the United States," America's Second Harvest, 2004, https://www.hungercenter.org/wp-content/uploads/2012/10/Hunger-in-America-Americas-Second-Harvest.pdf. In 2023, approximately 13.8 million children lived in food-insecure households. M.P. Rabbitt, M. Reed-Jones, L.J. Hales, and M.P. Burke, "Household Food Security in the United States in 2023 (Report No. ERR-337)," U.S. Department of Agriculture, Economic Research Service, 2024, 10, https://www.ers.usda.gov/publications/pub-details?pubid=109895.

26. 2002: O'Brien et al., "Hunger in America." In 2023, 47.4 million people lived in food-insecure households; Rabbitt et. al., "Household Food Security in the United States in 2023."

27. Peter cites the Bread for the World Institute for this data and notes that other relevant data from USAID and the UN Food and Agriculture Organization estimates the cost of reducing the number of hungry people in the world by half, from 800 million to 400 million, is in the range of $5 billion a year more than was being spent at the time. In 2016, Joel Berg, CEO of Hunger Free America, estimated we could end hunger in the US by "raising the food purchasing power of low-income Americans by $25 billion." Joel Berg, "How We Can End Hunger in America," Just Harvest, October 2016, https://justharvest.org/joel-berg-can-end-hunger-america-1/.

28. See the twenty-year record of accomplishment of the Local Initiatives Support Corporation (LISC) and the Enterprise Foundation in community development or the work of the Paul & Phyllis Fireman Foundation program to end homelessness for families in Massachusetts over a five-year period.

29. Bob Herbert, "Dark Side of Free Trade," *The New York Times*, February 20, 2004.

30. Peter C. Goldmark, "Before the Storm," in H. Peter Karoff, ed., *Just Money: A Critique of Contemporary American Philanthropy* (TPI Editions, 2004).

31. *A House Divided* is the title of Mark Gerzon's book that describes an American society deeply divided from seven sociological perspectives.

32. Joel Fleishman, "Simply Doing Good or Doing Well," in *Just Money*.

33. Shipler, *The Working Poor*.

34. Robin Toner, "The Culture Wars, Part II," *The New York Times*, February 29, 2004.

35. Cooper, "Nothing Has Been Used in the Manufacture of This Poetry."

36. Walt Whitman, "Song of Myself," Poetry Foundation, https://www.poetryfoundation.org/poems/45477/song-of-myself-1892-version.

37. Peter Frumkin, "Trouble in Foundationland: Looking Back, Looking Ahead," Hudson Institute, January 15, 2004, https://www.hudson.org/domestic-policy/trouble-in-foundationland-looking-back-looking-ahead.

38. Scott Harshbarger made these points in reaction to Peter's "Essay on the Issue of Trust."

39. 35.9 percent or $86.4 billion of the $240.7 billion Americans gave to charity in 2003 went to religion. "'Giving USA' Reports Increase in Charitable Giving," *Philanthropy News Digest*, June 22, 2004, https://philanthropynewsdigest.org/news/giving-usa-reports-increase-in-charitable-giving#:~:text=That%20represents%20an%20improvement%20over%202002%2C%20when,or%2035.9%20percent%20of%20the%20total%20%E2%80%94. In 2022, 29 percent of all donations went to religious organizations; Drew Lindsay, "'Pretty Scary': 7 Things to Know About Religion's Decline and Charitable Giving," The Chronicle of Philanthropy, December 12, 2023, https://www.philanthropy.com/article/pretty-scary-7-things-to-know-about-religions-decline-and-charitable-giving.

40. Peter references Phil Cubeta as the originator of this idea.

41. The work of the Tufts University College of Citizenship and Public Service, funded by a major grant for the Omidyar Foundation, is one exciting example.

42. The organization Ashoka, founded in 1980 by Bill Drayton, has supported more than 2,700 Ashoka Fellows who are hard at work in making the linkages between economic development, social action, and civic engagement.

43. Tyler Cowen, "Is Innovation Over?" *Foreign Affairs* 95, no. 2 (2016): 42–46, https://www.jstor.org/stable/43948177.

44. *Highlights of Social Justice Grantmaking: A Report on Foundation Trends*, The Foundation Center, 2005, https://search.issuelab.org/resource/social-justice-grantmaking-a-report-on-foundation-trends.html.

45. *Merriam-Webster Dictionary*, "radical," accessed January 2, 2025, https://www.merriam-webster.com/dictionary/radical.

46. Wheelis, "When the Void Is Not a Void."

47. Peter is referencing Aristotle on politics here.

48. John Rawls, *A Theory of Justice* (Oxford University Press, 1971).

49. David Brooks, "The End of Philosophy," *The New York Times*, April 6, 2009, https://www.nytimes.com/2009/04/07/opinion/07Brooks.html.

50. Brooks, "The End of Philosophy."

51. Wheelis, "When the Void Is Not a Void."

52. Peter C. Goldmark Jr., "The President's Letter," *Rockefeller Foundation Annual Report*, 1996, 5–8.

53. "CSBG Fact Sheet," Office of Community Services, U.S. Department of Health & Human Services, https://www.acf.hhs.gov/ocs/fact-sheet/csbg-fact-sheet. In fiscal year 2022, the government allocated a block grant of $755 million to state and local governments, migrant and seasonal farm worker organizations, tribes and tribal organizations, and Community Action Agencies (CAAs).

54. Steven Schroeder, "Does the Moral Arc of the Universe Really Bend Toward Justice?" *Journal of General Internal Medicine* 27, no. 11 (2012): 1397–1399, https://doi.org/10.1007/s11606-012-2146-x.

55. Schroeder, "Does the Moral Arc of the Universe?"

56. This quote comes from a previous version of the vision statement. The current vision statement is found at "About Us," The Annie E. Casey Foundation, https://www.aecf.org/about.

57. *Highlights of Social Justice Grantmaking: A Report on Foundation Trends*, The Foundation Center, 2005, https://search.issuelab.org/resource/social-justice-grantmaking-a-report-on-foundation-trends.html.

58. Rawls, *A Theory of Justice*.

59. Heaney, *The Redress of Poetry*, 3.

60. Heaney, *The Redress of Poetry*, 1.

61. Shirley Strong, interview in Peter Karoff, *The World We Want: New Dimensions in Philanthropy and Social Change* (AltaMira Press, 2008), 186–190, Kindle.

Section 5: Coming 'Round Right

1. "Simple Gifts," Song of America, https://songofamerica.net/song/simple-gifts/.
2. Midori Goto, concert program notes, January 2002, quoted in Peter Karoff, *The World We Want*, 17, Kindle.
3. Goto, concert program notes.
4. Seamus Heaney, *The Cure at Troy: A Version of Sophocles' Philoctees* (Farrar, Straus and Giroux, 1961).
5. Goto, concert program notes.
6. The Torah, Pirkei Avot, 1:15.
7. "Simple Gifts."
8. Richard Titmuss, *The Gift Relationship: From Human Blood to Social Policy*, rev. ed. (Policy Press, 2018), 1.
9. Titmuss, *The Gift Relationship*.
10. Whitman, "Song of Myself."
11. Titmuss, *The Gift Relationship*, 210.
12. Titmuss, *The Gift Relationship*.
13. Ian Parker, "The Gift," *The New Yorker*, July 25, 2004, https://www.newyorker.com/magazine/2004/08/02/the-gift-ian-parker.
14. Titmuss, *The Gift Relationship*.
15. Titmuss, *The Gift Relationship*, 191.
16. James D. Wallace, *Virtues and Vices* (Cornell University Press, 1978).
17. *Oxford English Dictionary*, "magic," accessed January 3, 2025, https://www.oed.com/dictionary/magic_n?tab=meaning_and_use/.
18. W. R. Spencer, "The Year of Sorrow," *Poems* (T. Cadell, W. Davies, Strand, 1811), 41–56.
19. *Merriam-Webster Dictionary*, "magic numbers," accessed January 3, 2025, https://www.merriam-webster.com/dictionary/magic%20numbers.
20. Heaney, *The Cure at Troy*.
21. Alan Broadbent, quoted in Peter Karoff, *The World We Want*, 67, Kindle.
22. For more on this, see: Randall Collins, *The Sociology of Philosophies: A Global Theory of Intellectual Change*, rev. ed. (Harvard University Press, 2009); James Hunter, *To Change the World: The Irony, Tragedy, and Possibility of Christianity in the Late Modern World* (Oxford University Press, 2010).

23. Stephen Jay Gould, "This View of Life: Size and Shape," *National History* 83 (1974): 20–26.
24. David L. Cooperrider, Jacqueline M. Stavros, and Diana Whitney, *The Appreciative Inquiry Handbook: For Leaders of Change* (Berrett-Koehler Publishers, 2008), 3.
25. Shirley Strong, interview in Peter Karoff, *The World We Want*, 5, Kindle.

Section 6: The World We Leave

1. Steve Smith, "What a Pianist Is Learning from 32 Sonatas," *The New York Times*, April 18, 2012.
2. "Simple Gifts."
3. Rabbi Shemuel ben Nachmani, the Talmudic tractate Berakhot (55b).
4. Mahatma Gandhi, quoted in "Five Historical Quotes That We Probably Misquote," BBC Bitesize, https://www.bbc.co.uk/bitesize/articles/zmvwwnb.
5. Bob Buford, interview in Peter Karoff, *The World We Want*, 215, Kindle.
6. *Merriam-Webster Dictionary*, "legacy," accessed January 3, 2025, https://www.merriam-webster.com/dictionary/legacy.
7. James Charles Collins, *Good to Great: Why Some Companies Make the Leap . . . And Others Don't* (HarperCollins, 2001).
8. "Simple Gifts."
9. Rawls, *A Theory of Justice*.